From :
John's staff
Teri, Firelei, ann,
Theresa, Georgia, Kathy
Christmas, 1994

A
Deeper
Walk

A Deeper Walk

A JANET THOMA BOOK

Thomas Nelson Publishers
Nashville · Atlanta · London · Vancouver

CONTENTS

SECTION TWO

A Deeper Walk in the Light   236

A Path of Your Own

by Barton Green

Several years have gone by and I've tried many times to tell Papa what I saw and heard that night, but to this day he dismisses it as a childish dream. He told me that there had to be another explanation for how and why Grampa just *disappeared*.

Everyone loved and respected Grandfather. He was a good man. And though he seemed a little eccentric at times, he was as predictable as a sunset. Each evening after dinner, weather permitting, Grampa would take a long walk down to the river and back. It's strange, but I never paid much attention to those late afternoon strolls, that is, until that night.

I remember that I was feeding the horses, around dusk, when I heard the familiar slam of our front door. Peeking over the top of our old mare's swayed back, I saw Grampa's tall frame standing on the porch. As I watched in amusement, his long, spindly legs paced off the land between the house and the barn in nearly half the time it would take me to run the distance. Pausing for a moment, he leaned on his cane and carefully surveyed the landscape of our farm. As I watched with curiosity I noticed an uncommon zeal in his inspection. It was as if he was trying to memorize every detail of the surrounding hills and trees. Soon, a trace of a smile crossed his face. Then tossing one end of his mantle over his stooped shoulders, Grandfather started off in the direction of the river.

He had taken only a few steps when I heard Papa's voice call out to him from the barn. "Father, wait!" Papa shouted. "Slow down, let me walk with you tonight."

Grandfather took another step, then turned around and held up his hand. "No, son, not tonight." Papa froze in his tracks. "No? What do you mean? What did I do?"

"Nothing, son," he said with a smile. And with that, he resumed his stride.

Papa seemed confused, hurt. Taking a moment to gather his thoughts, he inched forward in short, sporadic steps. Then scratching the back of his head, Papa called out again, "Why can't I come with you?"

Flashing an impatient look over his shoulder, Grampa responded, "When you were younger I let you come along, but now you are a man. It's time you found a path of your own."

"But you know I don't like to walk by myself!"

"Son, if you find the right path, you won't be alone."

As Papa wrestled for a reply, I dropped the bucket of feed, and moved closer. Slipping nearer to the conversation, I heard Papa ask, "Should not a son be with his father now and again?"

Straightaway Grampa looked in my direction and pointed at me with his long, twisted cane. "Yes, you are right. There is your son," he replied, "be with him." Then turning once more toward the river, Grandfather walked on.

Papa was shaken. He stormed up the porch stairs and slammed the front door behind him, causing the clay walls of our house to crack visibly. As for Grampa, I could just make out his lanky figure fading into the distant trees.

In that instant my curiosity awoke. I began to wonder where Grandfather went each night. What was so appealing about that winding river trail? Then the notion hit me; no one said that *I* couldn't tag along. So with a giggle, I took off down the path and into the trees.

By this time the sun was sinking behind the far hills and a hint of a breeze began to whisper through the thicket. I remember that the air was so calm I could hear the bleating of the sheep in the nearby village.

And being aware of this silence, I chose my steps carefully, so as not to alert Grampa to my presence.

However, after awhile of playing this quiet game of hide and seek, I, being just a child, began to lose interest. Although I had Grandpa in sight, I shrugged my little shoulders with indifference and impulsively turned back toward home.

As I retraced my steps, I recall thinking that Grampa's nightly walks were nothing more than an old man's way of passing time. Yet just as that thought crossed my mind, the wind began to pick up. In the space of a few seconds the whispering breeze became a tree-wrestling howl.

Freezing in my tracks, my mind began to race. *"A storm! From where? It was so quiet—how!?"* My eyes instinctively darted back and forth, searching through the rustling foliage for shelter. Then I saw it. A great light suddenly illuminated the forest. It seemed to be coming from behind me. Turning toward the sight, I wrapped my arms around the trunk of a nearby tree and yelled into the wind, "Grampaaaa!"

At that very instant everything stopped! And just above the subsiding wind I heard the voices of two men—talking! Releasing my grip on the tree, I slowly inched forward. From the sound of their pleasant chatter, it seemed that the two men were old friends. Then I heard a familiar chuckle. It was Grampa.

Peeking my head through the bushes, I saw the two sitting on a rock in the clearing. It was Grampa all right, but the other man I didn't know. I figured he was a friend from the nearby village. They seemed unaffected by the ebbing storm. Their common interest appeared to be focused on their conversation.

As I listened from the bushes, I found myself captivated by their dialogue. The questions Grandfather asked had nothing to do with our farm, or the village, but rather with greater things; subjects I didn't understand. The stranger's answers were even more confusing. Still, crouched in the bushes I listened, not knowing that the fascinating words spoken would be the last I would ever hear from my Grandfather.

". . . As always, I have enjoyed our time together, sir, but I must be getting back. It is late and the walk back home seems to get longer each time we visit." Using his cane to pull himself to his feet, Grampa let out

a weary sigh. *"I must say that your words continue to intrigue me. They make me burn with anticipation. It's as if, somehow, I know something wonderful is about to happen; but just what, I am not sure. I don't fully understand it all. Still, I wish to know more—much more."*

The stranger gazed up at Grampa as if pondering a decision. Then slapping his knee with resolve, he likewise stood to his feet. "My friend, you understand far more than you realize. You're closer to my house now than you are to yours. If you want to know more," he said, holding out his open palm, "come home with me." And with that invitation, I saw Grandpa's eyes light up with wonder. And with a boyish smile that I'll always remember, Grandfather leaned on his cane and took the stranger's extended hand.

Again, unexpectedly, the quiet evening turned into a sudden storm. And just as before, a great light filled the forest. Then, in an instant, all was quiet.

Stepping through the bushes and out into the clearing, I realized I was alone. Grampa was nowhere in sight. The evidence of all that I had witnessed had been swept away by the wind. Not knowing what else to do, I ran and ran until I reached the front porch of home. As I pushed open the door, I half expected to see Grampa sitting by the fireplace with Papa and Mama, as they always did this time of night—but only Papa was there.

"Where have you been? Isn't it enough that I have to worry about your grandfather?" Slowly closing the door behind me, I timidly asked, "Isn't Grampa here?" Papa's answer made my thumping heart beat even faster.

"No, he hasn't returned. He's never been away this late."

Slumping into Grandfather's chair, I sat silent and warmed myself by the fire. Finally, after debating in my head what I should do, I hesitantly began to recount for Papa everything I had seen and heard. He didn't believe me. He refused to listen. Papa sent me to my bed and told me to never speak of it again . . .

But that was many years ago, and I am no longer a child. Now the responsibilities of the family and the farm are on *my* shoulders. It is a heavy burden and I must contend with it daily. Yet when the weight of those hardships attempt to bend me into the shape of our old swayed-back mare, the memory of Grampa's path fills my thoughts.

"*. . . You are closer to my house now than you are to yours. Come home with me . . .*" The Stranger's words have never left me. Their meaning quiets the fear that often wakes me in the dark of night. And each morning as I rise to face another uncertain day, those reassuring words serve to bolster my resolve.

Eavesdropping on Grandfather's walk taught me an unforgettable lesson; I don't have to face my journey alone. If I am willing, God's Light can shine on my path, too. If I will take the time to listen to His words, He will meet me along the way and extend His helping hand.

There are indeed some folk, like Papa, who try to rationalize away the experience. I, too, once thought that Grampa's walks were just an old man's way of passing time. But then I saw the night turn to Light. I saw for myself the reward of grandfather's daily devotion. And by his example I have learned the value of setting aside a portion of the day to find my own path, and get a little closer to God's house.

I have passed on this important lesson to my son; who, like his great-grandfather, has begun taking that long walk down to the river and back. He says that, lately, he's felt the need to "*. . . know more, much more.*" He wishes the path didn't stop at the river. He wants to go farther. He reminds me of Grampa. I see the same zeal in his eyes.

Like that persevering old man, my boy's determination is as predictable as a sunset. And given that inbred tenacity I doubt even the boundary of the river will hold him back for long. In fact just today, as I watched his lanky frame fade into the distant trees, I saw Papa's woodsaw resting on his shoulder. Calling out to him I asked, "What do you plan to do with that, son?" He pointed off toward the river and called back, "I'm building a boat."

Every child of God feels the need to get closer to the Father now and again. It appears that my boy is no exception. Like Grampa, Noah's found a path of his own.

"*And Enoch walked with God: and he was not; for God took him.*"
Genesis 5:24 KJV

Weed the Path

Enoch's walk with God was so genuine and personal that it naturally brought both participants closer together. That day-to-day relationship between the Creator and His creation must have resembled, in some small way, the union originally envisioned for mankind in Eden's garden. The result of that model friendship was Enoch's divine invitation to bypass the portal of death, and physically enter the gates of heaven.

The Creator's rapport with this man was not preferential treatment. God is no respecter of persons. The Father cares for each of His children with the same loving attention He demonstrated to Enoch, his grandson Lamech, and great-grandson Noah. What made this particular fellow stand out in that Old Testament crowd was his unique willingness to display his mortal, yet mutual affection. Enoch noticeably went out of his way to make time for The One who created time. And because he did so, the Creator likewise went out of His way for Enoch.

This rare relationship is a prime example of why God created man. Yet it must be noted that His affection toward you, personally, is not measured by *His* desire for fellowship, but rather by the degree of *your expressed* yearning for Him. If you want a relationship with the Creator of all things, all you need to do is *actively display* your intent. You are made in His image. You share like feelings. You possess the same similar brand of emotions. Given such comparisons, isn't it logical that, just like you, God would choose to reveal Himself to those who show a genuine interest in Him?

But how does one actually go about getting close to God?

The answer can be found in an old adage, which Enoch obviously followed: *"The path between friends should never sprout weeds."* The implication is clear; the best way to maintain a road or a relationship is to keep it active, current, constantly in use. Likewise, when it comes to maintaining a close walk with God, you must not only establish a personal path to Him, you must also make such frequent use of your trail that no weed of interference would ever dare to sprout—for fear of being trampled underfoot.

Weeding your personal path is an important daily endeavor. And helping you reach that goal is the purpose of this devotional. Thought provoking and convenient, this commentary has been compiled to encourage your ongoing steps toward *A Deeper Walk* with God. Assembled from the published works of today's most prolific Christian authors, this inspiring collection offers you the same rare opportunity that is illustrated in the preceding story; the ability, like Enoch's curious grandson, to eavesdrop on spiritual insights that can only come from a genuine one-on-one relationship with God.

Through the study of this volume you, like young Lamech, will be able to "listen in" on the inspiring lessons realized by those who've traveled the path before you. The spiritual truths and illumination gained from these special devotionals will help you to maintain a deeper walk in the night; when life's darkest fears most often call. And if you are in need of direction to face another uncertain day, you will encounter in these pages enough words of hope and assurance to secure a deeper walk . . . in the light.

To accomplish this, all you need to do is actively display your desire to have communion with God. Don't allow weeds, rivers, or any of life's excuses to block your way. If you will set aside time for Him, He will do the same for you. God created time so that both of you might enjoy frequent walks together, in the cool of the day.

Place this volume nearby to assist in the maintenance of your personal, all-important path. Endeavor to keep that path weeded and your heart willing; doing so you'll soon find yourself wanting to know more, "*much more.*" And when you take that illuminating step of spiritual discovery you'll already be closer to His house than you are to yours.

A
Deeper
Walk

. . . in the
Night

"But then I saw the night turn to Light!"
Everyone knows that a day begins at sunrise; at least, that's the consensus of our modern world. However, in the first book of the Bible, that common notion is understood in an entirely different light. Upon a deeper walk through the Genesis account of creation, it's plain to see that "a day" does not actually start with the first rays of the eastern sun. As it was in the beginning, the miracle of a new day dawns in the dark.

> *And God said, "Let there be light"* . . . *And God called the light Day and the darkness he called Night. And the **evening** [1] and the **morning** [2] were the first day* (Gen. 1:3–5ᴋᴊᴠ).

On that first morning, the Creator gave us an example of how He works behind the scenes. He showed us that even when things seem to be the darkest and it appears that nothing can be done, He is able to speak a miracle into motion. To God, the dark void of impossibility is merely the fertile ground from which He creates wonders.

The miracle of Lazarus did not begin until his lifeless body had been placed in a dark, dank tomb. For all practical purposes it was "the end." Then, the Light of the world came walking up the path, and with His arrival things took a sudden turn for the better. Instantaneously, death was replaced with resurrection. And Lazarus' darkest moment became the start of a whole new life.

When the fears of the night have you questioning the uncertainty of tomorrow, take a walk with the One who created the light. And as sure as the sun rises in the east, your darkest moments will be just the beginning of a brand new day.

—Barton Green

If There Is Darkness . . .

And God saw the light, that it was good; and God divided the light from the darkness.
————————————**GENESIS 1:4** NKJV

*D*o you know what darkness is? It is the absence of light. Profound, eh? If you're sitting in a lighted room at night and open the door, does darkness flood the room? No. Darkness cannot chase away the light. Darkness can only enter the room when the light has been removed. The night does not force the day to leave; the day leaves and night follows.

If there is darkness, it is because God, for reasons known only to Him, has withdrawn the light. Making our own light frustrates the purpose of God.

There are some things you can see only in the dark. When you live in a big city as I do, it's hard to see the stars at night. One of the things I enjoyed most about the nights we used to spend on our farm in the country was how brightly the stars shone in the sky. Somewhere I read these words of Annie Dillard: "You do not have to sit outside in the dark. If, however, you want to look at the stars, you will find that darkness is required. The stars neither require it nor demand it."

Isaiah says that the one walking in darkness is to "rely on his God." The King James reads, "stay upon his God." The Hebrew word *rely* or *stay upon* means to "lean for support." In Psalm 23, the root of that word is translated "staff": "Thy rod and Thy staff comfort me." "Support me" is the meaning of the word *comfort*. It reminds me of the words of Proverbs, "Trust in the Lord with all your heart and *lean not on your own understanding*."

THOUGHT FOR THE DAY ——————————————
When God withdraws the light, He is trying to teach us that there is something better than light: faith.

Step By Step

Enoch walked with God three hundred years after he became the father of Methuselah, and he had other sons and daughters.
————————————————————————GENESIS 5:22 NASB

*S*omething happened to Enoch after he became a father. His walk with God became noticeably different. He allowed life's changes to produce in him dramatic spiritual growth.

As I watched my daughter learn to walk, I began to understand more fully what it means to walk with God. At first each step was almost a fall, until her strength improved and she learned to trust.

If we let them, life's changes can teach us about God's strength and faithfulness. Take your eyes off your changing circumstances and put them on the unchanging God. This alone will allow you to experience His strength and faithfulness.

THOUGHT FOR THE DAY ————————————————
Look to God. Watch your Heavenly Father and trust in His strength to guide you.

Jesus: Judge & Savior

"Go and sin no more."
——JOHN 8:11 NKJV

The story of the woman taken in adultery is unique in the New Testament. Some translations place a line before and after the passage to set it apart from the rest of the text. Others will footnote it with the statement: "The most reliable texts do not contain John 7:53—8:11."

I remember the first time I was made aware of the problem with the text in one of my Bible classes at the university. As the professor commented on the textual problems I could feel my face getting hot. I wondered if this was the time for me to stand up and fight for the authority of the Bible. I lacked the courage to speak up and challenge him, but I did research the passage later on my own. I discovered that what he said was right. The passage doesn't appear in the oldest and most reliable Greek texts. When it does appear in the later ones, it is found in different places. In one ancient text it even appears in Luke! For this reason scholars refer to it as a "textual floater." The textual commentary that accompanies the United Bible Societies' Greek New

Testament lists pages of problems with the textual authenticity of the passage, but low and behold, they include the passage in their Greek text of John, although at the end of the Gospel.

No one knows for sure just why this particular passage floats around and sometimes disappears the way it does. The explanation that makes the most sense to me proposes that the original manuscript of John did indeed contain the story of the woman caught in adultery. As time went on, however, the disturbing story of Jesus forgiving the adulteress, without belaboring her sin, without really even condemning her, became more and more of an embarrassment to the church, so the scribes began to simply leave it out. Adultery was a big problem in the early church, as it is today.

Despite its textual problems and the fact that it seems to disrupt the chronology of chapter 8, the passage is its own best witness for its authenticity. Few believers, even the most scholarly, are able to say it does not represent a true occurrence from the life of Jesus. Standing on its own, the way it does, the story of the adulterous woman has always spoken to me in an extraordinarily powerful way. The many details John provides make it easy to imagine the setting and the story. . . .

It was just after dawn. A large crowd had gathered around Jesus in the temple court. Just as He was sitting down to teach, the Pharisees brought in a woman. It was a trap, a "set up," both for the woman and Jesus. Perhaps that's why, from the start, He seems to be on her side.

There is little doubt that she was guilty. The law required witnesses. That's why the Pharisees kept insisting she was caught "in the act." "Now, what do you say?" they asked Jesus. The trap was set and the woman was the bait.

You have to give the Pharisees credit. They knew how to construct a trap. Whichever way Jesus answered, He would be in real trouble. If He said, "Let her go," then He would not be upholding the law, which prescribed death for adultery. If He said, "Put her to death," He would be in trouble with the Romans, who ruled the Jews and had taken the power of capital punishment away from them.

Jesus seemed calm. Having stood up He now bent back down again and began to write with His finger in the dust. The word that's used to describe His action literally means "to write down," so it's safe to say He wasn't doodling but actually writing something. Some speculate He was writing the names of people in the crowd who were also guilty of the same sin. Some think, because of a variant text, that He was making a list of their sins. We cannot tell from the text exactly what He was writing. Because of a passage in Jeremiah (17:13), I believe it was a list of names.

The Pharisees kept pushing Jesus for an answer. He stood up and calmly said, "If any one of you is without sin, let him be the first to throw a stone at her!" He then resumed His position on the ground and began again to write in the dust.

The power of conviction caused everyone to leave, the older ones first, until only Jesus and the woman were left, alone in the court-yard. The dialogue that followed contained an almost medieval simplicity.

Jesus stood up and asked a gentle question. "Woman, where are they? Has no one condemned you?"

"No one, sir," she said.

"Then neither do I condemn you. Go now and leave your life of sin."

Yes, it is a disturbing story. No lecture. No condemnation. Only a word of kindness and a simple command to stop. If we didn't know better (because of Jesus' other words on the subject), we might think that He was indeed being "soft" on adultery. But we do know better. As Malcolm Muggeridge said, Jesus would not condemn the woman because He would be condemned for her. It is impossible for us to imagine the relief of the woman, having just been snatched from death. Most of us will not know such a sense of relief until we stand before our Judge on the last day and realize that He is also our Savior.

But what about the other person who sinned with the woman? Someone will always bring up the subject of the man who had committed adultery with her. Was he one of the Pharisees? Is that why he was allowed to escape? After all, that particular sin requires two people.

There is a good reason for his not appearing. He is you and me!

We are, every one of us, as guilty as the man who got away. We think we have escaped, when, in fact, we are as good as dead unless we find our own way to that One, sitting alone in the temple court, with stones scattered at His feet, writing thoughtfully with His finger in the sand.

Burnout

*"Behold what manner of love the Father has bestowed on us,
that we should be called children of God!"*

—1 John 3:1 NKJV

Through the years, I occasionally said to Annie, "I sure would hate to die. It's not that I'm afraid to die. I'm just not ready."

One day I added, "There has to be more than I know. I have missed something. There's something I don't have this freedom in my heart. I know it's Your truth, but I don't know that I've missed, and I've got to find out what it is." At other times I said to her, "There's something between God and me, and I just can't identify what it is. But I know there's something between us."

The ache was especially evident after I preached a series from the Bible titled "The Truth Can Set You Free." Each week of the series, people throughout the church would come up to me and say, "Pastor, these messages have really set me free."

I'd go home, however, look heavenward on Sunday afternoon, and say, "But, God, what about me? I'm the one preaching the sermon, and I don't have this freedom in my heart. I know it's Your truth, but I don't know it as a full reality in my life."

The inner pain finally grew unbearable.

God in His mercy led me to call four friends—all of whom are very wise men, and all of whom are younger than I.

I knew without a doubt that the four men I was calling were men of the highest integrity. They would hear me out with empathy and trust God to help them to help me.

I asked the four men if they would meet me somewhere and just let me talk to them because I was at the end of myself. I didn't know what to do, I didn't know where to go, and I didn't know to whom I could talk.

The four men willingly agreed to meet with me, and we made arrangements to fly to a specific location two days later. When we had gathered together, I asked them if they would let me share with them my life. I told them that anything they advised me to do, I would do. I had that much respect for them. I conveyed to them how desperate I was. They knew I was extremely serious about receiving their counsel.

I talked with them all afternoon and all evening. I woke up several times in the middle of the night and wrote seventeen pages in longhand —legal-sized pages—of things I wanted to be sure to tell them the next morning. I told them everything I remembered about my early life and all the highlights—both painful and positive—of my adult life and ministry. I started with my first memory in life and brought it up to the very moment. When I was finished, I said, "Now, whatever you tell me to do, I'll do it."

They asked me two or three questions, and then one of the men who was sitting directly across the table from me said, "Charles, put your head on the table and close your eyes." I did. He said to me very kindly, "Charles, I want you to envision your father picking you up in his arms and holding you. What do you feel?"

I burst out crying. And I cried and I cried and I cried and I cried. I could not stop crying. Finally, when I stopped, he asked me again, "What do you feel?" I said, "I feel warm, loved, secure. I feel good." And I started weeping again.

For the first time in my life, I felt emotionally that God loved me. That may come as a shock to you. It shocked me, too. I had known God loved me as a fact of His Word. I had believed God loved me, accepting that as the nature of God. But I had never emotionally felt God loving me.

For decades, I had preached about trusting God, believing God, obeying God. But when I came home and looked through my sermon file, I discovered that I had preached only one sermon on the love of God (and it wasn't worth listening to). I hadn't preached on God's love because I didn't know what it meant to feel the love of God!

God used that encounter with those four men, and that one simple question, to begin to release me from years of excess baggage that I had been hauling around in my life. The full release didn't happen in a day. It was a process, little by little. But the more I explored the love of God, the more God began to reveal my true identity in Christ—that I belonged to Him as I had never belonged to anybody, that I was worth something to Him (and the Cross proved that), and that He loved me beyond measure.

The chasm that had separated me from God wasn't sin. It was a chasm of damaged emotions—emotions so hurt and raw that I had been unable to experience the love of God without the help of others who saw that what I really needed was not to try harder (in fact, not to try to do anything) but, instead, to relax and feel the love of God flowing in my direction.

Do you need help today? I've encountered many good people—including people in the ministry—who have been unable to say, "I really need help and I need it desperately." The first step toward getting the help you need is to admit it to someone. First and foremost, admit it to God. Let Him know that you are finally at the end of yourself and your efforts. It's at the point of being at the end of yourself that God can begin to do His work.

I discovered at the end of myself a kind and gracious God who had been loving me unconditionally all my life. There's nothing as liberating as that discovery! And with that discovery came an ability to help liberate others.

THOUGHT FOR THE DAY _____
God loves you just the way you are. Depend on His love to love others.

Peter's Potential

[Peter] denied Him, saying, "Woman, I do not know Him."

LUKE 22:57 NKJV

When Jesus predicted that Peter would deny him, Peter adamantly proclaimed that he would die before he would ever deny Jesus. Peter's good intentions were shattered that very same night when three times he denied being a follower of Jesus.

After he thought through his denial, Peter wept and was overcome with grief. I imagine that at that moment he felt totally hopeless, and he must have despaired that he would never serve God again. In that time of anguish, he could never have believed that God would choose to use him in the future in mighty ways and would inspire him to write parts of the Bible. It was through God's grace that Peter was restored to fellowship.

Remember the painful time when you felt your life was worthless and ruined? Attaining a closer walk with God you will come to understand your past and see that, like Peter, we all have the potential to improve.

THOUGHT FOR THE DAY
Search for God through the night and listen for His gracious call.

Life is built on character, but character is built on decisions. The decisions you make, small and great, do to your life what the sculptor's chisel does to a block of marble. You shape your life by your thoughts, attitudes and actions.

Warren W. Wiersbe
On Being a Servant of God

The Most Unbelievable Bible Verse

And we know that God causes all things to work together for good to those who love God, to those who are called according to His purpose.

——————————————————————————————ROMANS 8:28 NASB

I've been looking for loopholes in this verse.

I've read all the liberal commentaries, compared all the translations, studied the sentence structure and word definitions in the Greek in an effort to find something wrong with it—in short, to prove that it doesn't really say what it seems to say.

When you have experienced a great tragedy you may feel you've paid your dues and that's the end of it. But I found that the dues are never paid—or so it seems. Ronnie's death was only the first of many deaths, not physical deaths like his, of course, but deaths just as real that brought grief just as painful.

The writer of this verse, the apostle Paul, seems to be saying that if we love God and are called according to His purpose, that *all things,* not some things or even most things, but all things are working together for our good. "We know," Paul says, and he uses the word for certainty. This isn't guesswork. We know with absolute certainty that this is so.

Paul is not saying that whatever happens to a Christian is good. A lot of bad things happen to us. We cannot say that what happens is best. But it will be worked out for our good, the best. The bad things that happen to us have no weight in thwarting the good God intends for us.

If this is true it means that my complaints against life and God, no matter how understandable, are not legitimate.

If this is true it means that I have no right to cling to anger or to harbor bitterness against whatever injustices I may have suffered.

If this is true it means that if God subtracted one pain, one heartache, one disappointment from my life, I would be less than the person I am now, less than the person God wants me to be and my ministry would be less than He intends.

If this is true it means that I can climb over those hurts and disappoints, over the tears and heartaches, over the graves and sleepless nights, and stand on top of that ash-heap and declare, "All these things God is working together for my good."

As I write I am surrounded by stacks of commentaries on the book of Romans, the latest and the greatest; by piles of papers and notes I have searched through a hundred times; and I must tell you, *I have found no loophole.*

THOUGHT FOR THE DAY _____

God's power and authority are such that even the actions of the enemies of God and His people must subserve His will.

In the Night Turn On the Light

Fear not, for I am with you;
Be not dismayed, for I am your God.
I will strengthen you,
Yes, I will help you,
I will uphold you with My righteous right hand.
———————————————ISAIAH 41:10 NKJV

My life seemed to be an unending series of unknowns. All that had been familiar to me—my home, my family, my lifestyle, and my job—was becoming unfamiliar as the result of my sense of helplessness.

Nighttime was especially scary to me. In the dark quietness of my bedroom, I played all the unknowns in my mind over and over again. I dwelt on all that was ahead of me, and I knew I couldn't face it all.

One night, in the midst of my fear, I turned on the light and opened my Bible. In those pages, the Lord assured me that He knew what lay ahead. He would walk with me toward my future. He gently reminded me that I was not alone in the dark after all.

THOUGHT FOR THE DAY _____
Though I walk through the Valley of the Shadow of Death, I am thankful because You are with me.

This Is Not a Drill

"Whatsoever thy hand findeth to do, do it with thy might;
for there is no work, nor device, nor knowledge, nor wisdom,
in the grave, whither thou goest."

ECCLESIASTES 9:10 KJV

For a long time I had a distorted view of life. I would look at my life and think, *There are some good things going on, but there are also a lot of bad things. There's some good stuff coming down the pike, but there's some bad stuff too. And I know that's not how it's supposed to be. I'll just pull over here on the side and wait it out. And one of these days I'll get it all together and then there will be nothing but good things happening—which is the way life is supposed to be lived.* Right?

Don't tell me at times you haven't tried to put off your life. Put it on hold. Till you finish school. Till the kids are grown. Till you complete your apprenticeship and land the big job.

Most of us live our lives as though we were rehearsing for the real thing. But life is *not* a drill. As someone once put it, "Life is what happens while you are waiting for life to start."

We idealize life, reasoning that if God is really working in our lives, there will be nothing but good coming down. But as Lewis Smedes says, "We are always grateful for one thing in spite of something else.

Every silver lining must have a cloud." If we fail to understand this we will only curse the bad and deprecate the good.

THOUGHT FOR THE DAY _____

Begin with today by opening your eyes to see God at work.

*This is your life. You have the
starring role. It's either an Oscar or
obscurity. The choice is yours.*

Dr. Chris Thurman
*The 12 Best Kept Secrets for Living
an Emotionally Healthy Life*

With God, Losses Are Gains

Then Job answered the LORD, *and said,*
"I know that thou canst do every thing."
—————————————JOB 42:1-2 KJV

$\mathscr{I}$ love the words, "The Lord blessed the latter part of Job's life more than the first." I believe that is what God wants to do for all of us. He always saves the best wine until last.

God rewarded Job with twice as much as he had before his trial: Job ended with fourteen thousand sheep. *(He started with seven thousand.)* He accumulated six thousand camels. *(He started with three thousand.)* He eventually possessed a thousand yoke of oxen. *(He began with five hundred.)* And he concluded his life with seven sons and three daughters. Wait a second! Job started out with ten children, now he ought to have twenty!

Wait, I get it! He *did* have twenty children. Ten down here and ten in heaven. Because you never lose someone who has gone to heaven.

Dr. Vance Havner was a traveling preacher for forty years. He didn't marry until he was forty: He said he wanted to think about it first. He never learned to drive a car. But his wife, Sara, drove them to his meetings in the Buick when they didn't fly or ride the train. The two of them were inseparable until 1973 when Sara died.

After Sara's death, someone would occasionally say to Dr. Havner, "I hear you lost your wife."

"No," Dr. Havner would answer, "I didn't lose her. I know right where she is. You haven't lost someone if you know where they are." And then he would quote this poem:

> "Death can hide but not divide;
> She is but on Christ's other side.
> Christ with her and Christ with me,
> United still in Christ are we."

THOUGHT FOR THE DAY _____
Nothing you put into God's hand is ever lost.

What Should Have Happened Did

*For my part, whatever anguish of spirit it may cost, I am
willing to know the whole truth; to know the worst, and
to provide for it.*

—PATRICK HENRY

*L*isten to people talk and you will often hear them use the word
should or some variation of it:

"I shouldn't have said that."
"Jeff should have been on time."
"My parents shouldn't have treated me that way when I was
younger."
"Ann should have let me know about that yesterday."
"Things should be different from the way they are."

Whenever I hear (or use) the word *should,* a red flag goes up in my
mind that warns me that reality just got stiff-armed. What do I mean?
Well, think about it for a minute. *Should* is most often used in reference
to some sort of ideal setting in a perfect world.

Using *should* is our way of saying we don't like the reality we face.
To say, "He shouldn't have been so late" actually means, "I can't

accept the fact that he was so late." It means that we have a vision of some perfect world in which people are never late and we can't stand it when someone violates that world. Using the word *should* represents an unwillingness on our part to deal with reality as it is.

The reality is that if someone isn't being careful about the time, how could he be anything but late? Can a person who doesn't manage his time well and waits too long before leaving get somewhere on time? In a word, no. What I'm suggesting here is that it really doesn't make sense to say something like, "He shouldn't have been late," when everything the person did worked toward making sure he would be late.

One person who seemed to understand the real meaning of the word *should* was the late University of Alabama head football coach Paul "Bear" Bryant. The Crimson Tide football team was heavily favored to win a game against an inferior opponent. Instead, Alabama lost. During the postgame interview, Coach Bryant was asked, "How do you feel about losing a game you *should* have won?" His reported reply was, "What should have happened did."

What Coach Bryant was saying was, "Look, guys, throw out all of that 'the better team always wins' stuff. We fumbled the ball, threw interceptions, and missed a lot of blocks. The other team didn't. Given that we played badly and they played well, the game turned out just as it *should* have."

Coach Bryant had a pretty good understanding of reality and a willingness to deal with it rather than avoid it.

THOUGHT FOR THE DAY _____
When the truth of a situation is accepted and dealt with, your next step along the path will be placed with a more confident foot.

Remember to Forget

Therefore if any man be in Christ, he is a new creature: old things are passed away; behold, all things are become new.

─────────────────────2 CORINTHIANS 5:17 KJV

If you decide to have an enemy, choose a good one because enemies are very expensive luxuries. Some anonymous wit has put it this way: "If you're nursing a grudge, expect to pay some big doctor bills." Alas, most of the price is paid on the installment plan as little by little your grudge robs you of peace and power and makes you miserable.

You can't always help *having* an enemy, but you can help *being* an enemy. Each time I read Psalm 18, I'm impressed with the way the inscription separates Saul from David's enemies. Saul considered David an enemy, but David didn't consider Saul an enemy. David couldn't stop Saul from the foolish things he did, but he could control his response to them. *If you have an enemy eating away at your heart, it's probably because you choose to have that enemy there.* You aren't responsible for the way others treat you, but you are responsible for the way you respond. Whatever ego satisfaction you get from your secret meditations about your enemy just isn't worth the wear and tear on the inner person.

I've found that my first response has to be that of prayer. Maybe the people who declared war on me don't need my prayers, *but I need to pray for them.* Jesus instructed us to love our enemies, bless them, do good to them, and pray for them (Matt. 5:44). That is a surefire remedy for protecting a heart that's in danger of being poisoned by a grudge.

First, pray for yourself that you don't become bitter and start seeking revenge. Once you get over that hurdle the rest is easy. Second, pray fervently for your enemies.

Ask God to bless them with insight into His Word, that they'll see their own need and turn to Him for help. Furthermore, ask God for opportunities to do or say something good on your enemies' behalf. Say something good, or say nothing at all: *"For a bird of the air may carry your voice, and a bird in flight may tell the matter"* (Eccles. 10:20).

You must keep in mind *why* the devil wants you to have enemies: If you respond to your enemy in the wrong way, the devil gains a foothold in your life. Paul's warning about giving place to the devil (Eph. 4:27) is surrounded by additional warnings about the sins that help Satan establish a beachhead: lying, unrighteous anger, corrupt speech, malice, an unforgiving spirit, to name but a few. As long as your enemies are on the outside, you're safe; but when you let them get on the inside, you're in for trouble.

If the devil sees that your enemy isn't making headway in your heart, he'll usually do one of two things: either call the whole thing off, in which case you and your enemy can be happily reconciled, or increase the pressure and try to bring you to a breaking point. If that happens, remind yourself that your battle is not with flesh and blood (your enemy) but with the invisible satanic hosts that use flesh and blood to accomplish their purposes (Eph. 6:12). Be sure you put on the whole armor of God by faith every day and use the equipment God has provided for you.

The right kind of praying ought to lead to our forgiving our enemies from the heart, even if we can't yet forgive them in person, and asking God to defuse the painful memories that could explode within and do a lot of damage. This point reminds me of a story about the late

Dr. William Sangster, one of England's most effective Methodist preachers.

He was addressing Christmas cards, and a house guest was shocked to see an envelope addressed to a man who had brutally attacked Sangster eighteen months before.

"Surely you are not sending a greeting to *him*," the man said.

"Why not?" asked Sangster.

"But you remember," the guest began, "eighteen months ago . . ."

Sangster recalled the thing the man had done to him, but he also recalled that at the time, he had resolved to put it out of his mind. "It was a thing I would remember to forget," he said; and he did.

When Christians forget something, that doesn't mean they simply put it out of mind because sometimes that's difficult to do. The biblical meaning of *forget* (as in Heb. 10:17) is "not to hold it against the person and let it affect your relationship." Because He is omniscient, God can't forget anything; but

THOUGHT FOR THE DAY ⸻⸻⸻⸻⸻⸻⸻
He chooses not to hold our sins against us. He remembers to forget.

RONALD DUNN
When Heaven Is Silent

Judgement Beyond Our Judgement

"Let both grow together until the harvest."
——————————MATTHEW 13:30 NKJV

$\mathscr{T}$he mystery of good and evil is the mixture of good and evil. That's the point of Christ's parable of the tares:

> "The kingdom of heaven is likened unto a man which sowed good seed in his field: But while men slept, his enemy came and sowed tares among the wheat, and went his way. But when the blade was sprung up, and brought forth fruit, then appeared the tares also. So the servants of the householder came and said unto him, 'Sir, didst not thou sow good seed in thy field? from whence then hath it tares?'
>
> "He said unto them, 'An enemy hath done this.' The servants said unto him, 'Wilt thou then that we go and gather them up?' But he said, 'Nay; lest while ye gather up the tares, ye root up also the wheat with them. Let both grow together until the harvest: and in the time of harvest I will say to the reapers, "Gather ye together first the tares, and bind them in bundles to burn them: but gather the wheat into my barn"'" (Matthew 13:24–30 KJV).

"Let them grow together," Jesus says. During the night an enemy sowed tares among the wheat. *Among the wheat* is a strong Greek expression meaning, "all through the midst of the wheat, between and on top of." The roots had become so inextricably intertwined that any attempt to pull them out would have torn out the wheat also. You can't root out the bad without rooting out the good. Wait till harvest when they will all be rooted out, then separate the good from the bad.

The tares do not worry the Master. He will take care of them in due time. Make no mistake about it, God's control is never usurped. He is in sovereign control. It is *His* field, and He will tend it properly. It seems that the only reason Jesus gives for not weeding out the tares (*evil*) is the harm it would do to the wheat (*good*). We are simply not always able to discern the good from the bad. Judgement in these matters must be left to the end of the day, and committed to the hands of God.

THOUGHT FOR THE DAY _____
We can be thankful judgement is left to God, who knows good from evil.

Avoid the Jerks!

*"You also must beware of him, for he has greatly resisted
our words."*

───────────────────────── 2 TIMOTHY 4:15 NKJV

If you have been or are being victimized by jerks, take a tip from
the apostle Paul. He dealt with jerk abuse in writing to his pastor friend
Timothy. As he wound up his second letter to Timothy, Paul mentioned several people, some of whom had forsaken him, and some of
whom had stuck with him. And then he went on to say: "Alexander the
coppersmith did me much harm. May the Lord repay him according to
his works. You also must beware of him, for he has greatly resisted our
words."

Taking the very same advice that he gave to the Roman Christians,
Paul had left vengeance on Alexander to God; the Lord could repay
Alexander according to his works. Who knows? Alexander may have
repented and asked forgiveness. On the other hand, if he went unrepentant and an enemy of Jesus and the gospel, he would eventually
face the vengeance that belongs only to God, who deals with every one
of us in perfect fairness.

I believe Paul forgave Alexander, but he also learned from his experience. He had set some boundaries about dealing with Alexander, and what he was simply telling Timothy was, "Watch out for this guy. You are to love him, but don't trust him." In other words, beware of jerks who can do you harm.

In Paul's comments we can see all three steps in dealing with anger. First, Paul analyzed his anger, and it's fairly obvious that one of his legitimate rights had been violated—he had the right to preach the gospel, and Alexander was opposing his work in very jerky ways.

Second, Paul verbalized his anger by telling Timothy that Alexander had done him harm and that Timothy would be wise to beware of any dealings with this man.

Third, Paul neutralized his anger by turning vengeance on Alexander over to God. Paul forgave, but he also faced facts. To that point, at least, Alexander was an unrepentant jerk and needed to be dealt with cautiously.

This is a key lesson for anybody with masochistic tendencies to learn. Forgiving a jerk who abuses you doesn't mean that you have to cozy up to that jerk and become fast friends. In fact, in most cases, you will need to keep away from jerks who abuse you. Avoid them, if possible.

THOUGHT FOR THE DAY _____
As Paul put it, "Beware."

Be "Respondible"

And when he saw him, he had compassion.
————————————LUKE 10:33 NKJV

*W*e should all be "respondible" to others. No, that is not a mis-spelled word. Responsible is another trait. We need to think about "respondibility." The Good Samaritan showed "respondibility." When he saw someone in need, he stopped and helped. It is important that we respond to others and do so positively. We need to share with them the power that is great enough to free us from our self-will, the power that can help us see our strengths and weaknesses, the power that can forgive and lead us to forgiveness of ourself and others.

God responds to us and empowers us to respond to others. That is what "respondibility" is. It means looking around us and being aware of who has fallen and needs a steadying hand. As the miracle of the program works in us, we are compelled to respond by sharing this miracle of healing with others. As Good Samaritans we need to stop, look around, and extend our hand of love and kindness to those in need.

THOUGHT FOR THE DAY ————————————
Watch for those who need God's love communicated through you.

Jacob's Lesson

"I will not let thee go, except thou bless me."
——————————————GENESIS 32:26 KJV

God had Jacob right where He wanted him. He was alone; there was no one to rescue him. He was in the grasp of an unknown assailant. There was no escape.

Often we wrestle against the very things God sends to bless us. Like Jacob, we often try to throw away our blessings. But sometimes, like Jacob, we see junk turn into antiques right before our eyes, even as we struggle against it.

Jacob was fighting for his life, struggling to break the hold of his enemy, when suddenly everything changed. The attacker was now trying to get loose and Jacob was grasping. "I will not let You go unless You bless me," Jacob said. Jacob realized that he was not wrestling with a curse, as he first thought, but with a blessing.

This is one of the most remarkable things about the whole adventure: What Jacob at first sought to escape, he finally embraced. He began to cling to the thing he tried to throw down. This is how God transforms.

THOUGHT FOR THE DAY ———————————————

Stop. Think for a moment: The very thing you're wrestling against, may be the thing God wants to use to bless you.

Solitary Refinement

Jesus . . . spoke to them, saying, "All authority has been given to Me in heaven and on earth. . . . and lo, I am with you always, even to the end of the age."

————————————————————MATTHEW 28:18–20 NKJV

*W*ere there times when you felt lonely as a child? Maybe your best friend was out of town and you didn't have anyone to play with. Perhaps your parents went out and you were alone in the house. When I was a child and was disciplined for something I did wrong, I was sent to my room "to think about" what I had done. I felt alone and rejected. All I could think about was myself and how I was feeling, not about what I had done.

Now that I am an adult I find that there are still times when I need to go to my room and think about what I have done. Maybe I hurt someone's feelings by being unkind or impatient. Maybe I told a lie. Maybe I rejected God's love for me by putting myself down. Whatever the reason, I still find myself going to my room to think about my actions.

As a child I felt alone there. But now when I contemplate God's love for solitary me, loneliness is the farthest thing from my mind.

THOUGHT FOR THE DAY ————————————————
Lord, pull me out of the loneliness and into Your refining love.

Faith Determines Life

*. . . the substance of things hoped for,
the evidence of things not seen.*
————————HEBREWS 11:1 NKJV

*A*fter Sunday school one morning, a mother asked her little girl what she had learned. The daughter responded, "I learned how Moses built this pontoon bridge across the Red Sea, and how all these people were transported across with tanks and half-tracks. As soon as they were across, the bridge was blown up just as the Egyptians were coming across and they were all drowned in the Red Sea."

The mother was astonished and asked if that's what the teacher had told her. "Oh no," the little girl replied, "but you would never believe what she really said."

That little girl is like a lot of people. They think that faith is believing what isn't true. And for others, faith is little more than wishful thinking.

After Jesus claimed to be sent by God, some were seeking to seize Him, having come to the conclusion that He was not a good man. But others did believe in Him, "and they were saying, 'When the Christ shall come, He will not perform more signs than those which this man has, will He?' " (John 7:31 NASB). All the evidence was there. Some chose to believe; others chose not to. People do the same today. Yet to live within the will of God, you have to believe in the Lord Jesus Christ.

Faith is the operating principle of life. It is the means by which we relate to God and carry out His kingdom activity. Just think of the many ways faith must be operative in our lives.

> For by grace you have been saved through faith; and that not of yourselves, it is the gift of God; not as a result of works, that no one should boast (Eph. 2:8, 9 NASB).

We're not only saved by faith, but we also "walk by faith, not by sight" (2 Cor. 5:7 NASB).

Being found faithful is a prerequisite for ministry: "I thank Christ Jesus our Lord, who has strengthened me, because He considered me faithful, putting me into service" (1 Tim. 1:12 NASB). Paul later wrote: "And the things which you have heard from me in the presence of many witnesses, these entrust to faithful men, who will be able to teach others also" (2 Tim. 2:2 NASB). This is more than being reliable, since a person could be counted on to follow through on an assignment and not be a believer. The added ingredient in faithful people is that they know the truth and can be counted on to be reliable.

Really, the quality of any relationship is determined by faith or trust: "Many a man proclaims his own loyalty, but who can find a trustworthy man?" (Prov. 20:6 NASB). The words *faith, trust,* and *believe* are all the same word (*pistis*) in the original language. The man who has faith believes in something. The one who believes also trusts, or he doesn't truly believe. There is no concept that looms larger in life than faith because what we believe determines how we live.

THOUGHT FOR THE DAY _____

Choose to believe the truth and trust in Him who cannot lie.

God's Silent Lessons

"Be doers of the word, and not hearers only."
——————————————JAMES 1:22 NKJV

I've discovered that sometimes when we seek God's will on a particular issue, we experience silence on His part. For example, I got away a few weeks ago for a short retreat to pray and to write. I also wanted to get my spirit in tune for the many matters we were facing in our church. It was really a great time for reflecting and for getting in touch with myself and some of the real issues I was facing.

Although I really needed some direction from the Lord, I didn't seem to get any responses to the issues for which I was seeking answers. I just couldn't come up with any solutions, or even additional steps. The Lord just wasn't answering.

Finally, it dawned on me that the Lord was giving me a firsthand illustration. He was saying: "Doug, don't ask Me for any new guidance when you haven't done what I've already told you to do."

Part of the reason we get confused at times and don't know what to do is that we haven't yet fulfilled what He has already told us to do. God may, in fact, be saying: "Step back about three paces. Do what

I've already asked you to do, then let's talk about the new issue. Do what I've already asked you, and you'll then be in a position to be in My will for the next chapter of your life."

We usually have sufficient insight for the moment. Confusion comes when we don't fulfill what we know we're supposed to do today.

God may not reveal His purpose how or why when we would like it, but when we don't see the end clearly we must move ahead, simply because we feel the Lord leading us.

Everett L. Fullam
How to Walk with God

The Bible Contradicts

*They returned . . . strengthening the souls of the disciples,
exhorting them to continue in the faith, and saying, "We must
through many tribulations enter the kingdom of God."*

——————————————————————ACTS 14:21–22 NKJV

For some reason, we often think that people of real faith do not have problems. Then we make a false inference: Because we have such great problems, we must not have real faith.

But the Bible contradicts such thinking. All of the great characters of the Bible went through terrible times of difficulty and struggle. That is how we know they had real faith. They trusted in God despite the difficulties.

Hardships do not prove God to be false. They only prove that we live in a hard world. Trouble does not prove that God fails to love us. It only proves that we need God's love. Real faith never removes trouble, but draws us close to the One who can carry us through with peace and hope in our hearts.

THOUGHT FOR THE DAY ————————————————
Thank You for teaching me to lean on You, Lord.

No Illusion

"Blessed are they that have not seen, and yet have believed."
—————————————————————————————JOHN 20:29 KJV

A tour of Universal Movie Studios in Burbank, California, provided me with an interesting insight into one of Hollywood's greatest heroes, John Wayne.

The tour guide escorted our group through some of the local sets used for filming many of John Wayne's famous Western movies. As the tram wound its way through several of the ghost lots, it came to a halt in front of a local saloon which had often been used for Wayne's famous struts through the swinging saloon doors.

The tumbleweed props were still strewn about the porch. All of us felt the presence of John Wayne.

Our guide asked if we noticed anything unusual about the saloon storefront. With curiosity aroused, seventy-five pairs of tourist eyes surveyed the set without noting a hint of anything peculiar.

Then the illusion was revealed. The door of the saloon was constructed smaller than the standard eighty inches so that when John Wayne was filmed pushing his way through the squeaking doors, he would appear larger than reality to help enhance his image and character as one of America's giant stars of the screen.

The door's reduced size created an illusion, making John Wayne appear larger than reality. This simple fact burst all of our illusions regarding those whom we make our heroes. We can have no doubts about this fact of faith, however.

When the women stood in front of the tomb on Sunday morning, after Jesus died and was buried, there was no false illusion about the tomb's open door. The triumphant power of God had raised Christ from the dead. The empty tomb, the resurrected Jesus Christ, was no illusion created by biblical writers to give credibility to the character of Jesus.

It was the risen Christ whom Mary encountered in the garden, and who, despite all grave doubts about Easter, stood before her, magnifying God's promise of eternal life. Jesus stood before her as life magnified. Her words dispersed the clouds of doubt and are heralded to this day.

"I have seen the Lord! He is risen!"

She was standing in the presence of life's greatest power for living. Mary was held in the loving embrace of God.

The resurrected Lord was proof enough that He had come that we might have eternal life. If there were grave doubts about it prior to this moment, the resurrection appearance disputed them.

THOUGHT FOR THE DAY _____
Belief in Easter is belief in the abundant power of faith for living. The empty tomb is not a fantasy. Its open passage is our "visual evidence" that the promise of eternal life is no illusion.

The popular view espoused in some high circles is that all religions are basically the same. Don't believe it! That's a lie!

Everett L. Fullam
How to Walk with God

Time Heals

Do not say, "I will recompense evil";
Wait for the LORD, and He will save you.
————————**PROVERBS 20:22** NKJV

*W*hy is waiting so helpful?

Waiting allows us to gain *perspective*. You may have learned as a child to count to ten before retaliating. When someone has wronged us, we instinctively want to lash out, to repay evil. But why has the person done this? Are we at fault in any way?

Sometimes we must wait for *the opportune moment*. God has His plans, and we don't always understand them. God has His hands on the cogs of history, and He will act on our behalf.

And often we must wait for *natural healing* to take place. God has built the grace of healing into our own bodies and souls. The miracle will happen if we wait for it.

THOUGHT FOR THE DAY ————————————
Help us to see the good in waiting, God.

Three Kinds of Temptations, Four Reasons the Devil Wants You to Yield, and One Powerful Reason Why You Shouldn't

"Let us lay aside every weight, and the sin which so easily ensnares us, and let us run with endurance the race that is set before us."

———————————————————————HEBREWS 12:1 NKJV

"But," you say, "you don't know the temptations I face."

Yes, we really do. There are only three basic kinds, and the two of us face them all and so does everyone else.

There are three categories of temptations, and every one that comes up you can recognize and say, "Aha! I'm on to you, too, temptation! And I still say no."

For all that is in the world—the lust of the flesh, the lust of the eyes, and the pride of life—is not of the Father but is of the world (1 John 2:16).

"The lust of the flesh, the lust of the eyes, and the pride of life"—every temptation you'll ever have crops up in one or several of these three forms.

There was Eve, looking at the fruit of that tree in the Garden:

> When the woman saw that the fruit of the tree was good for food [the lust of the flesh] and pleasing to the eye [the lust of the eyes], and also desirable for gaining wisdom [the pride of life], she took some and ate it (Gen. 3:6 NIV).

To her it was a triple whammy, and she succumbed.

To be tempted is not wrong. Don't feel guilty when you're tempted! Eve did not sin until she yielded. Someone has said, "You can't stop a bird from landing on your head, but you can keep him from building a nest in your hair."

The Lord Jesus was "tempted in every way, just as we are—yet was without sin" (Heb. 4:15 NIV). We can say that Jesus lived *through* life. Most of us live a portion of life, but Jesus experienced it *all* for us. Luke says He "finished every temptation" (Luke 4:13 NASB).

Three punishing attacks of Satan upon Jesus are displayed for us to see. They summarize temptations we all face:

1. *"Tell these stones to become bread"* (Matt. 4:3 NIV). In Jesus' time of greatest hunger, Satan appealed to the lust of the flesh.

The Lord was soon to feed others miraculously; it wasn't that He couldn't follow Satan's suggestion. The temptation here was not to wait for God the Father to provide His food, but to act independently of the Father when He was hungry and to provide for Himself.

You will be tempted to fulfill your desires on your terms: "I want what I want when I want it!" You can ask for the right thing at the wrong time. (That's certainly true of sex; it's a good gift from God, but at the right God-given time—in the marriage relationship.)

2. *"If you are the Son of God, throw yourself down"* from the highest point of the temple (Matt. 4:6 NIV), appealing to the pride of life. His purpose? To get Jesus to go on an "ego trip." Let Him dive off the high temple and come swooping down like Superman.

But Jesus refused cheap heroics to get attention. He could wait for the glory that God would give, and not seek to drum up His own.

3. *"Bow down and worship me,"* said Satan, taking Jesus to a very high mountain and showing Him all the kingdoms of the world and their splendor, appealing to the lust of the eye. "All this I will give you if you will bow down and worship me" (Matt. 4:8–9 NIV).

And with this enticement the devil promised that he would make Christ a world power without the cross and all that suffering. He passed before Jesus' vision the world and all its glory, beauty, and strength— all its art, thought, and work. "Worship me, and all you see will be yours," said Satan.

But Jesus wasn't after earthly kingdoms; He was after *the* Kingdom. There could never be His ultimate crown without the cross. He kept His eye on the future! He knew what you and we must always remember: The temporary is no substitute for the eternal. And so "for the joy that was set before Him," He endured and resisted temptation.

Friend, so can you!

Satan will come after you in the fiercest temptations. He'll attack you in your three areas of weakness:

1. *The lust or the cravings of the flesh:* sexual immorality, overeating, addictive habits, laziness. . . .

2. *The lust or the cravings of your eyes:* excessive desires for beauty of any kind—cars, interior decorating, clothes, other persons of the opposite sex. . . .

3. *The pride of life:* overgrown appetites for money, status, or power, which lead to jealousy, slander, cheating, and "every form of malice" (Eph. 4:31 NIV).

Why won't Satan leave you alone? Because *he hates you for at least four reasons.*

One is that God loves you, and whatever is loved by God is hated by the devil.

Another is that the Christian, being a child of God, bears a family resemblance to the Father and to the household of faith. When Satan sees you, he thinks of Him!

A third reason is that a true Christian is a former slave who has escaped from the galley, and Satan cannot forgive him for this affront.

A fourth reason is this, as A.W. Tozer puts it:

> A praying Christian is a constant threat to the stability of Satan's government. The Christian is a holy rebel loose in the world with access to the throne of God. Satan never knows from what direction the danger will come. Who knows when another Elijah will arise, or another Daniel? or a Luther or a Booth? Who knows when an Edwards or a Finney may go in and liberate a whole town or countryside by the preaching of the Word and prayer? Such a danger is too great to tolerate, so Satan gets to the new convert as early as possible to prevent his becoming too formidable a foe.[1]

There you are: You're a sitting duck for the enemy's attacks.

But we want you to see a powerful reason why you shouldn't yield to him.

Mentally climb that tree again and get another panoramic view—this time not just of your own life but of the lives of generations before you and after you. Think big. Stretch your horizons.

As God looks down on the total human scene, He sees each individual, of course. (Aren't the genealogies in the Bible a comfort for that reason?)

But He does more. He also sees the whole human scene; He sees the connection, the mergings together, the patterns and the oneness of the generations that even from our treetop we can barely envision. Without the limits of time, looking down over all at once, God sees how you belong to your great-grandfather and how you affect your great-grandson and how in every particular detail you are part of the continuum of the human generations.

Who but God could think of this kind of logic?—He says that Melchizedek was even greater than the great high priest Levi, who lived three generations later—as proved by the fact that Levi, in the body of his great-grandfather Abraham, bowed down to Melchizedek and paid him tithes (see Heb.7:9–10)!

[1] "The Editorial Voice," *The Alliance Weekly* magazine, March 6, 1963.

Mysterious! Awesome!

What did *you* do in the body of your great-grandfather? And what are you doing today which is an action of your child, your grandchild, or your great-grandchild?

God gives hints of a commingling together of the behavior of generations which is unthinkable to us little people with limited perception. First Peter 1:12 says that God revealed to the prophets of old that when they wrote, they were not serving themselves but you! Centuries ago they thought about you. They wrote for you.

You and we are holding hands with a great host of unseen persons in unbroken chains.

What happens when you freak out and say, "Oh, heck, I quit"?

When you kick over the traces?

When you flee, when you say, "I've had it," when you give up?

What damage is that doing to the others—the whole chain of your ancestors and your desendants? What kind of permanent wound or scar are you making? What instability are you building into the line? How many will grieve? How many will be hurt?

Maybe at that Great Day we'll see larger reasons to weep over sins than we ever dreamed—or more glorious reasons to rejoice over temptations resisted and victories won!

Ask God for staying power, for determination, for patience, for gutsy courage to survive and survive well.

Everyone faces temptations. How will you handle yours? Will you blame others and crumple, or will you come out a winner?

THOUGHT FOR THE DAY _____
Your fortitude could have larger ramifications than you now know. Begin, persevere, win!

Keep Chasing Your Donkeys

"Seest thou a man diligent in his business?
He shall stand before kings."
————————————PROVERBS 22:29 KJV

*O*ne of the greatest illustrations from Scripture on how guidance has worked for me is found in 1 Samuel 9, where God chose Saul to be king of Israel. The prophet Samuel objected to the whole concept of having a king. In fact, at this point in the story, Samuel was still grumbling in his heart that Israel had not honored him as a prophet. He was also concerned that they would choose a mortal, human king over choosing God as their King.

At the opening of 1 Samuel, we find Saul, the son of Kish, and a servant pursuing several donkeys that had broken away from his father's ranch. The text says that they looked for days, climbing hither and yon through the sagebrush and the sand and, probably, the rolling hills of pasture.

The prophet Samuel started off for a nearby town, under the instructions of the Holy Spirit. Saul and his servant heard that Samuel was in a nearby town. The servant offered this insight: "Perhaps the prophet Samuel will know the whereabouts of the donkeys."

Both the young men scurried into town and found the sage old prophet. Upon setting his eyes on Saul, Samuel immediately knew that this was the young man he was to anoint as king. Now, catch the contrast. Saul thought he was chasing donkeys, but Samuel had been told by the Lord to anoint him king.

I really believe this is how most guidance works. I also believe it is how our lives stay the most stable. If we simply chase the donkeys that we have been assigned to pursue, God has a way of making us kings. The point is that Saul was obedient to the instructions of his father (and employer), and he fulfilled those instructions as the will of God. Saul's simple lifestyle of obedience led him right smack into the center of God's will—and the donkey chaser became king!

THOUGHT FOR THE DAY _____

If you will simply do what has been assigned to you, no matter how horrendous or painful the donkey chase may seem, there is no telling what kind of throne God has waiting for you.

Chip Off the Old Block

For whom He foreknew, He also predestined to be
conformed to the image of His Son.
—————————————————ROMANS 8:29 NKJV

*M*an was created in the image of God. That means that of all God's creatures, only man was made with the capacity to know God and enjoy fellowship with Him. As the catechism reminds us, "The chief end of man is to glorify God and enjoy Him forever."

When man sinned he did not lose God's image; it was marred but not destroyed. And with the marring of God's image in man, everything in man's life was marred, especially his relationship with God. Now, to be sure, there is still within us the capacity to know Him and the desire to fellowship with Him. But it has been crippled. By salvation, God intends to restore His image.

Notice that Paul, the author of this verse, does not say we are being conformed to the image of God, but rather to the image of His Son. And this is the emphasis throughout the New Testament.

Christ came not only to show us what the Father is like, but also to reveal what man, unfallen man, is supposed to be—to show us what it means to glorify God and enjoy Him forever. Christ is the God-man, the perfect example of what a person's relationship with God should be. In His humanity, Christ suffered loneliness, misunderstanding, hunger, thirst, abandonment and a death, the pain and humiliation of which defies description. Yet He remained in perfect fellowship with His Father and His brethren. Suffering was a part of His image; by it He was made perfect.

A man visited the studio of a sculptor and in the middle of the room sat a huge slab of marble.

"What are you going to sculpt out of that marble?" the man asked.

"A horse," answered the sculptor.

"How will you do that?" the visitor asked.

"I will take a hammer and a chisel and knock off everything that doesn't look like a horse."

I think it is fair to say that God's purpose is to chip off the "*old*" block—that is, to get rid of everything that doesn't look like Jesus.

THOUGHT FOR THE DAY ─────────────────────

Jesus was what God purposed man to be and what we will be. We who have been called according to His purpose will be transformed into the likeness of the inner character of Christ.

Your Heart's Condition

For as he thinks in his heart, so is he.
——————————PROVERBS 23:7 NKJV

We often speak of discernment as it relates to specific choices we make. Usually when we are unclear on a particular decision, discernment is that tool that weighs the evidence and brings clarity to thought. This can be of great value when we come in contact with people. And God has given us an extra hand when it comes to discernment with others. Many people are their own undoing. In a social or professional setting we can frequently "discern" the "fiber" of a man by his conversation and thoughts. I have heard it said that a man's words are a path to his heart. The inference is that if we could use his words as stones and follow them one by one, we could see what kind of condition his heart is in, not to mention where it lives. The heart's condition and where it lives are indicators of priorities—heavenly or earthly.

If someone were to take your thoughts and words and trace them back to your heart, what would he find? Would he find a home with a firm foundation supported by beams of God's Word, or would he find a loose, temporary structure, swaying with every wind of change?

God's Table of Grace

Ye all are partakers of my grace.
————PHILIPPIANS 1:7 KJV

$\mathcal{O}$ur family dinner was served daily with punctuality—5:30 P.M. sharp! Dad worked across the street from our home and arrived home each evening to the dinner Mom prepared. We were all expected to be at the table by 5:30 for this time of fellowship. I was the only one who broke this routine.

Often I stayed out after the 5:30 dinner call. Preoccupied with neighborhood friends one night, I finally pushed the curfew to its limit: 7:00 P.M. Then I was faced with the inevitable: returning home.

Even though a gentle hand turned the doorknob discreetly to open the door, the silence was pierced by a loud, "*Get yourself in here!*" I had no choice. There was no postponing this one. My dad's voice confronted me with the urgent "here and now," which was being fired at me point-blank.

Cowering, I made my way to the living room, regretting my disobedience and my soon-to-be pronounced punishment. *"You're grounded for a week!"*

Yet during this same encounter I discovered the embracing love of grace. For as I made my way through the kitchen, I glanced down at the stove. A delectable aroma came from the oven. I opened it. There under the glitter of aluminum foil was my supper, an evening meal, kept warm for one irresponsible, rebellious teenager.

While I deserved to be disciplined for my actions, I discovered grace in a meal that was fully prepared, kept warm, and placed on the table before me. Despite my doing wrong, my meal was not denied me.

The power of grace seen in an oven upon my late arrival home is an experience I recall each time I celebrate the Lord's Supper. All of us come to the Lord's table with our accumulated sins, our rebellious natures, which have offended God. Rightfully, we receive His kind and sometimes harsh reprimands.

But God never withholds the Bread of Life from us. For His grace always is an invitation to come to the table of fellowship with Him, to be embraced by Him. His grace always restores us to wholeness. In the breaking of bread we are redeemed by a grace that heals and forgives our sins.

THOUGHT FOR THE DAY ———————————————
God always allows us to come home. His grace gives the strength to overcome the old temptations.

In Sickness and In Health

*"Even though I walk through the valley of the shadow of death,
I will fear no evil, for you are with me; your rod and your
staff, they comfort me."*

—————————————————————————PSALM 23:4 NIV

$\mathcal{E}$arlier this year my wife's sister, Nancy, made an appointment for her annual checkup. Ever efficient, Nancy went in for a routine mammogram before her appointment. Her doctor called a few days later and said, "Before you see me, I want you to visit with a surgeon."

Shocked, Nancy made an appointment with a surgeon. It would be a slow, anxious journey for her to discover if anything was wrong.

Before making a recommendation, the surgeon wanted to review her previous mammograms. It took several days for them to arrive at his office. After reviewing them, the surgeon recommended a biopsy, which was performed two days later. Usually the labs can tell the next day if a malignancy exists, but in Nancy's case they had to send the tissue away. This added a week. The wait was excruciating.

Unknown to her husband, Hal, Nancy asked the surgeon to call him rather than her with the results.

The following week the surgeon phoned Hal at his office and told him his wife's breast showed cancer. At that moment Hal's whole world collapsed. *Why did he call me?* he wondered. A frightening feeling that he could lose her swept over him. It had not been that long ago that he had lost his mother to cancer, and his father had recently passed away. He had to leave his office to get hold of himself. He left the building and just started walking. He had to be alone, to think, to talk to God.

Nancy and Hal had made plans to go to dinner that evening with friends. Hal knew the timing for telling Nancy was not right, so he held the grim news inside.

The next morning Hal and Nancy put their two daughters in the car pool for school. When the house finally felt quiet, Hal said, "Honey, I need to talk to you."

Nancy recounts, "When he said that, I literally started shaking all over. I knew exactly what was coming."

Hal continued tenderly, "The doctor called me yesterday. We need to have surgery. They did find some cancer." Hal and Nancy sat down together and sobbed for fifteen minutes. Neither spoke a word. After gaining some composure, Hal looked into her eyes and said, "Nancy, I feel a love for you right now like I've never felt before."

Nancy elected to have the safest surgery, a modified mastectomy. As she says, "When you have a husband and two children you don't take chances. You want to live!

"One of the hardest moments of all came when Hal and I had to leave each other as they wheeled me into surgery. He went one way and I another. When it's just you, the surgeon, and the Lord, you feel a tremendous vulnerability."

After the successful surgery, Nancy had to remain in the hospital for two days. Hal slept in her room both nights. He had to help her out of bed and support her when she went to the bathroom. He cleaned up after some disagreeable medicine made Nancy throw up. Hal showed his love in a thousand ways.

"We felt a new closeness to each other," says Nancy. "For the first two months we would just hug and hold each other all the time. Hal said to me, 'You'll never know how much I love you and how courageous I think you are.' That really ministered to me. I think differently now. I realize how precious life is every day. I look at my husband and kids differently. I thank the Lord for giving me life!"

Some illnesses are routine and short, like colds and flu. One illness, morning sickness, is even a sign of joy. But other diseases—like cancer —are terrifying and may cause disability, infirmity, and death. Some of those diseases restrict themselves to the aged, but many strike in the prime of life. Heart attack. Stroke. Cancer. Mental disorders. Chemical dependencies. Alcoholism. Hepatitis. Chronic Fatigue Syndrome.

When the body of the wife is sick, so is the body of the husband. They are one flesh. When the body of the husband takes ill, so does the body of the wife. They are one flesh. We belong to each other, as we belong to the Lord. How important it is for your mate to have assurance that you will be there in the dark hour of illness.

THOUGHT FOR THE DAY _____
Lord God, we ask that You would protect us from sickness and disease. Help us to show such love to each other that we each have an assurance that we will always be there for each other. Amen.

Patience

He who is slow to wrath has great understanding,
But he who is impulsive exalts folly.
—————————————**PROVERBS 14:29** NKJV

"*A*nticipation." It was a great song from the seventies. It was also used as the sales pitch for a brand of ketchup, the premise being that the ketchup was so good and thick that it was worth the wait.

As long as I can remember, the virtues of patience have been extolled. Be patient because it's safer; it will save more money; it tastes better; you'll appreciate it more. When things are given the time necessary to be thought out and not rushed into, the chance of mistake is decreased.

Patience requires self-control. If you are patient you will control your temper. And if you are able to control your temper you will not exhibit embarrassing behavior and have to apologize for it. Most importantly, as patience is joined with prayer, you will mirror Christ, whereas impulse reflects folly.

Patience is a fruit of the Spirit, and like most fruit, it is at its best when nurtured and grown to maturity.

THOUGHT FOR THE DAY ————————————————
Pause before you react, *and you will* act *with patience.*

Waiting for Me

Better is a neighbor nearby than a brother far away.
——————————————PROVERBS 27:10 NKJV

*Y*esterday I began another business trip. As I walked alone through the St. Louis airport, I felt that now-familiar loneliness, almost smallness I always feel as I get my bags alone, rent my car alone, and check into a hotel room alone. It's not that people are unkind. The flight crew, the rental clerk, the desk clerk all call me by name, are kind and helpful. But they don't know me! There is no one I know waiting for me.

When I return home in a few days, I will feel different. I'll get my bags, get a ride home, all similar stuff to yesterday, but with a difference. Someone is waiting for me! Someone is counting on my return, so it matters whether I get home. I am important to them!

In those lonely times when you feel there is no one at home waiting for you, remember there is still someone who cares. In fact, you are so important to Him that He created time—just to spend it with you. Don't keep God waiting.

THOUGHT FOR THE DAY ——————————————
God knows us intimately. He longs for us to come to Him.

Do You Think "Biblically"?

To be carnally minded is death, but to be spiritually minded is life and peace.

ROMANS 8:6 NKJV

The Bible contains many specific principles of daily living. "Should I sue a fellow Christian? Can I divorce my spouse for abandoning me? Can I marry a divorced person? What should be my attitude toward an unethical employer?" These are not easy questions, but they do have answers—answers which are the will of God and found in the Bible.

The first step in finding the will of God is to simply ask, "Has God already spoken on this matter?" Where the Word of God has already spoken, the obedient child of God will immediately submit.

The crinkly pages of the Bible span from history to doctrine, from poetry to parables. The Word is the most comprehensive blueprint for successful living ever written. Guidance for living out the will of God comes from both the *commands* and the *principles* of God.

First, what God *commands* is *duty*. For example, "Honor your father and mother," "Love one another," and "Pray for your enemies" are not suggestions, but commands—therefore, duty. Once you have heard them your life can never be the same again. They are obligations, and all believers are bound by them. They are not only what we *ought* to do; to not do them breaks with the known will of God. It would be an act of open rebellion against Him. If we don't obey, then we sin. Obedience to the known will of God is the trademark of a biblical Christian.

Obviously, a distinction can be drawn between *what* we are to do and *how* we are to do it. *That* we must honor our father and mother is certain. *How* we show them honor leaves room for creativity, logic, and wisdom.

Second, what God establishes as a *principle* we must follow *wisely*. Consider, for example, this passage: "Folly is bound up in the heart of a child, but the rod of discipline will drive it far from him" (Prov. 22:15 NIV).

Few passages have led to more abuse than this "principle." It is not a *command* to spank, but a vein of thinking. The principle is that disciplining your children is important because they are foolish, and spanking helps them overcome that foolishness. Without wisdom the principles of God's will in the Bible can be distorted to fit our preconceived notions.

Do you think biblically? In other words, when you develop a *plan,* set a *priority,* solve a *problem,* or make a *decision* do you think in biblical categories? This is central. It is not possible to know the will of God apart from the Bible.

The people who make the greatest shipwreck of their faith are the people who don't think biblically—even though they are Christian.

THOUGHT FOR THE DAY _____
To learn the Bible is to learn the mind of God. To be willfully ignorant of the Bible is to invite disaster.

Purify Yourself

*Then Paul took the men, and the next day purifying himself
with them entered into the temple, to signify the accomplishment
of the days of purification.*

———————————————————ACTS 21:26 KJV

*I*magine a rocky windswept Alaskan shoreline—a place where
clear, cold Pacific waters daily cleanse the pebble-strewn beaches and
the tidal pools. The shoreline is aswarm with life. Sea otters play in the
surf, and various species of aquatic birds nest among the large rocks
along the beach. Many varieties of fish play beneath the sparkling surface of the waves. It is one of the cleanest, most beautiful environments
in the world. It is a place called Prince William Sound, and the date is
March 24, 1989.

On this day, a couple of miles offshore an oil tanker wallows off
course in shallow seas. Suddenly, the ship's hull strikes the rocky ocean
bottom and ruptures. Thick black crude oil pours out of the breach in
the hull and spreads toward the coastline. The churning seas whip the
oil slick into a gooey emulsion called mousse, which coats everything it
touches—rocks, pebbles, sand, birds, fish, and otters. It is filthy. It
stinks. Worst of all, it kills.

The shoreline is contaminated, and the contaminants destroy life
along the beautiful Alaskan shoreline. To preserve the life of the shore,

miles of rocky beaches must be *de*contaminated. They must be scrubbed, cleansed, and purified. Every inch of contaminated shoreline must be washed with steam or high-pressure water. Every oil-drenched bird or otter must be carefully scrubbed by hand.

Today, as I write these words, the decontamination of Prince William Sound in Alaska is nearly complete. Some scars of the oil tanker disaster remain, but the shore life and marine life that were once threatened by thick black crude oil have now returned pretty much to normal. The environment has survived, although the cleanup process has not been easy or inexpensive.

Spiritual decontamination is similar to the decontamination of an oil-stained shoreline. The apostle Paul counseled us to "cleanse ourselves from all filthiness of the flesh and spirit." Or as another translation puts it, "Let us purify ourselves from everything that contaminates body and spirit."

Although I believe this verse is primarily focused on the contamination of body and spirit resulting from sin, I believe the truth of this verse can also be applied to the contamination of the spirit resulting from toxic emotions, tainted beliefs, and poisonous memories since our minds and emotions are of the flesh and not of the spirit. I believe God genuinely wants all of His children to purify themselves from *anything* that would interfere with a pure trust relationship with Him—including emotional and mental contaminants such as shame, bitterness, fear, anxiety, and false beliefs about God. To preserve our spiritual life, we must bring our feelings and our memories into the open and hose them clean. We must carefully scrub the stink of shame and the poison of pain out of our inner being. The process may be costly in terms of the time spent and the effort it takes to face the truth about ourselves and our hurts. And even after we have undergone a thorough process of spiritual and emotional cleansing, some scars may remain.

But the poison and the stench will be gone. Life will return. We will feel pure and cleansed inside, and we will be able to taste the sweetness of the abundant life God wants for us.

THOUGHT FOR THE DAY ————————————————
God, give me a clean heart. Renew within me a right spirit.

Be Gracious and Receive Grace

So My heavenly Father also will do to you if each of you, from his heart, does not forgive his brother his trespasses.

————————————————————MATTHEW 18:35 NKJV

*T*hese are Jesus' final words after telling a fascinating story of an unforgiving man. It seems that the man owed the king millions of dollars. When the king demanded payment of the debt, the man begged and pleaded for mercy and time to pay. So the king graciously canceled the entire debt.

But the man's heart was not really touched by the king's graciousness. He went right out and met a man who owed him an insignificant debt of a few dollars. He grabbed the man and choked him, demanding payment, and then threw the poor fellow into jail. When the king heard how badly his servant had behaved, he had him arrested and thrown into jail as well.

Jesus said we cannot expect forgiveness from God unless we are truly willing to forgive other people.

THOUGHT FOR THE DAY —————————————————
Lord, give me a gracious heart so I may extend Your forgiveness to others.

Be Prepared to Wait

But they that wait upon the Lord shall renew their strength: they shall mount up with wings as eagles; they shall run and not be weary; and they shall walk and not faint.

——————————————————————————ISAIAH 40:31

Possibly the greatest sign of spiritual maturity is the ability to postpone rewards. The ultimate test would be to receive nothing in this lifetime, but to look forward to receiving our reward in the life to come. The writer of Hebrews expresses it this way:

> All these died in faith, without receiving the promises, but having seen them and having welcomed them from a distance, and having confessed that they were strangers and exiles on the earth. For those who say such things make it clear that they are seeking a country of their own. . . . And all these, having gained approval through their faith, did not receive what was promised, because God had provided something better for us, so that apart from us they should not be made perfect (Heb. 11:13–14, 39–40 NASB).

If I had known what my family would have to go through to get where we are today, I probably wouldn't have come. But looking back, we all say, "We're glad we came." Remember, God makes everything right in the end, though it may not even be in this lifetime. I believe with all my heart that when life is done and we're looking back, we will be able to say that the will of God is good, acceptable, and perfect.

It is not the critic who counts, nor the man who points how the strong man stumbled, or where the doer of deeds could have done better. The credit belongs to the man who is actually in the arena, whose face is marred by the dust and sweat and blood; who strives valiantly; who errs and comes short again and again; who knows the great enthusiasms, the great devotions, and spends himself in a worthy cause; who, at best, knows in the end the triumph of high achievement; and who, at the worst, if he fails, at least fails while daring greatly, so that his place shall never be with those cold and timid souls who know neither victory or defeat.

—**Theodore Roosevelt**

THOUGHT FOR THE DAY ——————————————
We may be in the arena, but we don't have to fear the outcome of the battle. I can say that with confidence, for the battle is not ours, but the Lord's.

Faith is not a means of getting man's will done in heaven; it is the means of getting God's will done on earth.

Dr. Neil T. Anderson
Walking in the Light

Submit—Without a Bit

I will guide you with My eye.
Do not be like the horse or like the mule . . .
Which must be harnessed with bit and bridle.
_____ PSALM 32:8–9 NKJV

When I was young I enjoyed riding horses. The only thing I disliked was putting the bit in the horse's mouth because it seemed cruel. My father explained that horses are large, high-spirited animals who require a bit and bridle for control.

There were many times when my horse, Beauty, was in a docile mood and allowed me to guide her with verbal commands. It pleased me when riding seemed so effortless and relaxed. Other times were difficult when Beauty had no desire to be ridden, and I had to pull firmly on the reins to keep her under control.

None of us wishes God to "bridle" us, and that will not be necessary if we come to Him in humble dependence on His power to help us change. We need to seek His will for our lives and obediently follow His direction by trusting Him in every situation. God wants to lead us gently, so let's humbly submit to His guidance.

THOUGHT FOR THE DAY _____
Realize that to submit to the Creator is to be at peace.

Trace the Pattern of Christ

"Christ also suffered for us, leaving us an example, that you should follow His steps."

———————————————————1 PETER 2:21 NKJV

*H*ave you ever bought your kids a coloring book with the figures already outlined, needing only for them to fill in the spaces between the lines with their crayons? Well, the Greek word which describes "a life that has been outlined" is *hupogrammos*. The pattern for our lives has been set by Christ. That is what it means to have Jesus as our model. To walk in His pattern means that He has already established the lines. We simply fill in His lines with our own lives.

Now, I'm no artist; I can't draw at all. What's more, I can hardly write, to which my wife and secretary will attest. So when I'm called upon to do anything artistic, I have to use see-through paper to trace the picture. To be honest, I traced my way through school. I remember one school project that my cousin did for me. It worked great because I got a good grade—he was a good artist and I was a poor one.

The idea here is that if you place your life over that of Christ's and fill it in with your own coloring, the outcome will be pretty exciting! Christ faced the worst mistreatment possible at the hands of sinful, worldly people; yet, He responded with the right spirit. Consequently, His response, using the opposite spirit to that of the world, has been changing the world ever since!

Hupogrammos can also describe a track that keeps one on course. It's a track-like groove. For example, those bumper cars at carnivals or amusement parks move around in grooves attached to the ceiling. No matter which way you turn the steering wheel, the cars will turn at the right time anyway. The same would aptly describe the point Peter was making. When we place our lives completely in submission to Christ, we simply follow His grooves, using His responses.

Though we can never change other people, we can oversee who it is we become. By responding in the opposite spirit to the mean spirit of this world, we actually become influencers and world-changers.

In 1 Peter 2:22–23, Peter recalled Christ's response to horrible abuse from Pilate, along with the harm and damage heaped on Him by the Jewish authorities. "Who committed no sin, nor was deceit found in His mouth"; who, when He was reviled, did not revile in return; when He suffered, He did not threaten, but committed *Himself* to Him who judges righteously. Even though His back was up against the proverbial wall, Christ chose not to retaliate but to entrust Himself to His righteous Father. And by doing so, He faced the ordeal and won!

THOUGHT FOR THE DAY _____

When you feel that your back is up against the wall, use Christ as your model and trace His outline on your wall; fill that image in with faith and you, too, can face the ordeal of each day with the assurance of victory.

Virtue Lies in the Struggle

Whatever you do, do all to the glory of God.
——————1 CORINTHIANS 10:31 NKJV

*P*ursuing the Roadrunner is what gives meaning to Wile E. Coyote's life. Catching and eating the scrawny little bird would almost seem anticlimactic after all those years of scheming and plotting for his capture. After the conquest, what next? It's the struggle that brings out the persistence and drive and ingenuity of the coyote: That's what makes us laugh. He's always getting smarter because he just doesn't know when to quit.

Neither do we, I hope.

We often love a struggle even more than the prize it offers us. It has always been that way. When Alexander the Great conquered the entire known world in 323 B.C., he sat down and wept. There were no more battles to be won. Nearly three thousand years later, just months after the July 20, 1969, date when Edwin "Buzz" Aldrin, Jr., became one of the first two men to walk on the moon, Aldrin realized that, as a pilot, there were no greater achievements he could strive for in his lifetime, and he had a nervous breakdown.

One of the great ironies of life is that people complain constantly about how hard it is to "get ahead"; yet when they no longer have to struggle, they seem either to go "stir crazy" and *make* work for themselves or they lose their inner sense of purpose and develop emotional problems. Few people seem able to "stand success" and enjoy the "prize" once they have it. The inability to enjoy the struggle along the way makes enjoying the prize difficult, if not impossible, for many of us.

This has been one of the recurrent themes of great literature throughout the ages. Throughout Victor Hugo's novel *Les Misérables*, a police inspector named Javert hunts the elusive criminal Jean Valjean. In the end, when Javert finally has a chance to capture and arrest Valjean after many years of pursuit, he cannot bring himself to do it. Instead, he hurls himself into the Seine River, committing suicide. The chase had given him a reason for living. For it to end was for life to end.

Consider the real-life parallels to that. Have you ever heard parents say that they can't wait to get their kids raised and out of the house so that they can have some time to themselves; yet once the kids are gone these same parents nearly go crazy with all the time they have on their hands?

My own tendency is to be so "prize-minded" that my efforts along the way get little or no credit. Graduate school felt like that. I felt as if contentment and "victory" were only to be obtained when I got my doctorate, not in my efforts to get it. Five years of graduate school was a long time to postpone victory. Writing my first book, *The Lies We Believe,* was the same way. I worked hard for over a year to write it, but I didn't allow myself many feelings of accomplishment until it was done. The effort to write it seemed to have no virtue to it; the actual "prize" of finishing the book was my victory.

In each case, I cost myself a great deal. In retrospect, I can see that the virtue was in the effort to finish a doctorate, not in getting one. I can also see that the virtue was in the effort to write a book, not in its finally coming out. This "scoreboard" mentality, where the effort on the field is considered less important than the final score, crushes a lot of us, though we may spend our whole lives denying it.

The virtue lies in the struggle, not the prize. Memorize that truth. Meditate on it. Keep it available for those times you are working diligently on something and the reward is nowhere in sight. When you are fighting a weight problem and not making much progress, remind yourself the effort to lose weight is your victory. When you are fighting being in financial debt, remind yourself that the effort to pay off your bills is your virtue. If your marriage is faltering and all your efforts to make it better seem to be failing, remind yourself that your struggle to make the marriage better is your victory. I hope "I tried" can become a satisfying statement for you.

THOUGHT FOR THE DAY ————————————————
More often than not, "I tried" will result in "I accomplished," which is the prize most of us want.

It is not for our defeat but our victory that God allows the pain.

Patrick M. Morley
The Rest of Your Life

Personal Value

*I beseech you therefore, brethren, by the mercies of God, that you
present your bodies a living sacrifice, holy, acceptable to God,
which is your reasonable service.*

————————————————————**ROMANS 12:1** NKJV

*R*ecall a possession of great value to you, either material or sentimental. It can be an heirloom, a collector's item, jewelry, or even an
automobile. You probably take special care to see that no one steals it,
and you make sure that it remains untouched or untarnished. If anything happened to it, you would probably be angry or upset. Now
recall a possession of no value to you. Think about how you care for it
and how you let others treat it. You treat something of value much
differently from something of no value.

Valuing yourself is one of the most important elements of successful
living. A man will only preserve and protect himself to the extent that
he perceives his personal value. Most people will not pour alcohol over
their sports cars, but they freely pour it into their tender bodies.

A person has to love and respect himself to be able to say no to
habits and behavior that is self-destructive.

THOUGHT FOR THE DAY ————————————————————
Listen to God's description of your worth to Him.

Purified by Fire

Beloved, think it not strange concerning the fiery trial which is to try you, as though some strange thing happened unto you: But rejoice, inasmuch as ye are partakers of Christ's sufferings; that, when his glory shall be revealed, ye may be glad also with exceeding joy.

————————————————————1 PETER 4:12–13 KJV

*A*re you being tested?

While the designation certainly doesn't fit every situation, *difficult times* may mean that we are being tested. Testing is a critical process of examination which determines stability and strength. Value and durability are established. As with steel, fire is the means by which strength is added to metal. Since God has already determined our infinite value to Himself and clearly knows our limits, we might conclude that the time in the fire is to demonstrate to us what He already knows is true.

The Greek original for testing, *dokimon,* means "to prove genuine." The root meaning suggests that testing is an ongoing process in human existence. Fiery periods are normal in everyone's life. Testing is the rule and not the exception. No, we have not been singled out for exceptional abuse. Testing exposes what our soul is made of.

In one sense each day of our life is part of the rating process. Being made gradually stronger by these daily "weight-lifting" exercises prepares us for the more difficult periods by adding increased capacity to our strength. Extended periods of difficulty are essentially everyday living given to us in very concentrated doses. Here's the real problem. Will we have the insight to receive testing as a gift from God rather than as an unjust imposition of cruelty?

Like a good parent, God's love is tough, not sentimental. Committed to genuine growth and maturity, the heavenly Father allows us to have the full range of human experiences that are necessary for the development of authenticity. Every parent knows that the test can be as hard on him or her as it is on the child.

Following high-school graduation, our second son, Tony, yearned to find his way into the world before he entered college. I recognized his need to establish himself as an independent person who was capable of making his own decisions apart from his parents. Highly creative, Tony had to find his own mind in much the same way that Indian youths found their bravery by going out into the wilderness armed only with a knife. To be an adult, a brave had to learn he could survive on his own. So we sent Tony forth for his time in the wilds. His decision was to take a six-month backpacking trip across Europe and into Greece. With sparse funds, he set out to see the world.

As we took him to the airport, I could see second thoughts mounting. At last we came to the final metal detector gateway and the moment of truth was at hand. The apprehensions in his mind were nothing compared to what his mother and I were thinking. Yet we feebly waved good-bye and with a forlorn look, Tony walked down that long hallway into the airplane and on to his destiny. Six months later a man came back down that same ramp.

The heavenly Father loves us too much to keep us from walking the long corridors of life. When the fires are kindled against us, we can know that we have reached the place where we are ready for the next step in the development of our soul.

Actually, testing gives meaning to life. We live each day in an arena where we demonstrate who we are. The test results are revealed in how we respond. The final judgment on our lives is essentially a gathering up of the data from all of these daily tests. Day by day, week by week, year by year, integrity and personhood are being measured. Purified or pulverized by life, we will generally be made stronger, more tenacious, and totally genuine.

Paul felt that God often gives us responsibility as a means to test our commitments (1 Thess. 2:4). We may be trusted with a divine responsibility in order that the very best will come forth in us. Through this testing, the authentic surfaces while the artificial and the unworthy are peeled away.

THOUGHT FOR THE DAY _____

At times testing may be extraordinarily painful, but we can take comfort in Paul's thoughts: What God produces is worth more than any difficulty caused by the ordeal.

Seek Wisdom

If any of you lack wisdom, let him ask of God, that giveth to all men liberally.

JAMES 1:5 KJV

$\mathscr{I}$ve always identified with the wise men. Not because I'm particularly wise, but because I've always wanted to be. I used to see wisdom as something to possess, as a commodity, a "thing." I suppose that's why I went to college to study philosophy. There was a hunger in me to know, to possess, something hard, if not impossible, to define. For the lack of a better term I called it *wisdom*.

Thankfully, early in those college years I began to discover that there was more to wisdom than the accumulation of facts and information. Although I hadn't found out what true wisdom was as yet, at least I was given the grace to recognize its impostor.

Wisdom is not the ability to be correct all the time, although I suppose people who are wise are right more often than people who are stupid. Now I've learned that wisdom is not facts or the accumulation of them, though that is what our educational system seems to believe.

Genuine wisdom is concerned with life, a life well-lived, perhaps. Wisdom isn't something we know as much as something we become.

Like life, wisdom is impossible to define or grasp. If the Magi were truly "wise men," they must have understood this. Perhaps that's why they left on their long journey in the first place.

It was a long, long journey. They came "from the east." Scholars think they might have been priests of Zoroaster, probably from Persia. They foolishly followed Jacob's star for months, perhaps even years, which doesn't sound like wisdom to me but rather foolishness or faith.

They are called "Magi" in the Gospels. Herodotus described the Magi as a special group of priests who had to be present at sacrifices to speak certain "sacred words," known only to them. When we finally come upon the Magi in Matthew, however, they don't seem to have much to say.

The Bible simply says they "bowed down and worshiped Him." Perhaps they were silent because they recognized in this little baby a Wisdom that went beyond their stammering words. Instead of pondering the mystery of this Wisdom, they fell on their knees and worshiped. They must have felt great relief at coming to the end of their long journey, for there is no true worship without that sense that you have finally found what you've been looking for all your life.

We assume there were three wise men because three gifts are mentioned. I'd like to think there were many more. They offered the baby gifts that were no doubt intended for some potentate: gold, frankincense, and myrrh. Upon seeing the young child (by now, Jesus was no longer a baby and the holy family was living in a house) the Magi's "priceless" gifts must have shrunk into worthless insignificance as they watched the toddler playing with gold, which meant nothing to Him and indeed never would.

It had been a long journey. For many of us it is a long journey still. The great writer Frederick Buechner described his life as a journey, a sacred one. So did C. S. Lewis, Malcolm Muggeridge, and others. Bunyan's famous metaphor of the Pilgrim's Progress is really only the story of a journey.

Our journey begins where the wise men's ended. Like them, we have found a Wisdom not to ponder but to worship, a wisdom that is not a matter of words but who is the Word. This Wisdom has everything to do with life because He is the Life. He gives us Wisdom because He gives us Himself.

THOUGHT FOR THE DAY _____
The Magi journeyed to Jesus, but our journey is with *Jesus, a sacred and a long, long journey.*

You're Not Alone

"I am with you always, even to the end of the age."
—————————————MATTHEW 28:20 NKJV

$\mathcal{I}$ have always struggled with loneliness. It's not because I don't have a wonderful family and friends. Sometimes it's precisely because they are so special and so numerous that I feel that way. Unless you suffer from the same feeling, you'll probably think that's a bit crazy. Someone once described such loneliness as being ill at ease with the world but at peace with the universe. There is no apparent reason, but feelings don't need reasons.

At those lonely times I often think about Jesus. It's no surprise that all four Gospels talk about His loneliness and preference for "lonely places." You can sense it between the lines of many of those passages, a holy melancholy. A lonely Messiah.

In the midst of His own disciples, whom He loved with so much tenderness, Jesus is so often misunderstood. They question. They doubt. They constantly miss whatever point He is trying to make.

When Jesus' family, believing Him to be out of His mind, come to take charge of Him, His response has a dull and lonely sound, "Who are My mother and My brothers?'' (Mark 3:33 NASB). When the crowd tries to force Him to become their "bread king," Jesus flees to the wilderness (Mark 6:45, 46). I can almost see Him wandering about there, talking to Himself and His Father, the only One who really understood.

John the Baptist, Jesus' cousin and friend, is senselessly murdered, and Jesus' response is to retreat, by Himself (Matt. 14:13). Luke tells us that He often withdrew to "lonely places."

When Jesus felt alone, it was because His Father was so visibly absent in the world. Jesus sought His presence in lonely places. I wonder if their hearts resonated together with loneliness . . . for each other.

We all know what it's like to be misunderstood by those we love the most, to feel as if we are the only ones in the world going through what we're going through, the feeling that life is meaningless. Yet in Christ everything has meaning. There is no darkness in Him, for He is Light. So where does loneliness fit in? The Gospels tell us that when Jesus retreated to those lonely places it was for prayer. In that, we can see a purpose in loneliness, both for Jesus and for us. That sense of "aloneness" forced Jesus to flee to a lonely place, to pray, to pour out His heart to the Father. One great conclusion is at the heart of Jesus' remedy for loneliness: If God, the Father of Jesus, really does exist, then none of us are alone, and indeed can never be.

Every time we let loneliness take over our feelings, we have lost sight of that personal, caring, and loving Father. He is "Abba," our Papa. Even if no other person understands or cares, He does. That is the God Jesus fled to when He felt lonely. The same caring Father is there for us.

THOUGHT FOR THE DAY _____

The humanity of Jesus might have caused Him to fear that He was alone. Our own flesh often speaks to us the same terrible message. Yet the voice of our Abba says, "Never will I leave you. Never will I forsake you. You are the apple of My eye, My chosen one, My beloved. How could you ever be lonely when I am here?"

There's Potential in Pain

"My yoke is easy and My burden is light."
————————————MATTHEW 11:30NKJV

It isn't what happens to us that makes us weak or strong. *It is who we become in the face of suffering.* The terrible thing about all suffering is that, in every pain, there is the potential for betrayal and for becoming a distorted and dysfunctional person. Also, in the face of every kind of suffering, there is the potential of becoming more Christlike—that is, becoming more powerful.

The apostle Peter said that not only is there the likelihood that we will suffer under the hands of harsh people in this world, but also that we are called by Christ to suffer. In fact, He left us an example: We should follow in His footsteps.

I tried to think of the types of suffering that would likely bring us the most agony in the kinds of situations Peter addressed. I can think of several. Perhaps you have some of your own to add:

- Suffering that comes from rejection
- Suffering that comes from being taken advantage of

- Suffering that comes from being manipulated
- Suffering that comes from needless ridicule
- Suffering that comes from indifference
- Suffering that comes from being forgotten
- Suffering that comes from deliberate attack

A number of persons have talked to me about the harsh environment at their workplace and in our culture today. One man described the lack of teamwork in his company as being "like a group of vultures working together, waiting for the first one to go down." The better jobs in the firm were so coveted that devious plans were put in motion to obtain them. Sometimes, two or three plans were set in motion to bring down a manager or an upper echelon employee in order to grab that person's slot.

One man lost his job after working for this company for nearly 20 years. Evidence was strong that his Christian beliefs became one of the reasons for his removal. You can imagine the trauma he experienced. He'd given tremendous amounts of energy to this company and was making a very high salary. Boom! One day, without notice, they fired him!

His temptation, at that moment, was to become retaliatory, to appeal his case with the same vengeance he had suffered. However, the Lord subsequently opened up a position for him in another company. To his credit, he never weakened in his Christian commitment, nor did he in any way "talk down" his previous company. Interestingly enough, in his interview process, that was one of the points his new employer brought up, knowing a little more of the details than the applicant realized. The new employer said that he admired this Christian man because he didn't run down his former company when he had applied for the new position.

Now, you may be thinking: "Great! You mean that, because I've received Christ, He has saved up for me all these terrible tortures, so that, once I say: 'Yes, Lord,' I'm in for a lifetime of misery? Is that what I'm called to?"

Let me reassure you. That's not what it means at all. It would be rather egotistical for us, as Christians, to say or to think that we're the only people in the world who suffer. It would be even more ridiculous to say that we suffer more than most people. In fact, my observation of American Christians is that we're all as addicted to comfort as anybody.

I personally know of many unbelievers who suffer a great deal! In fact, Jesus said the way of a Christian is easier than the person in the world; and He said, "My yoke is easy and My burden is light" (Matt. 11:30). He was saying that the spirit of this world is a heavy burden; it weighs you down. It is, in fact, easier to walk as a Christian than as a nonbeliever.

Yet, suffering has been a consequence of a fallen world since Adam's time. Conversely, it is a false gospel that, if you receive Christ, you won't suffer anymore and everything will be hunky-dory. That isn't true at all. Christ didn't promise that life would be any easier for Christians, but said that He would be *with* us in our troubling times.

Peter pointed out that Christians are called to face normal human suffering in a fallen world. Perhaps some persecution may come upon us as well. It's a rare privilege for us in our culture to experience that kind of suffering, so, when we do, we ought to rejoice about it and praise the Lord.

Please understand that we aren't necessarily called to suffer any more than others are, or to a higher plane of suffering. We are simply called to *face suffering with a Christlike attitude*. This kind of attitude not only brings victory to us, but also glorifies God.

THOUGHT FOR THE DAY _____
When we face pain with a Christlike attitude, we have the potential to become stronger and better equipped to overcome day by day.

Weakness Builds Strength

"My grace is sufficient for you, for My strength is made perfect in weakness."

—————————————————2 CORINTHIANS 12:9 NKJV

*A*s adults we have a prideful attitude that children don't have. Children ask for help because they have enough wisdom to know they need it. We have great difficulty putting aside our pride and simply asking God to be in control.

God desires that we come into a relationship with him with the heart of a child. Being childlike requires admitting our helplessness in many areas of life. We must recognize our need for guidance from someone who knows more than we do.

God promised that when we are weak, He remains strong. When we become empty of ourselves, He can fill us with His strength and wisdom. Just as loving parents delight in taking care of their child, so God finds great joy in providing direction for us.

Come before God and willingly ask Him to remove your recognized faults. As you hold up the deficits of your character before God, you can rest assured that there will be no condemnation. He will receive you as a loving parent and will provide the strength you need to continue to move forward.

I will view weakness as a positive pathway toward seeing my need for God's strength.

Listen to His Leading

The Holy Spirit intercedes with the Father to help us discern and do the will of God. "The Spirit intercedes for the saints in accordance with God's will."

ROMANS 8:27 NIV

*A*s the prophet Samuel finished anointing Saul the first king over Israel, he told Saul to go to Gilgal and wait there seven days for him to come. When Samuel did not arrive right on the button, King Saul felt "compelled" to perform the priestly duty and make the offerings. He heard a little inner voice, but it was not the voice of the Lord.

The Holy Spirit teaches us everything we need to know and also reminds us of everything we have already learned when we need it. Jesus said, "But the Counselor, the Holy Spirit . . . will teach you all things and will remind you of everything I have said to you" (John 14:26 NIV). Can you recall a single instance of already knowing but not remembering Christ's teaching on a subject? The Holy Spirit always reminds us, though we do not always obey Him.

The Spirit is our counselor both now and forever. Jesus said, "The Father . . . will give you another Counselor to be with you forever— the Spirit of truth" (John 14:16–17 NIV).

We must be extremely cautious in listening for leading from the

Holy Spirit. When Samuel arrived he told Saul, "You have not kept the command the LORD your God gave you" (1 Sam. 13:13 NIV). In the end it cost him his kingdom.

The apostle Paul also spoke of being "compelled," but "by the Spirit" (Acts 20:22 NIV). His leading was very different from King Saul's. Paul was led by the Spirit; King Saul was led by his own flesh. The strong leading of the Spirit must never be confused with the strong natural inclinations of our own flesh.

Do not be surprised if the Spirit's guidance only comes partially before it comes entirely. God rarely unfolds the whole field of vision before our eyes. The stage curtain is often (usually) partially drawn. God said to Abraham, "Leave your country, your people and your father's household and go to the land I *will* show you" (Gen. 12:1 NIV, italics added). Abraham obeyed, but he was "going, not knowing."

And don't be surprised if the Spirit's guidance leads you into a storm rather than out of one. After feeding the five thousand, "Immediately Jesus made the disciples get into the boat and go on ahead of him to the other side" (Matt. 14:22 NIV). Then Jesus dismissed the crowd and went up into the hills to pray. When the boat was in the middle of the Sea of Galilee, about three miles from shore, a fierce squall came up out of nowhere. Though not expected, such sudden storms were not that uncommon on this freshwater lake so much a part of everyday life in Galilee. When it seemed their oars would snap and their hearts would melt like wax, Jesus finally came to them in the middle of the storm.

Here's the curious point: Jesus only saved them *from* the storm after He had sent them *into* the storm. Storms are part of life. Sometimes storms just happen. Other times the Spirit leads us into storms. They are opportunities for us to rely upon Him, and for Him to bring glory and honor to the Father when He delivers us.

THOUGHT FOR THE DAY _____

If the Spirit leads you to cross a lake and, halfway over, it storms, know that He will sovereignly and lovingly guide you the rest of the way too.

Plan Your Private Pursuit

This book of the law shall not depart out of thy mouth; but thou shalt meditate therein day and night, that thou mayest observe to do according to all that is written therein.

——————————————————————JOSHUA 1:8 KJV

The Scriptures don't say you have to read the Bible and pray daily. Instead, they say we should continually meditate on the Word and pray about everything. The biblical concept is continual devotions. Actually, the concept of a daily quiet time is a cultural accommodation to busy, crowded schedules. Because most of us do have such hectic schedules, the idea of a few minutes devoted exclusively to Bible reading and prayer is valuable. Daily private devotions is not a *requirement,* but it is *wise.*

Personally, I have known many people who have had great struggles even though they maintained a close, intimate walk with Jesus. But I have never seen one of these go undelivered in due time. "The man who looks intently into the perfect law that gives freedom, and continues to do this, not forgetting what he has heard, but doing it—he will be blessed in what he does" (James 1:25 NIV).

On the other hand, I have known many Christians who suffered deeply simply because they did not pursue the presence of the Lord through regular personal devotions in their hour of adversity. Without regular time with God, the seeds of *syncretism* take root. Do you maintain a traditional time of private devotion? Without being legalistic, what kind of commitment to time alone with God is realistic for you?

Consider establishing a maximum time limit for your devotional life, not a minimum. This will keep down the guilt. If you have never had a quiet time before, start with a maximum of five minutes. Only allow yourself to go beyond your maximum if you are on fire for more. Read one chapter of the New Testament and pray a prayer (like the Lord's Prayer). Don't expect to make it every day, but pick a time and place regular enough that you can reasonably make it about five of seven days a week. If you read one chapter of the New Testament five days each week you will complete it in one year (260 chapters). Increase your daily time limit only as you feel you can't keep the lid on it anymore, but go slowly.

THOUGHT FOR THE DAY _____
If you will set realistic expectations, then you can design a personal program guaranteed to succeed.

Character: Life's Collateral

Search me, O God, and know my heart; try me, and know my anxieties; and see if there is any wicked way in me, and lead me in the way everlasting.

————————————————————PSALM 139:23–24 NKJV

Certainly God wants to use our talents. After all, He gave them to us. But along with the developing of our talents and spiritual gifts is the perfecting of our character. To use M'Cheyne's metaphor, we are God's weapons; and if the weapon is to be effective, it must be polished and sharp.

You may not think of yourself as a weapon, but the metaphor is quite biblical. In Isaiah 49:2, *Messiah* is compared to a sharp sword and a polished arrow; and Zechariah 9:13 compares Zion's army to bows and arrows and "the sword of a mighty man." Paul used the image in Romans 6:13 where he admonished believers to yield their bodies to God "as instruments of righteousness"; and the word translated *instruments* means "tools" or "weapons."

Christian service means invading a battleground, not a playground; and you and I are the weapons God uses to attack and defeat the enemy. When God used Moses' rod, He needed Moses' hand to lift it. When God used David's sling, He needed David's hand to swing it.

When God builds a ministry, He needs somebody's surrendered body to get the job done. *You are important to the Lord, so keep your life pure:* "A holy minister [servant] is an awful weapon in the hand of God."

There's no substitute for Christian character. No matter how much talent and training we may have, if we don't have character, we don't have anything. M'Cheyne said in 1840: "But oh, study universal holiness of life! Your whole usefulness depends on this. Your . . . sermon lasts but an hour or two—your life preaches all the week." He was speaking at an ordination service, but the admonition applies to any form of Christian service. A holy life is a useful life.

The media scandals of a few years ago gave us a painful reminder that there's a Grand Canyon of difference between *reputation* and *character,* and that popularity isn't always a guarantee of spirituality. It's possible to get a following but not necessarily promote God's work. You can fool many of the people some of the time, but eventually the truth comes out.

Life is built on character, but character is built on decisions. The decisions you make, small and great, do to your life what the sculptor's chisel does to the block of marble. *You are shaping your life by your thoughts, attitudes, and actions and becoming either more or less like Jesus Christ.* The more you are like Christ, the more God can trust you with His blessing.

The person who cultivates integrity realizes that there can be no division between "secular and sacred" in the Christian life; everything must be done to the glory of God (1 Cor. 10:31). God reminded two of His greatest leaders, Moses (Exod. 3:5) and Joshua (Josh. 5:15), that the servant of the Lord is *always* standing on holy ground and had better behave accordingly. If nobody else is watching, God is; and He will be our judge.

Character isn't the same as personality, although character affects personality. Too many Christians think they can "get by" in spiritual ministry because they have charisma and can attract and hold an audience. But it takes more than a winning personality to influence people for Christ; it takes godly character. It's been said that people are like trees: the shadow of the tree is *reputation,* the fruit of the tree is *personality,* but the roots of the tree are the most important part—*character.*

Somebody asked the wealthy banker J. P. Morgan what the best collateral was for a loan, and Morgan replied, "Character." What is true in the financial world is true in the spiritual world. God gives His best to those who most reflect the beauty of holiness.

THOUGHT FOR THE DAY _____
"For the eyes of the LORD run to and fro throughout the whole earth, to show Himself strong on behalf of those whose heart is loyal to Him" (2 Chron. 16:9 NKJV).

*God . . . will never sacrifice the
quality of our character to increase
the quantity of our circumstances.
God puts character ahead of stuff.*

Patrick M. Morley
The Rest of Your Life

Don't Deceive Yourself

Winking at sin leads to sorrow; bold reproof leads to peace.

PROVERBS 10:10 TLB

You are on your way, on a fresh new pathway surrounded by God's blessings. But don't deceive yourself. Take heed, you can step off the path and out of God's perfect will. In other words, you can still sin.

"What?" you may exclaim. "Didn't I leave that behind me when I declared my faith in Christ?" The answer is yes. But you are a voluntary recruit. You are not chained to God's chariot. You are still free to follow your own inclinations. You can disobey your King.

But who would want to go against Him? We may not really want to rebel, but Satan is constantly encouraging us to do so.

Who is this person who has such power over the world and over us? He is God's great enemy who goes about as a roaring lion, seeking whom he may devour. Some time in the past of eternity he was the highest of the angels, next in power to the triune God, until he revolted against God. With many of the angels on his side, he despised God and fought against Him, and he was dethroned and cast out of heaven.

Now he and his cohorts, the other fallen angels, are using every device possible to turn away mankind, whom God made for Himself, from following God. He is especially angry with those who turn their lives over to God. You are one of those Satan wants, and he is extremely anxious to help you disobey.

Your old nature is still there, and if it gets the chance it will take over. Can this really happen to a child of God? Yes, for the Scriptures declare to Christians, "If we say that we have no sin, we deceive ourselves (1 John 1:8)." This is a fact of the Christian life, and God tells us clearly, explicitly, what to do about it.

"If we confess our sins, He is faithful and just to forgive us our sins and to cleanse us from all unrighteousness(1 John 1:9)."

Disobedience saddens God's heart, but if we confess our sins and turn away from them, we receive abundant forgiveness and restoration from God. The sins are cleansed away by the death of Christ. It is perfectly fair for God to forgive us because of what Christ has done in paying our penalty.

Don't deceive yourself into thinking you can stay on the straight path on your own. Stop! Evaluate where you are. Examine yourself. List those things in your life that need to be forgiven—things displeasing to your heavenly Father.

Is there bitterness? Refusal to forgive someone? Lust? Impurity? Cheating? Stealing? Take this list to the Lord in prayer. Ask Him to forgive you and steer you away from deception.

THOUGHT FOR THE DAY _____
Though we have no right, whatever, Christ has made a heavenly path for us directly to the throne room of God. But that way is only revealed to those whose vision is free of deception.

TOM WHITEMAN
Flying Solo

You're Not About to Fall

Now to Him who is able to keep
  you from stumbling,
And to present you faultless
Before the presence of His
  glory with exceeding joy,
To God our Savior,
Who alone is wise,
Be glory and majesty,
Dominion and power,
Both now and forever.
Amen.
——————————JUDE 24–25 NKJV

*W*hen I walk with my young son, I usually hold tightly to his hand. We'll come to an uneven place in the sidewalk, and my son might trip—but I'm holding on. For a moment I am carrying the full weight of my boy, but soon he regains his footing. If I were not there, he would stumble and fall flat on his face.

The above text tells us that God is able to keep us from stumbling. We still trip. We still mess up. We still have problems in life, but none of them will last forever. God is holding us up. When our footing fails, He grabs on until we can regain our balance.

THOUGHT FOR THE DAY ————————————————
It is humbling if other people see me fall, God. Sometimes it hurts. But You are there to pick me up. Thank You.

The Miracle of Common Sense

Wisdom is better than strength.
—ECCLESIASTES 9:16 NKJV

*H*ave you heard about the devout Christian who heard an urgent news report on his radio that a flash flood was within minutes of entering the peaceful valley where he lived? Immediately he went to his knees and committed his life to the Lord and prayed for safety. The words were still on his lips when he became aware that water was gushing under his door. He retreated to the second floor and finally onto the roof of his house.

While he sat on the roof, a helicopter flew by and the pilot asked over the loudspeaker if they could lift him off. "It's not necessary since I have the Lord's protection," he replied.

Moments later the house began to break up and he found himself clinging to a tree. A police boat, braving the waters, approached him for rescue, but he assured the police that the Lord would save him. Finally, the tree gave way and the man went to his death.

Standing before the Lord, he asked, "Lord, I'm glad to be here, but why didn't You answer my prayer for safety?" The Lord responded,

"Son, I told you over the radio to get out of there. Then I sent you a helicopter and a motor boat!"

Nowhere in the Bible are we given the idea that God works only in the extraordinary. Much of the time He supernaturally works through His created order. Many people think God is present only when there is a miracle and that He leads only through signs and wonders.

This kind of mind-set is seen in John 7:25–27 (NASB). The Jewish people were commenting about Jesus: "Is this not the man whom they are seeking to kill? . . . Look, He is speaking publicly . . . The rulers do not really know that this is the Christ, do they? However, we know where this man is from; but whenever the Christ may come, no one knows where He is from." They were looking for a mystery man, seeking a sign when the real signs of Jesus' divine character and fulfillment of Scripture were there all the time.

Looking for signs is understandable. We usually are anxious concerning decisions we have made or are about to make. Naturally, we want to make right decisions and be in God's will, so there is the temptation to ask for some sign of confirmation from God.

Then, there are those people who *always* look for a sign. They walk by sight, not by faith. To them, God is present only in the miraculous. God was "really" at the church service if something unusual happened. Many desire and look for "visitations" from God.

But how does that square with God's omnipresence and the fact that He will never leave nor forsake us? Isn't God at every church service? Since God created the fixed order of the universe, would you expect Him to work primarily within that fixed order or outside of it? If God gave us an instruction manual, shouldn't we expect Him to operate within the confinements of it? If God gave us a watch, would we be honoring Him more by asking what time it is, or by simply checking the watch?

THOUGHT FOR THE DAY _____
God is God of the ordinary and *the miraculous. We can be thankful for both.*

Prayer: A Conversation with God

*"Whatever prayer, whatever supplication is made by anyone,
. . . then hear in heaven Your dwelling place."*

————————————————————1 KINGS 8:38–39 NKJV

*P*rayer should be a two-way communication. Since there is no voice of God speaking in the room, you need to learn how He speaks in the silence of your heart and mind. I believe this takes practice and experience. Ask God to help you to know His will. If a thought keeps returning to you, talk it over with others. Don't act hastily. Not every thought that pops into your head while you are praying is from God.

Sometimes when you are praying about a problem, the answer will suddenly occur to you, and you will wonder why you hadn't thought of it before. The reason is that you hadn't prayed about it before or hadn't prayed about it enough or it was not God's time to give you the answer until that moment. It is important, though, to bring the idea before the Lord to discover whether it really is from Him or whether it is your own idea.

What should we pray about? Very often part of my prayer time is spent talking to the Lord about the things He brings to my mind—things that may or may not be on my usual prayer list, or that He especially wants me to pray about that day. Sometimes I know why it is important to pray about it that day, and sometimes I don't; but I follow His direction.

How long should we pray? I don't know. I have found that when I pray little, my heart becomes cool toward the Lord, and answers to prayer don't come as frequently as when I pray more often. This is of course logical and scriptural. We are told to persist in prayer.

For many years I had a quiet time, presumably on a daily basis. I say *presumably* because often I would realize that I hadn't spent time with God that particular day or even the day before; and, in fact, it might have been several days since I had my last quiet time. I had become too busy, partly in Christian work.

Finally I got tough with myself. After several days of fearfully thinking about it, I decided actually to do what I felt was reasonable and to try to spend a longer time with the Lord. I hoped to succeed in spending about an hour a day in prayer apart from my Bible reading time.

I remember how frightening it was the first time I tried to spend such a long period in the presence of the Lord. It seemed as though I would quickly run out of things to pray about, so I had the book of Psalms open to help me, as well as a list of items needing prayer attention.

It was difficult at first; nevertheless, I survived! And I believe God was pleased. Anyway, I know that I have had some amazing answers to prayer and these times with God have become enjoyable and something I look forward to from morning to morning.

THOUGHT FOR THE DAY _____
God, teach us to pray.

Prayer is not helping God with an answer; it is asking God to help. It is not telling God what to do; it is telling Him (your) needs. It isn't so much for the disciplined as for the undisciplined.

Becky Tirabassi
Let Prayer Change Your Life

CYNTHIA SPELL HUMBERT
One Step at a Time

Learn the Lesson

Life is difficult.
SCOTT PECK

Fairy tales led us to believe that the beautiful princess is always rescued by the knight in shining armor, and then they live happily ever after. We grow up believing that the more successful we are in life, the easier it will be. Obviously, we aren't doing well if life is difficult.

The truth is that life is not easy, no matter how successful we are. Life will always be full of job losses, car wrecks, and poor health. If we continue to embrace the lie that life should be easy, we will grow to be resentful and bitter. We may even begin to question our faith in God.

God never promised us that life would be carefree. He promised to give us strength to face difficult times, and He reassures us that He brings good out of bad circumstances.

Once we learn that life is hard, we are no longer shocked when things seem unfair. We learn to accept difficulties as a chance for us to grow by allowing God to be in control.

THOUGHT FOR THE DAY _____
We can rest securely knowing that even in difficult times, God desires to take care of us.

Two Soles with Holes

"My people shall never be put to shame."
——————————JOEL 2:26 NKJV

$\mathscr{I}$ was not only embarrassed by my sad little drab dresses and my life in the store, but I was often upset over my shoes. Because of our poverty we could barely afford one pair of shoes a year for each of us. They were always too big at the start—we needed room to grow into them—and too tight for the last few months. There never seemed to be that magic moment when my shoes and feet met in harmony.

Besides the sizing mismatch was the fact that my feet were bigger than I was. I wore size 9 in eighth grade. In those days a child's size 9 had to be custom ordered and they only came in brown tie oxfords. I can clearly remember the shame I felt because I had to wear these ugly shoes. Once, in desperation, I painted the brown clodhoppers with white enamel paint only to be depressed when they looked bigger in white. Eventually they cracked and peeled, showing veins of dull brown through the shiny enamel.

Besides the wrong size and the ugly shape and color was what happened when the soles wore out before it was time for the year's new pair. At the sign of a hole in the sole, my mother cut cardboard to fit the shoe and inserted it for our protection. As the hole widened, the cardboard had to be replaced frequently until mother would sigh and say, "Chappie, you're going to have to fix these shoes."

Fixing was a major procedure. Daddy took a package of rubber soles from the nail on the wall where they hung for the customers' convenience. These soles looked like tire treads, black ugly rubber with waffle marks. They came in two sizes, men's and women's, and Dad had to cut them down to create a children's size. I remember him taking mother's breadboard and an ivory handled butcher knife to carve up the piece of rubber to make it fit the shoe. Interested customers would watch and make comments like, "The kid sure has big feet" and "Why don't you buy her new shoes? It would be a lot easier."

Once the new sole was carved to the correct size, give or take a jagged edge here or there, it was time to rough up the bottom of the shoe. Included in the set of soles was a "rough up" tool that looked somewhat like a little cheese grater. My brothers were assigned to scrape this vigorously across the shoe sole until it looked as if a dog had chewed it up. This mock destruction was such fun that they fought for the tool and attacked each shoe as an enemy.

When the shoe was gouged up enough, Dad would squeeze the cement out of the tube included in the set and spread the glue across the sole with a knife as if he were frosting a cake. There was an art to this step because not enough glue would cause the sole to drop off and too much would run over the edge and eat off whatever was left of the original finish. The final trick was to place the rubber treads onto the sticky soles and hold them down tight without gluing yourself to the shoe.

Once the procedure was complete, we were supposed to let the shoe and glue set for twenty-four hours. But usually I became impatient and would put my shoes on prematurely, causing my socks to be cemented into the original hole. I remember once pulling my feet out and leaving the socks in the shoes for several days because they were firmly attached to the sole by the hole.

But this procedure, which could give Bill Cosby a whole show's worth of material, was only a temporary solution. As the months went by the sole would loosen and the tread would flop with each step. How humiliating it was to be teased about the flip-flop of the phony soles as they came unglued. How I longed for a new pair of shoes more than once a year. How I wished for a fairy godmother who would wave her wand and give me glass slippers.

As I look back on the embarrassment of wearing tire treads on my shoes, I realize that most of us have had something glued onto us as children that made us ashamed of ourselves. It may not have been a rubber sole but perhaps you were given a derogatory name by an angry parent. Perhaps there was some failure that had been repeatedly pointed out so you couldn't get loose of it, or an abuse that made you feel you were wearing a Scarlet Letter on your chest.

THOUGHT FOR THE DAY _____
When you think back, what was glued on you that you've never been freed from? Until we uncover the phony sole over the hole, we won't be able to make the tough times count.

Providing Promise

Therefore I say to you, do not worry about your life, what you will eat or what you will drink; nor about your body, what you will put on. Is not life more than food and the body more than clothing?

————————————————————MATTHEW 6:25 NKJV

*W*hat's your biggest worry? Your job? Your children? A difficult relationship?

For many of us, food, clothing, and shelter are not givens. When we look at our debt, our rent, the spiraling costs of living, or perhaps an insecure job, we may be filled with anxieties about how we are even going to put food on the table. That is when it is important to refocus on God's promise to provide for us and determine to face our fears one day at a time. Overwhelming debt or an uncertain financial future is best confronted by faith in God, sound advice, and slow, steady, daily steps.

THOUGHT FOR THE DAY ————————————————
I need reassurance that You will take care of me, God. You are good. Help my unbelief.

Calm Down, Toughen Up!

"And let us not grow weary while doing good, for in due season we shall reap if we do not lose heart."

GALATIANS 6:9 NKJV

*H*ow do you explain the people who "calm down and toughen up" through tears and toil and trial until they finally make it?

How do you explain Glenn Cunningham, who was burned so severely in a school fire that doctors said he'd never walk again—but who in 1934 set a world's record by running a mile in 4 minutes and 6.8 seconds?

How do you explain Itzhak Perlman, born of parents who survived a Nazi concentration camp, and himself paralyzed from the waist down when he was four years old, who became one of the world's truly great concert violinists?

How do you explain a little fellow who was called a slow learner, even retarded, but who grew up to be Albert Einstein?

And how do you explain the unknowns, the little people you and we would like to relate to, who also go through hard situations and come out winners?

We know a pastor named Steve whose congregation gave him nothing but trouble for seven long years. Eventually this so discouraged his wife, Jane, that she escaped into alcoholism, drugs, and unfaithfulness.

But Steve just wouldn't quit. Through grit, through tears, he just kept on loving his congregation and loving his wife.

There finally came a point when Jane was willing to go for help, and their relationship, through a long, slow, tedious, and sometimes painful process, is getting beautifully healed. Steve and Jane are at last truly in love.

Meanwhile, several of his most "ornery" church members moved away, and some really supportive ones moved in! Gradually the majority of the congregation began to lean toward the new leadership, and the climate of the church as a whole has slowly shifted from hostility to allegiance.

It all took time. It's not perfect yet, but it's good, and Steve's a happy man.

"But," you may be saying, "how do you know if I stick out my situation I'd get a happy ending like these you've talked about? Maybe I wouldn't. And this is the only life I've got."

Maybe.

We don't want to lead you into unrealistic dreaming, but . . . hear another story.

We have a friend Julia; she's in her late sixties. Long ago when Julia was in her twenties, her husband had a stroke which left him permanently paralyzed and speechless.

It could have easily buckled her knees, but it didn't. For almost a quarter of a century—until he died—Julia faithfully cared for her husband. She raised her young family alone. She took an active part in community and church life. Julia just did what she knew she could do, and she kept going.

After the death of her husband, everyone was thrilled when Julia fell in love with a very eligible bachelor her age from a nearby church. Eventually they were engaged.

The very week of the wedding—unexplainably—the fellow took his life.

The grief was intense; the pain was terrible; but Julia just kept going. She gave herself to others; she never missed a beat in her civic and church responsibilities. She went through the right motions; she survived.

Today Julia is married to a silver-haired, vigorous, handsome fellow who fits her lifestye well. He loves to share with her the larger leadership responsibilities she's so good at. Julia is truly fulfilled, and all of us who have witnessed her life are cheering her on.

Well, on a scale of one to ten, how is life for you right now?

Is it a one—and you wish you could start running and never look back?

Is it a five—and you're feeling discontented and you'd like to switch to something fresh?

Is it an eight—it's pretty good, but there are one or two bad parts you'd like to get rid of?

Maybe your first need is for techniques of staying power. Maybe you need to learn how to tackle the bad situations where you are and turn them around for good.

The two of us are no heroes, like Glenn Cunningham or Itzhak Perlman, but we've had troubles, too. There have been periods when we've cried to the Lord that our marriage was a mistake. And there have been times when one or both of us—rightly or wrongly—have felt unneeded, unloved, rejected by the other.

But all in all, our forty years together have been wonderful, especially the last five! We're just crazy about each other now, and more in love than ever before.

Or take our career in Christian ministry. We've had thirty-six years so far, and sometimes we wouldn't have given you a nickel for the whole bloomin' business. There was a time when the entire governing board of our church was against our remaining as pastor, and another time when a few people got long lists of signatures petitioning our removal. You better believe it, those were times of bewilderment and depression.

Yet over the long haul we've seen, and we're still seeing, the realization of fabulous dreams, and we wouldn't trade careers with anybody in the world.

But plenty are quitting . . . around you and around us.

These are restless, unstable days, and everywhere jobs are quit too soon, schooling is cut too soon, marriages are severed too soon, friendships are broken too soon—switching and dropping out have become epidemic.

The two of us feel it's time to cry, "Hold it! Wait! Reconsider! You don't have to quit! There are techniques available for hanging on and letting God turn bad situations into good!"

Listen:

The best way out is usually through.

In a throwaway society, consider holding on.

THOUGHT FOR THE DAY _____

Learn ways to "calm down and toughen up"! Help us to develop staying power—so that in life's tough situations we can win.

*Let your feelings of inadequacy drive
you to God. You'll find your
adequacy in Him.*

Charles Stanley
The Source of My Strength

"Don't Get Mad, Get Smart"

A soft answer turneth away wrath: but grievous words stir up anger. The tongue of the wise useth knowledge aright.

————————————————————**PROVERBS 15:1-2** KJV

*A*ll through my life it has been necessary for me to chip away at the various kinds of walls that people built to exclude anyone who is the least bit different. Now as a world community, the extremes of ethnic warfare, ethnic cleansing, genocide, and many variations of tribal and gender conflict threaten to destroy any sense of community, state, and nation around the world. Breaking down the walls that divide us has become essential to the survival of the human race. In fact, this is one of the clearly stated ministries of Christ. The letter to the Ephesians describes the ministry of reconciliation, according to the purposes of God: "For he is our peace, who has made us both one, and has broken down the dividing wall of hostility" (Eph. 2:14 RSV).

Oppression breeds a certain amount of stoicism. When anyone does not have many avenues of redress or the power to defend oneself and family, the stoic response is to bear up gracefully and assume an air of rising above the suffering through the power of one's mind and spirit. This was the approach I saw my father take. He never seemed to let anything touch him. He was always a man of reason, and he taught me never to lose my cool. His advice was a marked contrast to the admonition of Joseph P. Kennedy to his children, "Don't get mad, get even." My father's advice was, "Don't get mad, get smart."

The concept of "getting smart" meant that one should think one's way through any difficulty or challenge. Anger only paralyzes the thought process and takes away one of a person's unique strengths. Animals are given to fight or flight, but human beings have the capacity to rise above any situation through the power of the mind and the spirit.

To reinforce this lesson my father would shadowbox with me. As long as I was controlled and disciplined in my approach, he would encourage and congratulate me. Whenever I began to get frustrated and swing wildly, he would tap me lightly but persistently on the cheek and say, "That's one knockout, two knockouts, three knockouts. How many times are you going to get knocked out before you learn to control yourself and think?"

That lesson came in handy later in 1962 when Martin Luther King went to jail in Albany, Georgia. Being a new arrival to the movement at that time, I was given the task of visiting him in jail twice daily to keep him informed of the movement's progress and problems. On my first visit, I entered the jail and said politely, "Excuse me, I'd like to see Dr. King, please." Without even looking up, the desk sergeant shouted to the jailer, "There's a little nigger out here to see those big niggers back there."

I was so taken aback that I didn't know what to do. To express my indignation would only get me thrown in jail or barred from visiting, and someone had to be able to move in and out of the jail to keep information flowing if it were at all possible. Violence was no answer. The sergeant was a six-foot-five, 250-pound former football player with a stick and a gun. I did, however, make note of his name on his uniform. When I came back the next day, I addressed him by name. "Good morning, Sergeant Hamilton, how are you doing today?"

Now, he seemed shocked, and grunted, "Okay."

From that time on, I never went to the jail without addressing Sergeant Hamilton by name and engaging him in some brief small talk before asking to see Dr. King. He never again spoke disrespectfully to me, and we actually became familiar with each other's families and sports interests. Of course, as everyone in the southern farm belt does, we talked about the weather. I not only survived, I accomplished my mission and visited the jail daily until Martin was released.

Sparring with your adversaries accomplishes nothing. When trouble crosses your path, rise above it. *"Be wise as serpents and harmless as doves"* (Matt. 10:16). Don't get mad, get smart.

THOUGHT FOR THE DAY _____

Love your enemies, bless those who curse you, do good to those who hate you, and pray for those who spitefully use you and persecute you, that you may be sons of your Father in heaven; for He makes His sun rise on the evil and on the good, and sends rain on the just and on the unjust. (Matt. 5:44–45 NKJV*)*

Clean Your Closet

"Has no one condemned you?"
"No one, Lord."
"Neither do I."
———JOHN 8:10–11 NKJV

*C*loset cleaning is a necessary part of your household upkeep and an important part of your spiritual maintenance. Often the Lord has led me to search the closets of my spiritual house. There, I found one closet labeled "guilt & shame," filled with the skeletons of my painful past.

No matter what our sins, we need to give God full ownership of all sin items in our spiritual closets. They belong to Him. After all, He has fully paid for them, and the blood of Jesus has washed all our dirty laundry—it's whiter than snow! His spirit will breathe new life as we witness His neverending grace. There are no bones about it!

THOUGHT FOR THE DAY ————————————
Thank You, Lord, that we do not have to live with skeletons hidden in our closets. Give us the grace to let You walk through them with us and to clean them together.

Where Does Your Love Lie?

For where your treasure is, there will your heart be also.
———————————————————MATTHEW 6:21 NASB

In Genesis 22, Abraham was placed in the excruciating bind of having to consider killing his son Isaac as a living sacrifice. The story begins by God either testing or tempting Abraham depending on how one chooses to translate the passage. Because Abraham was faced with a clear choice to respond to a command, I would translate this as a story of temptation. Child sacrifice was common in that day, and Abraham could have well reasoned that should this son be taken, God could easily provide another. This great chosen leader was hurled into a staggering conflict of great fury. Whom would he love the most? His son? His God? Because Abraham was confronted with a choice about his ultimate values, he was being tempted to decide who occupied the place of final loyalty in his life—God or the family.

There's nothing out-of-date about Abraham's story. While none of us would ever have to ponder the idea of human sacrifice, we are constantly tempted to put many things, situations, and people in the place that should be reserved only for God. Whatever is our final source of meaning and happiness is actually our god. Often people have lost their souls giving them away to something or someone who is less than our heavenly Father. In effect, we have placed God on the altar of achievement, power, romance, family and have tried to slay Him. However, we, and not a ram, are the ones who end up caught in the thicket.

THOUGHT FOR THE DAY ————————————————
In the dark of night when all the unseen forces of disaster are closing in, what do you cling to? family, friends, or the Father? What are you willing to sacrifice? Your momentary relationships, or your eternal connection to God?

Integrity is a one-on-one correlation between my Bible, my beliefs, and my behavior.

Patrick M. Morley
The Rest of Your Life

No Bitterness

Do not rejoice when your enemy falls,
And do not let your heart be glad when he stumbles;
Lest the LORD *see it, and it displease Him,*
And He turn away His wrath from him.
—————————————**PROVERBS 24:17–18** NKJV

This proverb says something important about the Lord's nature. It assumes that the Lord is on your side and that your enemy is someone who has wronged you. So what does this tell us about God?

1. He cares about our attitudes.
2. He cares for those who have fallen.

When our enemies stumble, we are to react soberly, lovingly, confident in the justice of our God, but also sharing in His mercy. There is no place for bitterness. God turns our mourning into dancing. As you grow closer to His merciful heart, yours will become less embittered. And in time you'll even be able to invite your worst enemy to dance.

THOUGHT FOR THE DAY ————————————
I don't feel like dancing today, God. Help me believe that someday
I will be glad again. And give me the grace to love my enemy.

WARREN W. WIERSBE
On Being a Servant of God

Obedience Gives You Wings

If ye will obey my voice indeed, and keep my covenant, then ye shall be a peculiar treasure unto me above all people: for all the earth is mine.

————————————————————EXODUS 19:5 KJV

God has a specific plan for you. He wants to share His plan with you and help you to fulfill it. At least that's the way I interpret Paul's words in Ephesians 2:10: "For we are His workmanship, created in Christ Jesus for good works, which God prepared beforehand that we should walk in them."

" '*For good works*' is not a narrow phrase referring merely to specific acts of so-called Christian service," said G. Campbell Morgan in a sermon on this text. He explained that "it refers to the whole life. . . . He has foreordained the works of the man He is making. He has been ahead of me preparing the place to which I am coming, manipulating all the resources of the universe in order that the work I do may be a part of His whole great gracious work."

Since God made you the way you are (Ps. 139), He must have had a purpose for you. Everything in the universe accomplishes some divine purpose; and it seems unreasonable that you, who are made in the image of God and redeemed by the sacrifice of His Son, should be left out. John of Damascus defined *providence* as "the care God takes of all existing things." If not one sparrow is forgotten before God (Luke 12:6), surely the Father cares for and guides His own children!

God indeed has a plan, and it requires your compliance. But obedience to the will of God gives you wings, not chains! You are never more free than when you fulfill the plan God has for your life. This plan is not an impersonal, unreparable machine that will break down when you disobey. It is an unrelenting understanding that remains as flexible and forgiving as pliable clay. Likewise, God should not be thought of as a mechanic fixing your mistakes, but rather as a master potter lovingly reforming the life and the will you have turned over to Him. "And the vessel that he made of clay was marred in the hand of the potter; so he made it again [refashioned it] into a another vessel, as it seemed good to the potter to make" (Jer. 18:4).

Moses began his ministry by defending a fellow Jew and then fleeing for his life, but God refashioned him again. When things got tough, Abraham ran off to Egypt, and twice lied about his wife, but God refashioned him again. Isaac, too, lied about his wife, and Jacob schemed his way through life; but upon their return to God, their hardened clay became submerged in the water of obedience, allowing God to refashion them again.

Their sinful human actions should not have happened, but they did. Nevertheless, their failures didn't stop God from accomplishing His divine purpose, because He refashioned each of their repented lives into the very men we call "the patriarchs" of the Hebrew nation.

Most certainly there are things in your life that should not have happened. Yet no matter how "marred" you have become, you can begin again. All it takes is your compliance. All that is necessary is your willingness to draw closer to God; to follow His laws and the specific plan He has designed just for you.

THOUGHT FOR THE DAY _____
Daily devotions and a diligent desire to please God can and will refashion you, and give you wings to fly.

Obedience to the will of God gives you wings, not chains.

Warren W. Wiersbe
On Being a Servant of God

W. MATTHEW REED, JR.
Flying Solo

Proof Through People

> *Now the LORD said to Moses, "Go in to Pharaoh; for I have hardened his heart and the hearts of his servants, that I may show these signs of Mine before him."*
> —————————————EXODUS 10:1 NKJV

When I found myself alone because of my wife's sudden departure, I asked, "Why, Lord? Why have You permitted her heart to get so hard? Why haven't You broken her and caused her to return to me?" If you have wondered the same thing about your spouse, you can find an answer in this verse.

Pharaoh's heart was hardened so that all Egypt would see God's miraculous power demonstrated in ten plagues. The plagues were proof of His existence and lordship.

God does the same thing today, but He uses people, not plagues. He hardens hearts to demonstrate power and lordship in our lives.

THOUGHT FOR THE DAY ————————
God has a hand in some of the most unusual places. Look for His power everywhere.

All My Problems Are Caused By My Sin

And we know that all things work together for good to them that love God, to them who are the called according to his purpose.

—ROMANS 8:28 KJV

*E*ver since the days of Job, people have been hearing and believing that problems are caused by sins. Logic holds no sway with this lie, which says, "God messes up our lives to punish us for our sins." Harold was the victim of this old lie.

"I know why I'm having such trouble," he said. "I'm being punished." Harold was a distinguished older man I'd been working with for only a short time, and he opened one of our sessions with this statement.

"Punished? For what?" I said.

"Well," he hedged, "I don't know for sure. But I'm sure it's something we can find out. It's the only thing that makes sense."

"Harold, you believe, then, that the only time people have problems is when they sin?"

"Yes, it makes sense."

"Then that means that bad things only happen to bad people. Good people never have any troubles."

"Well, no, that's not what I said. Good people seem to have trouble . . ." He thought about that for a second, then clicked his fingers. "But maybe they're not as good as they seem to be!"

"And bad people who get away with awful crimes, they're not really bad?"

"No, no, no. Look, I don't know. There's some explanation for that, I'm sure," he said, with a wave of his hand.

We humans like to explain things. We like to explain the universe to each other, to have some tiny grasp of the future. Everything must happen for a reason, we feel. If we just know that reason, we can control the future somehow. To believe we cause all our own problems is a very easy lie to believe. If it's true, then all we have to do to keep out of trouble is be good. The problem is we cannot always *be* good, and, when we believe this lie on top of that inevitability, we doom ourselves to a guilt-ridden life we wouldn't wish on anyone.

Of course, as always, this lie has a toehold in reality. If you are carrying on an affair with someone at the office, problems can result from that sin. Other people's sin can hurt you too. If your partner decides to funnel off your business profits into a Swiss checking account, you will suffer. But what about the problems resulting from no sin at all? For example, our friends' home was struck by lightning. It burnt a hole in their roof, "fried" some of their electrical wiring, and ruined some appliances. Yet even in a situation like this, some Christians would start to think, *I must have done something wrong because otherwise God would not let that lightning strike my house.* If God used lightning to get back at us for our sins, every house in America would have been torched long ago!

We can see the truth, once again, in the ministry of Christ. When He and His disciples saw a man blind from birth, Christ's disciples asked Christ in so many words, "Rabbi, who sinned? This man or his parents? Who caused his blindness?"

"Neither this man nor his parents sinned," said Jesus, "but [this happened so] that the works should be revealed in him."

Sometimes God allows bad things to happen to good people because He wants to display His power. Sometimes He allows it, as we discussed earlier, to help us mature. Sometimes, through free will, as the Valley Girls say, "Stuff happens." The only truth we can grasp is that God can bring good out of bad. That's the truth behind the passage, "in all things God works for the good of those who love him" (Rom. 8:28 NIV).

The challenge we face is to examine honestly the root of a given problem. If the root is personal sin, then that sin does need to be dealt with before the problem can be solved.

If, on the other hand, a problem is the result of someone else's sin or no sin at all, then we need to let ourselves off the hook and solve the problem as best we can. The alternative is to spend our lives feeling guilty over something we didn't cause, all because of a lie.

THOUGHT FOR THE DAY _____

I will examine my heart, and pray for God's insight. If I can find nothing wrong, I will let myself off the hook.

ANNE AND RAY ORTLUND
You Don't Have to Quit!

Whatever Your Situation—"Stick It Out till June"

"Therefore He is also able to save to the uttermost those who come to God through Him."
———————————————————————HEBREWS 7:25 NKJV

*W*hen Nels was in early high school, he wasn't applying himself and studying well. Having lunch one day with a friend, we were telling her how we were going bananas over our happy, unstructured, unmotivated, and unconcerned boy.

"I know what you mean!" said Marian. "Our Johnny was exactly the same. I don't think he ever would have turned out so well if we hadn't sent him to Stony Brook."

Stony Brook! We knew that fine Christian school outside New York City, and we asked Nels if he'd like to go. He was thrilled. Fifteen-year-old Nels dreamed of the glamour of an Eastern prep school and of wowing them with his personality and his tennis. . . .

It took him about a week to get thoroughly homesick. He decided that he was a true California beachboy and that from September to Christmas certainly ought to be as long as anyone should endure the East Coast.

Boy, did we have phone bills! He kept begging to come home at

Christmas to stay, and we kept telling him he must complete that one school year.

"Nels," we said, "if you want to finish high school in California, we will love having you at home. But you really must stick out Stony Brook until June. You don't want to remember this as the year you were a quitter."

At Christmas he came home. He'd had a deep cold for three months, he was unbelievably skinny, and his face was all broken out. He looked terrible.

And he announced he'd sold his furniture, given up his dorm room, told everybody good-bye, and shipped home all his belongings.

"Well," we said, "we love you, Skipper, and when you're gone we miss you terribly, but you'll have to pay to ship your things back again. And you can just do without room furnishings until June."

He couldn't believe us! We said, "We don't want to spoil Christmas by arguing. Let's not talk about it until the Monday after Christmas, okay? Then we'll go spend the day in the desert and talk and pray together."

On December 29 the three of us drove to Palm Desert. By the end of the day Nels knew he'd lost, and it's a wrenching thing to see a skinny, six-foot-one lad cry. We sat there watching in agony as he paced back and forth in the sunshine he loved, and then he ended the discussion like this:

"All right, Mom and Dad, I'm going back. I hate it; I don't want to go, but you guys are forcing me."

(He wiped his runny nose with his hand, and when he heaved an uncontrollable sob, it just tore us apart.)

"But I just want you to know one thing. Even though I'm going back and I don't want to, we still love each other, and nothing is ever going to change that!"

Can't you believe how we were absolutely melted and how our hearts went out to him?

At that moment, and through the next six months, we prayed night and day for our dear boy. His cold continued to go in and out of pneumonia until spring, and he never did well scholastically. But can you imagine how continually and intensely we prayed over our dear, skinny, fragile, fifteen-year-old Nels? *He had surrendered himself in love to our will, and because of that he was in a distant and (to him) difficult place.*

"Lord," we prayed day and night, "ease his pain! Lord, give him godly friends! Lord, help him study! Lord, help him know we love him! Lord, help him see how those dear teachers and staff are on his side! Lord, dry up his cold! Lord, turn his thoughts to You! Lord, strengthen and help our dear boy! Lord, comfort him! Lord, help the time pass quickly until he's home!"

With April and May came thawing and more sunshine and more tennis, and Nels began to like it a little better. By June he was glad he'd stuck out the year, and by midsummer, at home, he had trouble deciding whether to go back and finish high school at Stony Brook.

He didn't—but he tells us that year was his most necessary and most life-changing year so far. We know it; we see it.

A little epilogue to the story came several years later when the three of us were dining in a local restaurant. Nels, rested, handsome, happy, and growing up, commented, "Mom and Dad, look across the room. There's _____, who went back East to school the same fall I did and dropped out at Christmastime. Boy, I'm so glad I don't have to look back on that year and remember myself as a quitter."

And here you are, and here are the two of us—Jesus Christ's dear, fragile, immature kids. Our schooling is in a difficult place, and we're far from our heavenly home. *But we've surrendered ourselves in love to His will—and don't you think that melts Him?* Don't you think His heart goes out to us? Don't you think that makes Him intercede for us continually and intensely, "with groans that words cannot express"(Rom. 8:26 NIV)?

See from the book of Hebrews that

1. *He sympathizes with you.* (He's not looking down on you ready to belt you one with a big stick.)

For we do not have a high priest who is unable to sympathize with our weaknesses, but we have one who has been tempted in every way, just as we are—yet was without sin. Let us then approach the throne of grace with confidence (4:15–16 NIV).

2. *He is right there to help.* (And He's far more able to help than California parents with a son in New York.)

Because he himself suffered when he was tempted, he is able to help those who are being tempted (2:18 NIV).

3. *And He can bring you through in triumph.*

Therefore he is able to save completely those who come to God [the verb means "who make a habit of continually coming to God"] through him, because he always lives to intercede for them (7:25 NIV).

THOUGHT FOR THE DAY _____
Friend, whatever your tough situation is right now—Stick it out till June.

Run from Fools

Go from the presence of a foolish man,
When you do not perceive in him the lips of knowledge.

PROVERBS 14:7 NKJV

A friend of mine told me about a recent trip to the golf course. Tom was in a foursome with a group of influential men whose conversation was deteriorating with each hole they finished. He had a choice to stay and listen, to speak up, or to leave. When Tom shared his feelings about the level of conversation, the others became hostile and defensive. Tom figured it wasn't worth listening to the garbage through the final nine holes, so he left. It was a tough choice. Just because Tom could recognize the men as fools in their manner of conversation, he didn't want to be thought badly of by anyone, not even by a fool.

The need not to appear "too Christian" or "too different" leads many men to stay around the fools and sometimes to fall into trouble. God suggests that we leave, lest the foolishness rub off on us.

THOUGHT FOR THE DAY
It takes courage to run from fools.

Be Still!

Too many irons in the fire make the fire go out.
————————————————JOHN W. WHITE

Many of us move toward activity. We volunteer for every commit-tee, serve on every board, plan and attend every church function, and still put in more than forty hours each week on our regular job. We acknowledge that we aren't taking time for ourselves, but still we never slow down.

Have you ever stopped long enough to figure out what purpose the compulsion of drivenness serves for you? It looks so wonderful on the surface because you're such a servant and give your time so freely. How-ever, God calls us to "be still, and know that I am God" (Psalm 46:10).

Being still would mean you face your fears, your pain, and the anxiety that you continue to run from through your load of activities. You have two choices: either to slow down and face yourself or stop completely when you reach burnout.

THOUGHT FOR THE DAY ————————————————
God, give me the courage to slow down today so that I can get to know myself and You.

It's Always Too Soon to Quit

> *Blessed be the God and Father of our Lord Jesus Christ, the Father of mercies and God of all comfort, who comforts us in all our tribulation, that we may be able to comfort those who are in any trouble, with the comfort with which we ourselves are comforted by God.*
>
> 2 CORINTHIANS 1:3–4 NKJV

God is as concerned about the servant as He is the service. If all God wanted to do was get the work done, He could send His angels, and they would do it better and faster. But He not only wants to do something *through* us, He also wants to do something *in* us; and that is why hurdles clutter the path of our lives. God uses them to encourage us to pray, trust the Word, and depend on the Spirit for love and grace. Difficult people and difficult circumstances can be used by the Spirit to help us grow and become more like Christ.

However, when these difficulties come, our tendency is to pray for deliverance instead of growth. We ask the Lord, "*How* can I get out of this?" instead of "*What* can I get out of this?" When we do that, we miss the opportunities God gives us to develop spiritual maturity.

Sometimes you may feel like quitting and running away. That's the worst thing you can do. Resigning your job, abandoning the task or leaving town altogether will never solve your problems or satisfy the needs of your heart. In fact, you'll probably end up meeting the same people (with different names) in that next town. Why? Because God won't let His servants run away. God is determined that His children be "conformed to the image of His Son" (Romans 8:29), and He will keep working until He has accomplished His purpose.

It's human to want to run away from a tough situation. Many believers have done it, and many more have wanted to do it. Moses had such a difficult time with Israel that he wanted to die (Numbers 11:10–15), and Elijah became so discouraged that he deserted his post and went into the wilderness where he asked to die (1 Kings 19). Dr. V. Raymond Edman used to tell the Wheaton (Illinois) College students, "It's always too soon to quit." On the flyleaf of my copy of his book *The Disciplines of Life,* Dr. Edman wrote, "Remember always to keep chin up and knees down!" Good counsel!

You'll meet problem people and problem situations wherever you go, so make up your mind to expect them, accept them, and let God use them in your life. The devil wants to use problem people as weapons to tear you down, but the Spirit can use them as tools to build you up. The choice is yours. If you stay on the job and trust God to work, you'll experience His grace in a wonderful way; and you'll be a better servant.

THOUGHT FOR THE DAY ————————————————
One of the best ways to discover the divine resources that others need is to need them yourself and trust God to supply them.

We tend to ask God "How can I get out of this?" instead of "What can I get out of this?"

Warren W. Wiersbe
On Being a Servant of God

Don't Judge— Befriend

Let all bitterness, wrath, anger, clamor, and evil speaking be put away from you, with all malice. And be kind to one another.

——————————————————EPHESIANS 4:31–32 NKJV

"**D**on't worry about it! He's a jerk," Art said when I told him I felt bad about not liking Jim and talking behind Jim's back. Jim was obnoxious—loud, brash, and forward.

Art's answer didn't reassure me. I still felt bad about the way I treated Jim, so I called, and Jim was most gracious. He even invited me for lunch at his office. When we sat down, I told him that I had been cutting him down behind his back. I told him I was sorry and hoped we could be friends. Jim's eyes moistened as he answered, "You know, I've done just about everything I could to make friends. I even bought a big-screen TV and asked the guys over to watch the game, but no one came. I've just about given up. I guess I just don't fit in."

I was shocked—I had pushed away someone who needed my help. Jim wasn't a bad guy, only different. He and I agreed to be friends, and we still are. That was good for him . . . and even better for me.

THOUGHT FOR THE DAY ————————————
Help me see behind the masks people wear, God. The people I count my enemies may want to be my friends.

Face Up to It

When You said, "Seek My face,"
My heart said to You, "Your face, LORD, I will seek."
————————————————————————————**PSALM 27:8** NKJV

*M*ost of us like to look into the faces of other people. When we have something very difficult to say, though, it is hard for us to look at a person's face. We are afraid of what we will see there. How do we feel when the look we see on someone else's face is *not* the look we want to see? Sometimes we feel inadequate.

There's a big difference when we seek our Lord's face. When we make a mistake and we seek His face, we can know we are forgiven. When we are hurting and we seek His face, we are assured of His comfort. Even when we close our eyes to sleep, we can seek His face and rest in peace. We each need to be aware of whose approving looks we value. The looks of people may disappoint us, but when we seek God's face, we will find acceptance and guidance.

THOUGHT FOR THE DAY ————————————————————
In the time of trouble, You Hide us, Lord. You are gracious and kind.

" 'Tis Death That Makes Life Live"

"I was dead, and behold I am alive for ever and ever!"
—————————————REVELATION 1:18 NIV

*V*iewed from the heights of grandmotherhood, life tends to hide its shadows. When eyewitnesses are gone, older women tend to "forget" failures. And little-girl fantasies, wrinkled with age, can come alive to retouch family histories.

I am tempted to downplay my early tussle with the concept of death because for so long it held me by the throat. But I crave an ability to recall the way it really was because only then can I tell you what I learned about living and how I learned it from what Job called "the king of terrors."

For years I didn't even know I needed to learn a lesson about people. Like every newborn baby, I arrived into the world and people were there, talking and being who they were. I imitated them and didn't ask questions. But when suddenly some were not there any longer, that got my attention.

Robert Browning's words describe my experience: "You never

know what life means till you die. Even throughout life, 'tis death that makes life live."

Death has made its statement in our world. It is the irreversible closure, the period—or exclamation point—or question mark, at the end of the human sentence. It is the most profound lights out, the end of the road, the final crush, the last ultimate humiliation of humanity. And it struck paralyzing fear into my six-year-old being when I met it head-on for the first time.

Aunt Carrie lived close by; she was my frequent baby-sitter, the mother of four favorite cousins, and it was at her home in suburban Philadelphia where our family ate nearly every Sunday dinner. Then came a stormy spring night when I sat on my daddy's lap in her darkened living room and saw her corpse.

Nobody could explain why to my satisfaction. My cousins seemed as confused as I was, and the adults in the family just didn't say much. At home Dad told me that she had too much fat around her heart; nevertheless, Aunt Carrie was gone and nothing was the same.

A decade passed, years in which uncertainty about life and death grew for me. During that time, I made a personal commitment of my life to Jesus Christ. I understood, at least in theory, the ultimate answer to death, but the churning torment of loss when a loved one was irretrievably gone had not been alleviated. I had no label for my inward terror, much less did I understand my real need. In no way was I prepared for another shattering loss.

This time I was alerted, but I plugged my ears. A childless couple who had become family friends when I was about eight years old began to invite me to spend time with them. Uncle Floyd and Aunt Grace enchanted me as they took me with them in their shiny car to visit their wonderful German relatives. One of his uncles owned a candy shop; another one had a small farm. All of them were marvelous storytellers and happy, friendly, and kind. My difficult early teen years were highlighted with these loving and high-spirited people who introduced me to having good clean fun. Then without warning, Uncle Floyd pulled me aside during a weekend retreat and told me he loved me and wanted to say good-bye; he was having heart surgery on his "leaky pump."

"No!" I protested. "You'll get better; I know you will!"

But he knew intuitively, and about a week later, the dreaded call came from Aunt Grace. I wanted to run away and scream, to somehow undo the personal knot that was choking me, to change it all. Instead I had to stand beside the casket and face the truth, but I could not bear to look at Uncle Floyd's face. I closed my eyes and tried to deny; I simply had no coping mechanism.

Every year we celebrated Christ's resurrection. I had memorized parts of 1 Corinthians 15. I had sung often, *"O death, where is thy sting? O grave, where is thy victory?"* But the monster kept pursuing me and moving in ever closer. As a young adult I tried to become a bit more philosophical. When three of my own babies died before they were born, I pretended that it hadn't really happened. But there was no escape; the day came when Mother told me that Dad was terminally ill with cancer.

No, not my daddy! He's too big and strong and warm and loving—God will make an exception. I believed it and I went home and sat with Mother in the living room and pleaded in prayer for Dad's miraculous recovery. But the disease persisted and took its deadly toll. Dad's ready wit and engaging personality faded. He whispered hoarsely and scanned me with serious and piercing eyes. I knew him well because we had often talked together, and he had many times given me advice that was filled with uncanny insight and common sense. Now it was his last opportunity, and God allowed him to share with me the most important counsel he had ever given to this second daughter with whom a mutual trust had grown over the years. Dad held out his wasted arm to me and began to fill in my blanks.

"Honey, don't be sad. God gave me many years and that's what counts. Now, He's letting you and Howie and your youngsters carry on. So, you just use your life for the Lord. Just do what He tells you. And I'll be seeing you again . . ."

With months to prepare, I was still not ready for the icy words, "He's gone." Never had I wept with tears so bitter, so unable to be turned off. Never was there a colder, more bleak October day than that dreadful afternoon when Dad, my source of comfort and consolation since birth, sank into the sod.

Aunt Carrie had left a mysterious emptiness. Uncle Floyd had said he loved me, but I resented his absence. Dad had tried to prepare me, and finally I was beginning to understand. Death *is* bigger and stronger than I am, but I don't have to be its victim. I can learn from it.

Falling asleep has always been one of my best accomplishments. But after Dad died, I found myself lying awake in bed with a deep sense of loss and sadness. I often woke up in the middle of the night and cried bitter tears because he was no longer available to me—or was he? I began to think back over the words he had spoken.

First, there was the hope—"I'll see you again . . ." Of course, that is exactly what Jesus told His disciples when He was going to the cross. Death was not the end, not the real end.

Second, Dad was gone, but I was still here with my family. He had said that it was now my turn—he handed me the torch.

A new resolve began to set into my thinking. The little oft-repeated couplet surfaced: *"Only one life; 'twill soon be past. Only what's done for Christ will last."* Gradually I began to gain strength from remembering that parting scene by the bedside. Like a transfusion of spiritual vitamins, my goals crystalized. I began to see what Paul meant by the defanging of death and the grave.

Death is neutralized by life when that life continues in another warrior who "fights the good fight." The grave is a mere formality in the total scheme of God's grace.

When Mother died in my home, after twenty-three years of widowhood, I was sad, but also full of a deep joy that I had been privileged to come into the world as the product of her—and Dad's—love. The emptiness and void were there, but they were overshadowed by a sense of challenge: It's my turn now.

Jesus speaks to me with full force: "He who loves his life will lose it . . . Unless a grain of wheat falls into the ground and dies, it remains alone; but if it dies, it produces much grain" (John 12:24, 25). And so with full speed ahead, I aim to pour myself into other lives so that Christ may say of me, "Well done, good and faithful servant."

Aunt Carrie's death left me with a fear, based on ignorance, of people. I simply did not know how important they were and I took them for granted. Uncle Floyd's passing left me with a fear based on unwillingness to allow people to come in (and go out) of my life. Dad helped me look my fear in the face, to break it and melt it by using death as a harsh, but very effective, teacher.

Aunt Carrie had cared for me; Uncle Floyd had reached out to a quiet little girl and shared with her the mainstream of his life. Dad dispelled for me the seeming impossibility of facing death's horror.

Possibly the most amazing fallout from these three significant deaths was the implant of love for people. I was known as a shy child, a painfully insecure, timid, and self-conscious teen. Always concerned with what people would think of me, constantly avoiding public visibility, I was slow to realize that my purpose in life was simply to relate to other people. Like the payload on a three-stage rocket, I found myself catapulted into a life of serving people, touching them with the love and confidence I received from Christ. Best of all, funerals were no longer the numbing horrors of my early years.

Whether human beings divert attention from funerals with political parades or try to drown them with laughter and liquor, we all cower in the presence of death. It is impossible not to. Jesus Christ sweat drops of blood and suffered incredible agony in contemplation of His death; He took it seriously and so should we. No one escapes its clutches, but we can escape its consequences. Salvation through Christ means victory over the grave. His words to John are my ultimate consolation:

Do not be afraid. I am the First and the Last. I am the Living One; I was dead, and behold I am alive for ever and ever! And I hold the keys death and Hades (Revelation 1:17–18 NIV).

THOUGHT FOR THE DAY ————————————
Thank You, God, for the victory over death we have in Jesus Christ.

You Can't Please Everyone

*I cannot give you the formula for success,
but I can give you the formula for failure—
try to please everybody.*

——————————HERBERT BAYARD SWOPE

In 1975 singer Rick Nelson recorded a song called "Garden Party." In the song, Rick Nelson told of being invited to sing in an "oldies" concert at Madison Square Garden. When he got on stage, he sang several of his newest songs and the crowd booed and hissed at him. That wasn't what they had paid to hear. They wanted him to do "Hello, Mary Lou" and "Traveling Man" and his other hit singles from the 1950s and 1960s. In the song "Garden Party," Rick Nelson surmised, "You can't please everyone, so you've got to please yourself."

Whereas I am not so sure about the "so you've got to please yourself" part of that phrase (it sounds a little bit too self-centered for my tastes), I do think the "you can't please everyone" line is one of the great truths we need to recognize and practice in order to lead emotionally strong lives. To some extent Rick Nelson must have come to this realization, for the last line in his song was, "If memories were all I sang, I'd rather drive a truck."

"You can't please everyone" is a one-liner you've already heard a million times. But hearing it and believing it are not always the same thing. Most people are out there every day trying to please most everyone. Consider how much you worry about whether or not people like you and if they are happy with what you do. Why does it put a knot in your stomach whenever someone is upset with you? Why are you willing to do almost *anything* to insure that people will be pleased with you?

The answer is that we all have a basic need of approval. We want people to tell us we are all right, acceptable, special, worthy of love and admiration and trust and respect. In fact, if we *don't* receive adequate approval from people, we find it hard to get through life. A problem arises, however, when we think we need to earn the admiration and approval of every human being we meet. That simply is impossible and we can emotionally wipe ourselves out proving it.

Emotionally healthy people often walk a sort of tightrope. They need to do a certain amount of things in order to receive a needed amount of approval from other folks. However, they realize they also need to try to please themselves in certain areas. Where Rick Nelson made his mistake at Madison Square Garden, was that he didn't divide his performance between the new songs he wanted to share with the audience and the older songs they wanted to hear. We need that same balance in our relationships.

THOUGHT FOR THE DAY _____
Help me to be considerate of others, Lord, while I appropriately care for myself.

Requests Denied

God shall supply all your need according to His riches in glory by Christ Jesus.

PHILIPPIANS 4:19 NKJV

In the late 1800s a woman was traveling with her four-year-old son on a train. She had brought along the boy's nanny to take care of him. At one point, the boy began to fuss and cry. The mother was annoyed and questioned why the child was upset. The nanny responded, "He is crying because I wouldn't let him have something that he wanted." "Give him whatever he wants and keep him quiet," replied the mother.

Several moments passed, and suddenly the boy screamed in pain. Angrily the mother yelled, "I told you to give him whatever he wants." "I did," replied the nanny. "He wanted a wasp."

We are often like this child. We see something or someone we want, and we beg God to let us have it. It is difficult for us to understand that God is not trying to deprive us when He tells us no.

God sees the big picture. He knows that if we received some of our desires we would find a sting of pain. Because He loves us He withholds some of the things we desire. He is wise enough to know what we really need.

THOUGHT FOR THE DAY _____

Help me discern, Lord, between the desires of mine that will cause pain and those that will bring about good.

Too Busy?

But if from there you seek the LORD your God, you will find him if you look for him with all your heart and with all your soul.

DEUTERONOMY 4:29 NIV

The alarm didn't go off. The kids rolled out of bed in a cranky mood. The toaster burned breakfast. Someone forgot to plug in the iron. The neighbor's dog chewed up the newspaper again. It's raining. It's your day to carpool, and the car engine won't start.

When the Bible teacher says, "and the most important part of the day is a quiet time," it sounds good, real good. But as the momentary and immediate problems of everyday life set in, making the transition is no easy task. Why is a quiet time so important? What is supposed to happen there? And how does one pull it off?

The quiet time often becomes a hollow convention of religious structure, instead of a holy meeting with the personal Christ. We read a verse or two of the Bible, pray a little prayer and—oops! It's 7:30. Amen, and off to work again. That's one more item checked off the daily to-do list, another installment payment on a spiritual insurance policy.

Our quiet times often become yet another perfunctory duty of the

Christian life, another activity to verify our Christianity to ourselves. When this happens, the quiet time has become secularized. We cannot apply worldly methods to spiritual needs.

We are too busy. The suffocating pace of secular society subtly strangles our personal devotions. We must come apart to meet with the Lord. But, it seems we can barely function without the dull drone of a radio or a television in the background.

Some of us have forgotten *why* we take time, and with *Whom* we spend it. Instead of thinking of devotions in terms of what we want from God, perhaps some of us need to reevaluate. Let us go and meet with God and humbly quiet ourselves before the throne of His grace. Leave the religious party horns and hats to others.

A great tragedy of our era is that only ten percent of Americans read their Bibles daily, according to a 1986 Gallup poll. A far greater tragedy is that many of us who do read them do so out of a sense of duty and without much joy. Yet the Word is everything to the life of a Christian.

There is an order to life, a continuity, a progression. It is from *faith* to *obedience,* not from obedience to faith. Paul's mission was to call people "to the obedience that comes from faith" (Rom. 1:5 NIV). And how do we acquire the bedrock of faith? We meet with God. "Faith comes from hearing the message, and the message is heard through the word of Christ" (Rom. 10:17 NIV). Do you meet with and listen to God?

There is such a thing as a dry quiet time. When we walk upon deserts of disobedience, our thirst for God goes unmet. When we are caught up in a rat race, we must live out of the reserves. Yet our loving Father entreats us to come, no matter how far we have strayed. "But if from there you seek the LORD your God, you will find him if you look for him with all your heart and with all your soul" (Deut. 4:29 NIV).

Are you depending upon the religious structure of your life instead of your personal relationship with Him? Go and meet with God. You will find Him "if you look for him with all your heart and with all your soul."

THOUGHT FOR THE DAY _____
Are you looking, or just punching the clock?

Let Go and Grow

Even as Christ forgave you, so you also must do.
_____COLOSSIANS 3:13 NKJV

A man went to the doctor and found out that he had rabies. He immediately pulled out a pad and pen and began to write frantically. The doctor explained that there was no need to write out his will because he was not going to die. The man quickly responded that he was not making out a will; he was writing down a list of people he was planning to bite!

Some of us spend years waiting to get back at people. We keep a mental list of people we plan to "bite" the next chance we get. We waste a lot of energy keeping our anger fueled, ready for attack.

Holding a grudge in our hearts breeds bitterness. Carrying resentment is like dragging around a fifty-pound anchor. It tires us out and steals the joy of living. Bitterness damages us more than the people we are angry with. To grow, we must let go of our past grudges and move forward to the joy of living each new day.

THOUGHT FOR THE DAY _____
Joy returns when we throw away our grudges.

Plant a Thought Reap an Action

I would have you learn this great fact: that a life of doing right is the wisest life there is.

*———————————————*PROVERBS 4:11 TLB

*H*ow in the world can you suddenly stop sins and wrong habits that have gripped your life, perhaps for a long time? The answer lies in the fact that Satan is no longer your master; he has lost control of your life. You belong to Christ, and He lives in you now. Satan can still tempt you, but in Christ's power you can say no and walk away from the temptation. The Holy Spirit is now in your heart to help you.

All by itself, our determination to do right just doesn't seem to work, for we are fighting against Satan's power.

He entices us to do wrong, and he is too strong for us to stand against—unless we have God's help.

God's help is what God gives us when we become His children. He plants the Holy Spirit within us, and we can ask the Spirit to send Satan's power reeling into the corner.

The most important thing to remember is that you can't be what you want to be and what God wants you to be without the Holy

Spirit's help. What you want to be is kind, good, loving, strong, and fearless. These qualities are the results of the Spirit living in you.

It has been well said that if you plant a thought, you reap an action. Plant an action and reap a habit. Plant a habit and reap a character. It all begins with the thought life, and who can wrest the thought life from Satan's wiles except the Spirit of God?

The Holy Spirit now lives within you and is willing to take over and make you the person you have always wanted to be—the one God expects you to be. Yet He can't do it unless you let Him. No wonder we are told, "Don't you realize that you can choose your own master? . . . Thank God that though you once chose to be slaves of sin, now you have obeyed with all your heart the teaching to which God has committed you" (Rom. 6:16, 17 TLB).

But don't expect the Holy Spirit to transform you if you refuse to let Him have all of you to work with. "I plead with you to give your bodies to God. Let them be a living sacrifice, holy—the kind he can accept. When you think of what he has done for you, is this too much to ask" (Rom. 12:1 TLB)?

THOUGHT FOR THE DAY _____
If you are holding back part of yourself from Him, you are limiting His power in your life. How much of you does He have? Who really runs your life?

Run for Your Life

Do you not know that those who run in a race all run, but one receives the prize? Run in such a way that you may obtain it.
—1 CORINTHIANS 9:24 NKJV

*S*ome people seem to live a healthy Christian life. Things are even and balanced, with priorities intact. They seem to negotiate life's hurdles without breaking their stride. Sometimes they don't even appear winded. How do they do it?

Fitness experts agree that regular exercise increases one's energy level. The runner who trains consistently is always ready for the race. Similarly, the child of God who trains regularly in prayer, meditation, and Bible study has more energy for Christlikeness, vitality for the gospel, and zest for walking and talking the Christian life.

Training is essential. The person who is in shape and knows the course is equipped with stamina and confidence. Attitude, however, may separate those who merely run the race from those who run to win. The Christian's attitude is shaped by his relationship with Christ. By grace we are free from the tyranny of the law.

As we are freed from encumbrances that so easily entangle us (Heb.

12:1), we have space to stride, room to stretch out, and freedom to live.

Being Our Best

"But now God has set the members, each one of them, in the body just as He pleased."
————————————1 CORINTHIANS 12:18 NKJV

For most of life, i think we fight God. we keep trying to show Him what we were made for. we keep giving Him better ideas. we keep working for something bigger & greater than anything He seems to have in mind. for many of us, by the time we are in midlife, we feel we somehow have missed out on some of the great things we were born for. we fight with God over this.

God made me with special ideas in mind, but i wish i could have been in on the planning. my skin would have been more olive-colored, & flawless. my hair more coarse, with some curl in it. my shoulders broader. my eyes wider-spaced. i would have completely removed the lazy part in me that i have to fight with all the time.

i come to you, however, knowing God made me not to impress you. not to be on book covers. not to be an authority. not to be perfect or a genius. not to make a million dollars!

God made me to be uncomplicated in my faith. to watch children & kites & sunsets & rainbows & enjoy them. to take your hand regardless of who you are or how you look. to listen to you. to accept you right where you are. to love you unconditionally.

God made me to be real. to be honest. to be open. to never compare myself to you, but to strive to become my own best person. to have character & dignity.

THOUGHT FOR THE DAY —————————————————
God, help me to be myself, the way You made me, and to be happy in this.

The Bible uses three key words to guide us in our quest for serenity in a shattered world: Heart, Spirit, Soul. These ideas are lamps for our dark nights.

Robert L. Wise
When the Night Is Too Long

Turn "Why?" Into "What"

All things work together for good to them that love God.
ROMANS 8:28 KJV

I warn you that Confusion first appears in a most deceptive form. Seemingly disheveled and in total disarray, his disconnected demeanor is a complete facade. As a matter of fact, Confusion is an efficiency expert. He knows how to gather up all of our accumulated knowledge and experiences and in the shortest amount of time reduce their collective meaning to nonsense. While he appears to move aimlessly, actually he is carefully scrambling all of the data we carry in our heads until what we know becomes quite useless. Nourished by gossip and rumor, he uses suspicion as a primary tool in causing distortion. Once he has created paranoia, our soul is in deep trouble.

Confusion first appears when we cannot make sense out of what has befallen us. He poses one particularly difficult question. "Why has this happened to me?" When we cannot find an adequate or satisfactory answer, the work of Confusion begins. Therefore, it is of critical importance that we face this question with confidence.

"Why me? Why us?" a young mother asked sadly. "All we ever

wanted was a child that we could love and cherish. And now look at what we have." Maggie and I bent over to peer into the windows of the incubator, squinting to see the tiny baby with tubes running in every direction, who was slowly turning purple even as we talked. "We tried so hard for so long to have a baby." Her tone of voice revealed the desperation of many years of frustration. "We truly believed the hand of God brought this pregnancy to pass. So why is it now ending because of carelessness?"

While running an amniocentesis test, the doctor had punctured the placenta and caused a hemorrhage. Although the hospital had reacted immediately, the damage was irreversible. We both knew that within a few hours, this premature infant would be gone.

With confusion in her eyes Maggie asked again, "Why me?" Obviously she felt deeply and profoundly betrayed.

I must tell you in all candor—there is no complete answer to her question. The best we have is the tabulation of the results of cause and effect that chemistry, physics, and psychology offer. However, our hearts want a response that is satisfying.

Why did it happen? On one level the answer is obvious. A needle was stronger than tissue and when the membrane broke, blood pressure created a hemorrhage. The doctor made a mistake.

Why the car wreck? Well, when tons of metal fly out of control toward a metal post, the speed creates a deadly impact. The road was slick.

Why the stroke at age forty? Aneurysms can only last so long and then the elasticity of the blood vessel snaps when the blood pressure is too great. The body proved fragile.

Will any of those answers speak to the nagging fears of the heart and satisfy the deepest levels of the soul?

Not a hair!

"Why?" can often be answered with biological facts, formulas, equations from physics, or psychological studies about why people do crazy things. But very seldom can "why?" be answered so completely that the heart is relieved and the soul consoled. No, our query is wrong.

We must change the question. Paul actually turned *why* into a *what*.

He implied that the better inquiry is, "What can happen if I turn the whole matter over for God to use?"

THOUGHT FOR THE DAY _____

Once you begin to look for some positive use for devastation, Confusion can be converted into creativity.

Give It Your All

And whatever you do, do it heartily, as to the Lord and not to men, knowing that from the Lord you will receive the reward of the inheritance; for you serve the Lord Christ.

COLOSSIANS 3:23–24 NKJV

A great coach once said, "There's only one thing we practice for and that's to win; there's only one thing we play for, and that's to win; there's only one thing we live for, and that's to win; and there's only one thing we do to win —*everything*." Everything his team did was for victory. They practiced and played with precision and intensity. To do any less was to prepare for defeat. Every part of their lives had to be trained on winning, never second best—it wouldn't do.

Another aspect of this story is the players' love for their coach. He had instilled in them this great work ethic and motivated and inspired them to win. As a result they grew to love the coach for his leadership.

Similarly, our lives must be driven to holiness in every aspect. When God speaks of "whatever you do," He means all, our motivation being eternity, our inspiration being the Cross. Out of this is born a growing love for the Savior and willingness to give Him our all.

THOUGHT FOR THE DAY —————————————
This one thing I do, Lord: love You with my heart, mind, and soul.

Overcoming Bitterness

*"Jesus said, 'For if you forgive men when they sin against you,
your heavenly Father will also forgive you. But if you do not
forgive men their sins, your Father will not forgive your sins.'"*
——————————————————MATTHEW 6:14—15 NIV

$\mathcal{H}$appy-go-lucky: That's the only way to describe him. He's never
met a stranger; loves everyone; quick with a smile; works hard.

Bitter: That's the only way to describe her. She's an angry person;
shriveled up like a prune; rarely has a good word about anyone; real
unhappy with her life. She can't seem to let any offense go, no matter
how petty. Everything her husband does wrong rankles her, no matter
how minor. She rarely forgives, and certainly never forgets.

Middle-aged, she had to have some surgery, which put her in bed
for several weeks of convalescence. With time on her hands, she decided
to write down every slight, offense, wrong, and sin her husband had
ever committed against her. Instead of feeling better, she became more
bitter than ever.

Admittedly, this example pushes the limits of bitterness. Yet, if we
are completely honest, in every marriage there are roots of bitterness
that take hold—some seen; some unseen. Sometimes we know what
makes us bitter. Other times, the reason remains obscure. Sometimes
we may even like feeling that way, like a martyr.

Bitterness is a sinister enemy of marriage. Bitterness strangles the lifeblood out of a marriage—literally dries up our bones—and makes the words of our mate like fingernails on a chalkboard. Bitterness and intimacy cannot grow in the same heart. The one is poison to the other.

Where does bitterness come from? Bitterness is the fruit of a harbored grudge, the odor produced by pettiness, the product manufactured in the factory of unforgiveness. Like a field gone fallow, an unforgiving heart will yield to weeds of bitterness.

The root of bitterness, however, cannot take hold in a forgiving heart. Feelings of bitterness toward our mate send us a signal that we have something yet to forgive. What is it? We may not even know. It may require much thought, meditation, and prayer to come to grips with the source of bitterness against our mate.

Not only does an unforgiving spirit make us bitter, it cuts us off from fellowship with God. Jesus said, "If you do not forgive men their sins, your Father will not forgive your sins." Why? Because not forgiving each other is sin. (For a thorough explanation of this truth see Jesus' words in Matthew 18:21–35. Sobering.)

You may have been hurt deeply by your spouse. No one may know or understand how you feel. As the proverb says, "Each heart knows its own bitterness, and no one else can share its joy" (Prov. 14:10 NIV). The only way out is to forgive. When Peter asked Jesus how many times he must forgive the brother who sins against him, Jesus said, "I tell you, not seven times, but seventy-seven times." Jesus used hyperbole to say, "However many times it takes." Don't be bitter, forgive. Will you?

If you have hurt your spouse, you can make this process exceedingly easier by saying you are sorry and asking forgiveness. Will you? Mark Twain said, "Forgiveness is the fragrance the violet sheds on the heel that crushed it."

THOUGHT FOR THE DAY _____

Our Father in heaven, hallowed be Your name. We pray Your kingdom will come and Your will will be done in our lives here on earth, as it is in heaven. Give us this day all our needs. And forgive all our sins as we have just now forgiven one another. Amen.

Check Your Response

Do not repay evil for evil or abuse for abuse; but, on the contrary, repay with a blessing . . . that you might inherit a blessing.

──────────────────────1 PETER 3:9 NRSV

"*I* want justice!" If you've said these words, you know your human desire is to get even or see the wrongdoers punished. After all, isn't it only right to give back to others exactly what they give to you? If they're rude or mean to you, they'll see that you can dish it out too.

But what do you gain from your repayment? Do you solve the problem? Do you feel any better? The truth is, you probably make the problem worse. You may feel a slight sense of satisfaction, but that doesn't last. No, the real solution is not to respond in like manner but to stop, regroup, and then respond in a more positive and productive way. Stop—check your initial natural response. Regroup your thinking, get a healthier perspective, and then respond in kindness. This formula, proposed some two thousand years ago is still the best way to "get even."

THOUGHT FOR THE DAY ────────────────
I need perspective, God, to see this situation clearly. Help me be still while I gain the insight I need to move on.

*Don't Be a Pig
with Time*

"It is appointed unto men once to die."
————————HEBREWS 9:27 KJV

At the risk of stating the obvious, death is the ultimate limitation placed on life. And such limitations make our time here important.

The fact that life comes in limited quantities can be used to motivate us to lead quality lives. Because of the reality of death, we are pushed to see life as something precious and, thus, to live accordingly.

Now, before you get too self-assured that you are already time-conscious and leading a quality-filled life, consider these statistics: If you get eight hours of sleep a night, you will spend approximately 122 days a year sleeping. If you spend one hour each for breakfast, lunch, and dinner every day, you will spend 47 days a year in these activities alone. Sleeping and eating combined cost you half of each year you are alive. Add to that all the time spent in personal grooming, travel to and from work, bill paying, shopping and other life maintenance requirements, and you can see how much time "slips away," virtually undetected.

There is the story of a man driving by an apple orchard when he happened to see a farmer lifting his pigs, one at a time, up to the tree branches so that the pigs could eat the apples. The man stopped his car, got out, and approached the farmer. "Excuse me," he said, "but isn't that an awfully time-consuming practice?" The farmer looked at the man, shrugged his shoulders, and said, "So what? What's time to a pig?"

Sometimes we are all just as blind as the farmer when it comes to recognizing the true quantity and worth of our time. The notion that placing a limitation on something makes it more valuable came through loud and clear to me during a recent vacation. My wife, Holly, and I took a trip to Jamaica prior to the birth of our third child. (It was one of those "we'd better go have some fun *now* while we still can" kind of vacations.) While there, I decided to ride a jet ski, which was something I had never done. The rate I had to pay the hotel concession was $30 per half hour. That struck me as being pretty expensive, but I paid it anyway.

With the time limitation of just thirty minutes hanging over me, I tried to get as much enjoyment out of that ride as I could. I rode at all different speeds, turned the sharpest corners I could turn. And I even purposely fell off a few times just to increase the excitement.

All during the ride I constantly kept an eye on my watch, knowing that my time would be up relatively soon. This time constraint motivated me to try to squeeze all the enjoyment possible from that ride.

Now suppose I had been given unlimited use of that jet ski. Do you think I would have found it as intense, challenging, and exciting? Not hardly.

I'm convinced the same principle applies to life. Those who truly recognize and respect that life has a time limit will make an effort to get the best ride they can. They will experience life fully and will appreciate what is available to them.

If death can motivate us to maximize our time, it can be seen in a positive light. If there were no death and everyone just stayed on the planet forever, do you think people would have a sense of urgency about anything? Would the experience of life be as intense? Would we work as hard to enjoy it? For most of us, the answer would be "Probably not."

If death is a prime motivator for life, why aren't people determined to have a fuller existence; knowing that their days are numbered? Life is not a dress rehearsal—this is the real thing. Lights, camera, action! You're *on,* friend! This is your life. You have the starring role. It's either an Oscar or obscurity. The choice is yours.

So why isn't everybody shooting for an Oscar? I think people are so terrified by the prospect of death, they will do anything to avoid facing the notion. Like children who put their hands over their ears and say over and over, "I'm not listening," these adults say, "I'm not acknowledging the truth of death." The more terrified people are of the concept of death, the more they will stay preoccupied with "things to do" rather than live with purpose and fullness.

Woody Allen once remarked, "I'm not afraid of death. I just don't want to be there when it happens." Too many of us feel that same way. But death awaits us all. It's inevitability can motivate us to attempt to live minute-by-minute. Knowing death is pending can actually challenge us to spend our days well. If we do so, death loses much of its sting. As Leonardo da Vinci put it, "As a well-spent day brings happy sleep, so life well used brings happy death."

THOUGHT FOR THE DAY _____
Time may mean nothing to a pig, but you can't afford to be a pig with your time. Because it is appointed unto man once to die.

Wonderfully Made

For You formed my inward parts;
You covered me in my mother's womb.
I will praise You, for I am
fearfully and wonderfully made.
——————PSALM 139:13—14 NKJV

*H*aving been present at the birth of each of my three children, I will never forget how awesome it felt to witness this miracle of God. We are all very incredibly complex persons. Yet how often do you ever think about how complex you are? Let me challenge you to think about three things you like about yourself and three things you don't like. Of the things you don't like, which one do you most wish to change? Determine today to start working on that area of your life.

If you can examine yourself in this manner more frequently, I believe you can become more and more conformed to the image of God, not in a perfectionistic pursuit but in a way that honors how fearfully and wonderfully you were made.

THOUGHT FOR THE DAY ——————————
Take a moment and realize the wonder of whose image you were created in and are being created daily.

From this day forward I will base my self-worth on what God says about my worth to Him.

Paul Meier, M.D.
Don't Let Jerks Get the Best of You

Life Without Work

Count it all joy when you fall into various trials, knowing that the testing of your faith produces patience.

—————————————————————JAMES 1:2–3 NKJV

𝒰nemployment has to be one of the most difficult valleys a man or woman can walk through. The effects of being laid off or fired run right to the heart of a man's identity, pride, and self-worth. When I once was unable to find work, I felt more depressed and worthless than I ever had before. I felt guilty for not providing for my wife and useless around the house. My manhood was further threatened as I was turned down by employer after employer.

I was much harder on myself than I needed to be. One of the reasons I felt so worthless is that I based my self-worth in my work. I also entertained some false guilt. It was not my fault that I was out of work, and I continued to look for work daily even though I was depressed. I must not have trusted God a lot back then. That's why I did so much worrying. In fact, I distinctly remember being angry at God.

If you are unemployed and are waiting to enter the workforce again, do not add injury to your self-worth by condemning yourself, and do not feed your own guilt unless you're not trying.

THOUGHT FOR THE DAY _____
God has not abandoned you. He cares for you amidst your frustration and anger.

Be Like the Widow

The widow who is really in need and left all alone puts her hope in God and continues night and day to pray and to ask God for help.

—1 TIMOTHY 5:5 NIV

$\mathcal{S}$everal men went on a mission trip to Haiti where they met a nineteen-year-old boy who loved Christ deeply. He impressed them so profoundly that they invited him to visit the United States.

Upon arrival a whole new world opened up before this young Haitian's eyes. He had never slept between sheets, never had three meals all on the same day, never used indoor plumbing, and never tasted McDonald's.

While traveling the U.S., this godly young man made many new friends. At the end of a six-week-long visit, his sponsors hosted a farewell dinner in his honor. After dinner several members of the group offered warm parting remarks. Then they asked the young Haitian if he would like to say anything.

"Yes," he said as he rose, "I would. I want to thank you so much for inviting me here. I have really enjoyed this time in the United States. But I am also very glad to be going home. You have so much in

America, that I'm beginning to lose my grip on my day-to-day dependency on Christ."

Do you have "so much" that you find it hard to keep a grip on your day-to-day dependency on Christ? Or worse, have you lost your grip?

When we don't need to depend on Christ, we will not. It is part—maybe even a curse—of human nature. Our natural tendency is to depend on self, not Christ. Depending on Christ is an act of the will by faith, not the natural disposition of our heart.

I have prayed that God will always keep some major unmet need in my life so that I will always depend upon Him. To be really in need, like the widow in 1 Timothy 5:5, creates dependency. To have so much, as the young Haitian observed, creates self-sufficiency. When our lives prosper, the natural tendency is to lose our grip.

Someone called my prayer courageous. I disagree. It is not a prayer of courage, but of fear—the fear of a holy God. For God has the power to give us what we deserve, whether good or bad. I have come to fear, with reverence and awe, the God who is, for He is a consuming fire.

The Scriptures teach that "the widow who is *really* in need . . . puts her hope in God and continues night and day to pray and to ask God for help" (v. 5). Are you in need? Do you put your hope in God? Do you continue to pray night and day and ask God for help? Or do you have so much that you don't need to depend on Christ for the details of your life?

If you have lost—or are losing—your grip on your day-to-day dependency on Christ, ask God for an unmet need. When you are "really in need," you will put all your hope in God, not your own ability. You will pray night and day and ask God for help, you will not depend on your own resources. You will *use* your ability and resources, but you will *depend* on Christ.

A friend of mine frequently says, "You will never know Jesus is all you need until Jesus is all you have." God loves people who depend upon Him, people who stop pursuing the God they want and surrender to the God who is.

First Timothy 5:6 continues, "But the widow who lives for pleasure is dead even while she lives" (NIV). Is your faith in Christ dead or alive?

When we live for pleasure, we lose our grip. When "so much" gets in the way of our day-to-day dependency on Christ, we grieve the Holy Spirit.

Ask God to make you more like the widow who put her hope in God alone and continued to pray and ask God for help. That is day-to-day dependency on Christ. If you do this, you will never lose your grip. She depended on God because she was "really in need."

THOUGHT FOR THE DAY _____
There is safety in an unmet need. That's not courageous; that's just smart.

Rebuild

"And the rain descended, the floods came, and the winds blew and beat on that house; and it did not fall, for it was founded on the rock."

—MATTHEW 7:25 NKJV

*J*esus told a story of two men who built houses in different locations. One man foolishly built his house on sand. When the storm came and the wind and rain beat upon the house, it fell. The second man wisely built the foundation of his house on solid rock. The floods came and the winds blew, but the house did not fall, because it was set on the rock.

In our troubles we have been like the foolish man. Our own wisdom and ingenuity never brought us the results we hoped for. We looked to ourselves for solutions and were unable to solve life's problems. For many of us who built our house on sand, the realization of our own powerlessness came slowly. Often after a storm of destruction, we sought to rebuild in exactly the same spot. We repeated the patterns of our addictive behavior over and over again.

Sanity can be restored as we realize the futility of our efforts for control. Seeking God's wisdom and guidance, we can begin to rebuild our lives on a solid foundation that will stand through the storms of life.

Balance Your Account

Do not weary yourself to gain wealth,
Cease from your consideration of it.
When you set your eyes on it, it is gone.
————————PROVERBS 23:4–5 NASB

*H*ave you ever noticed that you never seem to make enough money? I heard on a recent news report most people surveyed felt that they would need to double their salaries to live comfortably. In other words if you make $15,000, you probably think that about $30,000 would be enough for you. But those who make $30,000 believe that they would need *$60,000* to be satisfied!

The apostle Paul indicates that you need to learn to be satisfied with what you have today (Phil. 4:11–12). Stop living for someday, and begin to focus on today. Balance your need to live within your budget with your need to enjoy your life. Make the most of what God has given you.

THOUGHT FOR THE DAY ————————————
You honor Him when you enjoy your life and make the most of what you have.

Heavy Baggage

If you have been foolish in exalting yourself,
Or if you have devised evil, put your hand on your mouth.
For as the churning of milk produces butter,
And wringing the nose produces blood,
So the forcing of wrath produces strife.

——————————————————**PROVERBS 30:32–33** NKJV

Some of us carry a lot of baggage full of memories from the past. One suitcase may hold our anger at another person's broken promises, unfair treatment, or verbal put-downs. Sometime we packed the anger in a suitcase and we still carry it around with us. Maybe another suitcase contains fear of another's anger, fear of abandonment, or fear of physical pain. The fear stems from the past but we still carry it around with us today. Guilt for our past behavior may fill the third suitcase. Here again, the suitcase we carry is full and feels heavy.

No wonder we feel tired and weighted down! We carry a heavy load. Set the suitcases down and begin unpacking them. We need to talk with a friend, minister, or counselor in order to get it all out.

THOUGHT FOR THE DAY ————————————————
God, help us unpack the bags of anger, fear, and guilt, and leave those feelings at Your feet. We want to travel lightly.

Vengeance is God's—He keeps perfect books.

Paul Meier, M.D.
Don't Let Jerks Get the Best of You

DR. CHRIS THURMAN

The Lies We Believe

Missing the Forest for the Trees

Whatsoever things are true, . . . honest, . . . just, . . . pure . . . lovely, whatsoever things are of good report; if there be any virtue, and if there be any praise, think on these things.
——————————————————————PHILIPPIANS 4:8 KJV

$\mathcal{D}$o you ever focus on a small thing to the exclusion of all else? For instance, have you said something fairly goofy in a crowd at a party and spent the rest of the night worrying about your remark?

Leigh, a friend of mine, had just gotten a nice promotion. The promotion, though, involved some added pressure she wasn't sure she could handle. One day I ran into her, and I could tell she was upset.

"I blew it! I know I'll lose this job," she exclaimed. "You should have seen it. There I was, at this fancy restaurant with my boss and a big client. And what do I do but drop my fork. I mean, I don't just drop it; I fling it! It made a big stain on my dress and then bounced about fifty times on the floor. I couldn't speak above a mumble the rest of the meal."

She went on like that for another ten minutes or so. Finally, I said, "Leigh, come on! Nothing *nice* happened?"

"If you call laughing 'nice.' That's what the client did. He said,

'Don't you worry about it.' And then he called the waiter over and got me another fork."

"And?"

"And we got the contract, but I bet my boss won't trust me again in a situation like that."

"Leigh, it sounds like everything worked out fine. You might even have humanized the whole meeting."

"What?! How? I just can't agree. It was awful!"

In spite of all that had gone right, Leigh could only focus on the one thing that had gone wrong.

THOUGHT FOR THE DAY _____

Take a step back from the tree you're examining—the one negative event of your day—and thank God for the forest.

Peace of Mind

God, grant me the serenity to accept the things I cannot change.
—————————————————————REINHOLD NIEBUHR

$\mathcal{S}$erenity is a state of mind in which your thoughts are not running in thousands of directions at one time or your mind is not so vacant and confused that there is nothing rational coming out. Serenity is a state of feeling whole and at peace and thinking clearly.

We pray what is called "The Serenity Prayer" by Reinhold Niebuhr, and we ask God for serenity. How do we know when He answers our prayers? How do we know when we are serene? Do we have to be serene before we can accept things? Or do we have to accept certain things to be serene? What is this acceptance business?

Let's look at the other side of this question. If we can become serene enough, we can accept without trying to change others. If we can become serene enough, we can tend to our own business and let others take care of themselves. If we are serene enough, we have love, patience, kindness, gentleness, joy, peace, and self-control.

THOUGHT FOR THE DAY ————————————————
Help me let go and trust You to take care of me, God.

Don't Create Zeros

"Death and life are in the power of the tongue."
_____**PROVERBS 18:21** NKJV

*S*peak words of hope and blessing every day. Not just for your own positive outlook, but for the well-being of those around you, as well. Many people who miss out on hearing such life-giving words tend to give up and wander down the road that leads to apathy, depression, and withdrawal. And at the end of that road, they usually find themselves teetering on the edge of a terrifying, yet beckoning cliff.

A classic example of a child that took this silent road is illustrated in a film that circulated several years ago:

Standing by himself at the edge of the group, Roger stares down at the ground. In the next few moments, you almost get the feeling that Roger is invisible. Several children run right by him in excited conversation; others crowd around him when the bus finally comes. But Roger never looks up, and the other children never speak to him or acknowledge his existence.

The children rush to see who gets on the school bus first. Glad to be in out of the cold, the children happily take their seats—that is, all except Roger. The last one on the bus, he wearily mounts the steps as if climbing each one requires a monumental effort. He stops briefly and looks up expectantly into the faces of the other children, but no one beckons him to join them. Heaving a sigh, he slumps into a seat behind the driver.

The sound of compressed air is heard being released from the bus's hydraulic system, and the door slams shut. With one look behind him to make sure everything is in order, the bus driver pulls slowly away from the curb and onto the country lane.

They have traveled only a few miles when suddenly Roger drops his books and staggers to his feet. Standing next to the bus driver, steadying himself on a metal pole, Roger has a wild and distant look in his eyes. Shocked by his sudden ill appearance, the bus driver asks, "Are you all right? Are you sick or something? *Kid, what's the matter?*" Roger never answers, and half out of frustration, half out of concern, the bus driver pulls over to the side of the road and opens the door.

As Roger begins to walk down the steps of the bus, he pitches forward and crumples into the snow. As the opening scene ends, we see the bus driver standing over Roger's body, trying to discover what has happened. As the camera pulls away, we hear an ambulance siren begin to whine in the distance, but somehow you know its coming will be too late.

This scene is from the excellent educational film *A Cipher in the Snow,* a film designed for teachers but that speaks to anyone concerned about giving the blessing to others. The movie is a true story of a young boy who actually died on the way to school one day and the resulting confusion over the reasons.

Medical records indicated no history of problems in either Roger or his family. Even the autopsy shed no light on his death. Only after an interested teacher looked into his school and family background were the reasons for his death discovered.

This teacher found that Roger's life had been systematically erased like a blackboard. In his first few years at school, he had done well, up until problems began at home. His parents' marriage had disintegrated, and a new, preoccupied stepfather never had time to fill any of the missing gaps. Resentful of any attention his new wife gave Roger, the stepfather would limit their time together. His mother loved Roger dearly, but soon she was either too busy or too intimidated by her new husband to give Roger any attention at all. Like being pushed away from a seat near the fireplace, Roger was now left with only the cold ache of indifference.

As a reaction to his home life, Roger's schoolwork began to suffer. Homework assignments were either turned in late or not at all. Tired of his apparent apathy, his teachers gave up on him and left him to work alone. He also began to withdraw from the other children at school, and he lost the few friends he once had. Roger would not begin a conversation, and soon other children wouldn't bother to try. Slowly but surely he was retreating into a world of silence.

In only a few months, everything and everyone of value to Roger had either been lost or taken from him. With no place of shelter and no words of encouragement, he felt like a cipher—an empty zero. This sensitive child was unable to stand the pain for long.

Roger was not killed by an infirmity or a wound. He was killed by a lack of words of love and acceptance. Roger withstood the painful silence as long as he could. Ultimately, however, the lack of a spoken blessing from family and friends acted like a deadly cancer. After months of pursuing its course, it finally ate away his will to live. He died a cipher in the snow, believing he was totally alone and unwanted.

Are words or their absence *really* that powerful? Solomon thought so. Like throwing ice water in our faces, he shocks us into reality with his words, "Death and life are in the power of the tongue" (Prov. 18:21).

If we struggle with speaking words of love and acceptance to our family or friends, another proverb should encourage us. Again, it is Solomon writing:

> Do not withhold good from those to whom it is due, / When it is in the power of your hand to do so. / Do not say . . . , "Go, and come back, / And tomorrow I will give it," / When you have it with you (Prov. 3:27–28).

If we can open our mouths to talk, we have the ability to communicate blessing.

THOUGHT FOR THE DAY _____
Don't be silent. Spoken blessings stir up life. Silence creates zeros.

Don't Cross the Line

See to it that you do not refuse him who speaks.
—HEBREWS 12:25 NIV

*O*ne of the great dreams is to build a business and be your own boss. As in every endeavor, there are risks as well as rewards, possible downsides as well as potential upsides.

The most common way to build a business includes debt. Debt can have personal liability, or (at least in real estate) property itself can often stand as sole collateral for repayment. In the early days of building our company, I resisted the lure to take on personal liability. Everything we did contained a "no personal liability" clause. Then one day the irresistible deal came along. I stepped across the line. After that I signed regularly.

One morning, sometime later, I discovered a verse during my personal devotions: "Do not be a man who strikes hands in pledge or puts up security for debts; if you lack the means to pay, your very bed will be snatched from under you" (Prov. 22:26–27 NIV).

This was not the truth I had been looking for. In fact, to follow that principle would have stopped all of my plans dead in their tracks, for I was building a real estate business, and everyone knows you can't do that without mortgage debt. And much of the debt required my personal liability—meaning that *all* my assets were pledged to repay the debt, not just the asset against which the money was borrowed.

I tried everything to dilute the meaning of that verse. *Well, it's not a command, only a principle. . . . It doesn't say I will have my bed snatched; it only says if I can't pay. I will be able to pay. . . . This applies to a different time and place. Our laws don't permit losing everything—'my very bed'—the risks are different today.*

Oh, how I wished I had never seen that verse. It tortured my mind. God had spoken to me, but the best deals all seemed to require personal liability. I had a clear choice to make: my plans or the Word of God. Build the business based on mortgage debt which required personal guarantees; or change my plans, go slowly, and refuse to strike my hand in pledge.

"See to it that you do not refuse him who speaks" (Heb. 12:25 NIV). Don't cross His line. The problem with crossing the line—refusing Him who speaks—is that once you have done it, each successive temptation to cross it again becomes easier and easier. Finally, your dulled senses no longer even distinguish that you are refusing Him who speaks.

THOUGHT FOR THE DAY ⸻⸻⸻⸻⸻⸻
What is the line He has shown you? Have you stepped across it yet? "Do not refuse Him who speaks."

MICHAEL CARD
The Name of the Promise Is Jesus

Jesus: Man of Sorrows

And God shall wipe away all tears from their eyes.
REVELATION 7:17 KJV

$\mathcal{I}$ had just finished giving a talk on the poverty of the nativity of Jesus to a group at a small country church when one sweet lady walked up to me. I could tell by her expression that she was bothered by some of the things I had said and that her "guns were loaded." I braced myself.

"I simply do not agree with your picture of the birth of Jesus, young man!"

"What exactly troubles you about it?" I asked.

"Well," she paused as she searched for the right words, "I don't believe He cried the way you said."

I gently pressed her to show me a passage from the Bible that would lead her to believe such a thing. She thought for a while and couldn't come up with anything. Finally, out of desperation, I suppose, she retorted, "Well, what about 'Silent Night, Holy Night'?"

That dear sister is only an extreme example of a tendency we all have to incorporate our traditions into Scripture. We sing "Away in a

Manger" and believe what we sing: "No crying He makes." So He must not have cried.

We thereby dismiss the examples we see every day from a multitude of newborns. I wonder if, way back in our minds, we believe He never soiled a diaper!

We celebrate the birth of Jesus in December, so we sprinkle snow on our nativity scenes and sermonize about Joseph and Mary's struggle with the cold. In truth, the Bible says nothing about the season, apart from a reference to the fact that the shepherds were "keeping watch" in the fields all through the night, which might mean it was the season when lambs were being born, the only time shepherds stay in the fields all night. If that is so, Jesus was probably born in the spring. I'd like to think it was April, since that is the month of my own birthday!

These false images of the Nativity have provided the foundation for a distorted picture of Jesus' entire life, which simply must go if we are to try to grasp the real picture, given in the Gospels, of the nativity of Jesus.

We know from Scripture that Jesus wept as a man. It is naive to think He did not cry as a baby. Tears are a basic part of what it means to be human. It is one of the sad signs of our fallen world that the first sign we give to show that we're alive is a cry. It was to this fallen world that Jesus came, not an imaginary one without tears. For the "Man of Sorrows" it would seem that tears were an even more integral part of His life than ours. He came as much to weep for us as to die for us.

My response to this realization of the weeping baby Jesus was to write Him a lullaby. It seemed only natural. For me it was a way of coming closer to His birth, to feel the darkness of that night, to smell the smells of the stable, and to hear that fragile newborn voice crying out in the night to His mother, Mary, and in a way, to me as well.

THOUGHT FOR THE DAY _____
He came as much to weep for us as to die for us. No matter what the reason for your tears may be, Jesus understands.

Get Focused

> *So we fix our eyes not on what is seen, but on what is unseen.*
> *For what is seen is temporary, but what is unseen is eternal.*
> —————————————————————2 CORINTHIANS 4:18 NIV

In grade school we were taught about how the eye focuses. We were told to hold a pencil directly in front of our eyes and to focus on a distant object. As long as we did so, we could not see the pencil clearly. But if we reversed the focus and concentrated on the pencil, we could not see the distant object clearly.

This Scripture encourages us to pay attention to our spiritual focus. We must make a point of "fixing" our eyes on things that last, the things of God's kingdom. If we do, the things that are temporary will not seem so important. They will not drag us away from the things that matter most.

THOUGHT FOR THE DAY ————————————————
I'm having trouble seeing beyond what is in front of me—my business, my home, my education, my friends. Help me focus on You, God.

Whom Do You Trust?

"Now on whom dost thou trust."
—————2 KINGS 18:20 KJV

*W*hile we often describe the story of Job as one of supreme testing, there was a very important temptation he had to face. The ancient story begins as we learn that Job is a righteous man. When his calamities fell, some friends came begging him to repent of his secret sin so that the heavy hand of God could be removed from him. These so-called comforters were spokesmen for what is generally referred to as the Deuteronomic Code of Retribution. Simply put, this was the idea that God always blesses the good and chastises the evil. Therefore, righteous people will always prosper and bad people will always get it in the end. The friends of Job were convinced that he was in trouble because of hidden sin.

As a matter of fact, Job was a righteous man in the eyes of God. His friends were wrong and Job stood his ground with them. He maintained that his punishment did not fit the crime. Yet here was a hidden personal issue Job had to face before the dark night would come to an end. Standing toe-to-toe with the Lord, Job proclaimed his righteousness and his right to vindication. Job was simply too good for such shabby treatment.

If we place Job in the terms of the last chapter, we can begin to see his problem in a different light. While he certainly wasn't a bad man, Job had become an ego-possessed person. He had lost his perspective. Who of us, even the very best, should stand before the holy and perfect God and tell Him what goodness looks like? Job had fallen to the temptation of believing his own press clippings. Mr. Ego had completely seduced him.

Sound familiar? It hits me between the eyes. How many times have I protested to God about how fortunate He is to have me on His team? Doesn't He understand that someone who has done as many good things for the cause as I have deserves first-class treatment? How can I be in this kind of difficulty being as wonderful and spiritual as I am? And when one is truly trying to be all of these things, the temptation comes with almost irresistible force. We become trapped by our own self-righteousness.

Job was finally forced to see that the answer was not to be found in his righteousness, but in a relationship with God. With all of his high character, he was to discover that nothing in his goodness exempted him from the trials of humanity nor gave him the right to question God. Only as he repented of his presumption was he able to find a new, life-transforming vision of the Divine. His only hope was in the constant care of the heavenly Father that comes to all of us as grace. Job's temptation was to trust in himself. In the long night, he learned how to trust in God alone.

THOUGHT FOR THE DAY _____
Who are you trusting in this long night?

Keep Life Simple: Pray

The steps of a good man are ordered by the LORD,
And He delights in his way.

—PSALM 37:23 NKJV

The more stressful life becomes, the more some of us are driven to handling stress in unhealthy ways. Sarah is a competitive person. She wants to achieve, so she pushes herself to perform at top efficiency. When she gets involved in a project, she forgets about time and becomes totally absorbed with what she is doing. Then when she is reminded to stop and attend other responsibilities, she feels stressed out. Her compulsion to work on only one project at a time creates stress when there are several things that need attention at the same time.

We all attempt to deal with stress in many different ways. We blame others for creating stress for us. We keep it inside us and let it create physical distress. To overcome this we can learn how to set realistic goals, plan and organize our time, and follow a basic life principle, "Keep it simple."

By planning ahead and relying on the power of God rather than acting impulsively, we can gain a healthier way of dealing with stress in our life, thus eliminating the unhealthy ways we handle stress.

THOUGHT FOR THE DAY _____
Work on the structure of your life and discipline your patterns of coping.

Know Yourself First

Jesus answered and said to them, "Those who are well do not need a physician, but those who are sick."

———————————————————————————LUKE 5:31 NKJV

*W*e wear masks every day to keep people from knowing us. Shyness is a mask we wear, hoping to be invisible. Maybe we hide behind a mask of caretaking. Taking care of others, making all the decisions, and dominating conversations are all ways to control a situation. Controlling gives us a sense of power we did not have as a child. We also wear masks to protect us from hurt in intimate relationships, cover our inferiority complex, or make us feel better than others. Many of us wear the mask of Goldilocks: We're always searching for just the right person, thing, or event to make us happy or give us comfort.

Living behind these masks becomes more difficult as we get older, but we are afraid to take them off. We fear that if others knew us they would abandon us. Still, continuing to wear the masks keeps us apart from intimate relationships. It is risky taking our masks off with another person, so it helps to get to know ourselves first. As we love, nurture, and care for ourselves we begin to feel safer in letting others get to know us.

THOUGHT FOR THE DAY _____
Help me to think of one thing I can do to take care of myself today, God.

Knowing God's Will

"Nevertheless not what I will, but what thou wilt."
————————————————MARK 14:36 KJV

"What is God's will for my life?" Few words occupy so much of our thinking or burn up so much of our energy. J. I. Packer said, "To many Christians, guidance is a chronic problem. Why? Not because they doubt that divine guidance is a fact, but because they are sure it is."

What is the will of God? The will of God is the sum of the choices and determinations God has made in His mind from an infinite number of possible choices. God's will is the confluence of those choices into an order of things, into a system. God's will is what God wants to do. He is God. He can do whatever He wants.

The picture of a single life must necessarily fit into the big picture of God's character (what He is like) and purpose (what He wants to do). Finding the will of God is not a matter of persuading God to our way of thinking, but of coming to a complete, total surrender of our will to His will—His good, pleasing, and perfect will.

The overarching will of God for every Christian is this: "For those God foreknew he also predestined to be conformed to the likeness of his Son, that he might be the firstborn among many brothers" (Rom. 8:29 NIV). Whatever happens, and however it happens, the reason *why* it happens is to conform us to the image of His dear Son and our Savior, Christ Jesus.

How do we go about finding the will of God for our lives?

Our main job is to get our hearts right. George Mueller captured the idea when he said, "I seek at the beginning to get my heart into such a state that it has no will of its own in regard to a given matter. Nine-tenths of the trouble with people is just here. Nine-tenths of the difficulties are overcome when our hearts are ready to do the Lord's will, whatever it may be."

In Bristol, England, George Mueller cared for ten thousand orphans over a span of sixty years, relying only on faith and prayer to feed and house the children. He never once asked for money, though he regularly asked for more orphans.

One morning with no food or milk on hand Mueller seated his orphans around the breakfast table and prayed, "Father, we thank Thee for the food Thou art going to give us."

Just then a knock came at the door. A baker told Mueller, "I was awakened at 2:00 A.M. and felt I should bake some bread for you."

Within minutes came another knock. A milkman said, "My milk wagon just broke down in front of your place. I must get rid of these cans of milk before I can take the wagon for repairs. Can you use this milk?"

Mueller meticulously recorded thousands of similar instances in his journals. To what did Mueller attribute God's continual provision? He always satisfied himself that He was doing God's will before he started a project. Then he stood on the promises of the Bible and continued to ask God for help in prayer.

If getting your heart right is nine-tenths of finding God's will, what's the other one-tenth? Diligently studying God's Master plan; the Bible. The more you know the more you'll grow into His will.

THOUGHT FOR THE DAY _____
What is God's will? It is the path you would choose if you knew all of the facts.

Do the Next Right Thing

*Jesus said . . . , "No one, having put his hand to the plow,
and looking back, is fit for the kingdom of God."*

LUKE 9:62 NKJV

On his hundredth birthday, a well-known cynic was interviewed by the local newspaper. The young reporter, expecting to tap a lifetime of experience, asked: "In a hundred years, Mr. Smith, you must have seen many new things."

"Yes," the old man replied, "and I was against every one of them!"

Do you have a closed mind? Do you struggle with the notion, "No, that can't possibly work"? When you refuse new things, you are tempted to look back. Here are some ways to keep looking forward:

1. Stick with the winners (those who stay straight, who will lead you forward), not the losers.
2. Stay away from old friends, the ones who may not be good for you, and make new friends.

3. Do the next right thing. If you don't know what that is, ask someone who does.

THOUGHT FOR THE DAY ⸻

Dear God, help me to open my mind to Your better way of living and thinking today.

Disconnection

"If You, LORD, should mark iniquities,
O Lord, who could stand?
But there is forgiveness with You,
That You may be feared."

—————————PSALM 130:3–4 NKJV

*O*n a recent trip, I stayed several days in the same hotel. One particular bellhop seemed to be on call each time I needed my books carted down to the front door. Joe was a very friendly young man and always seemed happy to help me. His gentle spirit seemed to belie his burly appearance which was aided by his long, shaggy hair and his tatoo-laden arms.

The day I left, as he set my baggage in the lobby, I thanked him and gave him a copy of my book *When Your Dreams Die.* Joe knelt down beside my chair and very quietly asked, "Can God be mad at you?"

I asked, "Do you feel God is mad at you right now?"

Joe nodded. "I've done some bad things, and now everything is going wrong in my life. God must be mad at me."

Joe presented a very strong reason why many of us quit praying: Unconfessed sin puts distance between us and God. God is not mad at us; it's more that we're mad at ourselves and assume He must be, too.

We're going in the wrong direction and we don't know how to get turned around.

Years ago I heard Dr. Henry Brandt describe knowing he was going in the wrong direction on the freeway, but he kept going that way because he couldn't figure out how he could get turned around without admitting to his wife and other passengers in the car that he had been going the wrong way.

Many times we are like that: We keep trying to figure out a way to change directions without admitting we have gone the wrong way. Confession of sin is seldom easy but it is vital to our walk with the Lord.

Recently, I came home from a short trip and routinely checked my answering machine. The voice on one message was that of a young man perhaps in his early twenties. He said, "Hi, this is Peter. I'm trying to reach Cheryl. I think this used to be her number, but I'm not sure if it is now or not. I just wanted to tell Cheryl that I'm sorry for the way I treated her in high school, and I hope she'll forgive me."

Bless his heart! How I wish I'd been home to take that message. Peter needed someone to hear his confession. He needed to be heard so badly he confessed to an answering machine!

In the past few years, I have begun to understand the value of the confessional. Not that we necessarily need to confess to a priest or a minister, but James 5:16 states, "Confess your trespasses to one another, and pray for one another, that you may be healed."

When I was a little girl, it was not uncommon for people to walk forward at the end of a church service to confess sin and pray with the pastor or a prayer counselor. While only God can cleanse us of our sins, being willing to confess our sin to another human being is very healthy. Not that we should broadcast our sins to the world, but admitting to someone else the areas where we are struggling to live the Christian life is important. In the Christian community, however, we have moved away from any kind of public accountability. Because of this we seldom become aware of how even a close friend struggles against sin until he loses the battle and his sin becomes public.

A few years ago I attended a week-long prayer and emotional healing seminar. On the second day, the leader announced she felt God was telling her she should not continue with the seminar until there was confession of sin among those who were in attendance.

First, I was absolutely amazed at her forthrightness, but then I thought, *Well, we'll all bow our heads, pray and confess our sins privately, and then we can get on with this seminar.*

You can imagine my shock when the leader said, "I want everyone to whom God is speaking to please stand. Then I want you to come down here where my team is waiting. Speak with one of them, confess your sin to them; then the two of you can take your sin to the Father, place it at the cross, and proclaim it forgiven."

I thought, *No one will do that. It's too embarrassing.* Then I looked up and realized over two hundred people were making their way to the front of the church!

Recently I conducted a seminar attended by over four hundred women. At the end of the day, I made a similar invitation. I was a little nervous since I had never given an open invitation before, but I felt very strongly that God knew that some people in the audience needed to have someone else hear their confession of a particular sin or that they needed to state their declaration of forgiveness toward a particular individual. During the last song, I stood near the front and was thrilled when three women came forward. While the rest of the audience was leaving, I was absorbed in praying individually with these three women. When I was concluded with them, I assumed my counseling time was over, but as I looked up, I saw a sea of faces looking at me.

I innocently asked, "Are you waiting for me to sign books?"

One of the ladies in the front of the group said, "No, we're here to confess!"

I spent the next two and a half hours praying with each lady and hearing her confession. We then prayed together and placed her sin and her repentance at the cross and thanked God for the cleansing and freedom He is waiting to give us when we confess our sins.

THOUGHT FOR THE DAY _____
We are a hurting, sinful people, in need of a Savior, but we also need a body of flesh and bones to whom we can admit our sins and our struggles, a fellow struggler to whom we can be accountable.

Your Greatest Cause

There is one alone, without companion:
He has neither son nor brother.
Yet there is no end to all his labors,
Nor is his eye satisfied with riches.
But he never asks,
"For whom do I toil and deprive
    myself of good?"
——————ECCLESIASTES 4:8 NKJV

Single folk need to think about these words of wisdom from Solomon. Singleness has many advantages and disadvantages. We need to have purpose in our life, and this purpose must go beyond ourselves.

If we set our eyes on God, He can direct our life goals. I worked with a single man who had been successful in business and had all the material blessings a person could want. As we discussed the true meaning in life, he recognized he had not been living for God. He realized he did not have a cause greater than himself. His commitment to God's purposes for his life brought him peace.

THOUGHT FOR THE DAY ————————————
Do you have a greater purpose than yourself as you live your life?
We all need to think about this whether we are married or single.

Circumstance vs. Character

Trust in the LORD *with all thine heart; and lean not unto thine own understanding. In all thy ways acknowledge him, and he shall direct thy paths.*

PROVERBS 3:5—6 KJV

$\mathcal{I}$n times past I took great pride in telling people, "I always go through the open door." But I left out one minor detail. I neglected to add that many of those doors opened only after I had blown off the hinges.

We can walk with confidence through the door that God opens. If the door is stuck, shut, or locked, however, don't force it open—pray it open. If it still doesn't shake free, put some oil on the hinges. If it still won't jar loose, then go ahead and picket. Maybe do a sit-in. And if you have to extend your vigil late into winter—go ahead, do it. That's fine. But whatever you do, never, never break through the door God has left closed.

Think of the hundreds of hours we spend trying to undo the damage of the doors we have forced open. God is at work in your circumstances. *"For it is God who works in you to will and to act according to his good purpose"* (Phil. 2:13 NIV).

When God circumstantially opens a pleasant door and gives you the desire to go through it, receive the blessing of God, whether humble or exalted, with reverent gratitude. If your circumstances are a bed of nails, you should try to improve them. If you cannot, then you can trust in your loving, holy Father to work it out for good in the end. Where we can exert no influence, we should accept whatever God sovereignly allows or causes to happen.

We should ask God to guide us to success in our circumstances. We can ask Him to help us in our priorities, our relationships, and our finances. It is honorable to consider what the likelihood of success will be. It is not likely to be God's will for you to undertake a job, a marriage, or a ministry that seems doomed to failure from the outset.

Though God's message about material blessings has been distorted by the manic teachings of the "health and wealth" gospel, let's not throw the baby out with the bathwater. The Scriptures do say that God wants to give material blessings to His children. But He will never sacrifice the *quality of our character* to increase the *quantity of our circumstances.*

God is more interested in the success of our character than the success of our circumstances. He puts character ahead of stuff. Don't misunderstand. God is vitally interested in our circumstances. But He will never *sacrifice* our character to *improve* our circumstances. Instead, He frequently reengineers our circumstances to get at our character.

THOUGHT FOR THE DAY _____
Rest in the assurance that your Father will guide you in right ways. Trust His open doorway and respect the door He closes.

Release!

Create in me a clean heart, O God,
And renew a steadfast spirit within me.
——————————PSALM 51:10 NKJV

When we feel there has been an injustice, we become angry. That is a natural response. However, many of us continue to harbor the anger long after the event is over. Bitterness, discontent, and negative thoughts pollute our minds, and life looks pretty bleak. Harboring angry, bitter thoughts soon creates a bitter, lonely person.

Is that what you have chosen to be? "But you don't understand what the other person did to me!" you say. The question is, What are you allowing this to continue to do to you? God tells us to forgive others as He forgave us. He held nothing back! As you forgive, an inner space fills you. As the hate is released, the tension eases, and a new joy is found again. The choice is yours.

THOUGHT FOR THE DAY ——————————————
O God, please forgive me for the thoughts I have continued to hold on to. Create in me a new spirit.

Be Grateful for the Journey

Then Noah built an altar to the LORD and took of every clean animal and of every clean bird, and offered burnt offerings on the altar.

—————————————————GENESIS 8:20 NKJV

𝒫rior to building the altar mentioned in this verse, Noah had been through a very traumatic series of events. A flood had covered the whole earth, killing everyone and everything except him and his passengers. The flood's devastation left Noah's life totally changed but also afforded him the opportunity to experience God's preserving grace. When the flood finally receded, he took time to build an altar on which he could praise and thank God.

No doubt you, too, have been through a series of traumatic circumstances. Although you have experienced devastation, take a few minutes to reflect on the grace God has shown you. Thanking the Lord for life's difficult circumstances has a way of giving you a positive outlook on the past, present, and future.

THOUGHT FOR THE DAY ———————————————
Revere God by recognizing His plan of grace for you.

Virtue lies in the struggle, not the prize.

Dr. Chris Thurman
The 12 Best Kept Secrets for Living an Emotionally Healthy Life

Difficult People

A man who has friends must himself be friendly,
But there is a friend who sticks closer than a brother.
_____**PROVERBS 18:24** NKJV

*O*ne of the most difficult pressures I have faced in my career has been having to deal with difficult people. I used to believe that if only I could get away from these people, I would be happy. This of course was impossible. There were difficult people in every department and job I went to. So I concluded that I could never work again or I could learn how to deal with them.

Difficult people are miserable inside and want everyone else to be as miserable as they are. They are insecure and compensate by controlling others. Difficult people bring out the worst in all of us; they remind us of people we have not liked before. They tell lies, gossip, and like to manipulate others.

Maybe you have to face a difficult person or persons every day on your job. Sometimes you may dread waking up in the morning to go to work because you know they're waiting for you.

These are several ways to lighten the blow of having to work with difficult people. Don't take them personally. What they say is merely their opinion. Avoiding these people when possible is not a bad idea either. Try to be assertive, and avoid being aggressive or reactive because they can always be more so. Finally, turn to the Lord, remembering that He is the master at dealing with difficult people.

THOUGHT FOR THE DAY _____
Lord, give me the strength and patience to handle difficult relationships.

Keep Walkin'

Jesus said to him, "If you can believe, all things are possible to him who believes."

————————————————————————MARK 9:23 NKJV

*H*ave you ever watched toddlers learning how to walk? They take a step or two and then fall down hard on their bottoms. They sometimes cry and sometimes laugh, but they always get back up and try again.

Why is it that the older we get, the longer we stay down when we fall—sitting there, feeling sorry for ourselves? Oh, to have the faith of that toddler, to just take one step at a time, and when we fall, to get back up and try again and again.

God offers us that faith—faith that can perform miracles, faith that when we are down, we can reach up to Him, and He will give us the strength to try again. All we have to do is believe in Him. He tells us that faith will move mountains.

The grace of God allows us to pick ourselves up, dust ourselves off, and start all over again.

THOUGHT FOR THE DAY ————————————————
Believe in the Author of hope and action.

A Deeper Way

The LORD is my strength and song.
—————————EXODUS 15:2 NKJV

*W*hen I think about how I leaned on my wife, I have to say that her support helped me function in some immature ways. Her strength and support continued the illusion that I was a strong man inside.

And unfortunately, my leaning on her let me keep at bay the pressures of life. The pressures ultimately overwhelmed me and I had to lay whole new emotional and spiritual foundations. I learned to be satisfied with being alone with myself; I gave up trying to please everybody; and I learned how to be appropriately assertive. I finally stopped trying to meet my father's excessive expectations, and I tried to do what I could with the gifts God has given me.

THOUGHT FOR THE DAY ———————————————
God, I am pleased to see the changes in my heart. Thanks for continuing to craft me. Thank You for allowing me to believe in a truer and deeper way.

Deception

*And no wonder! For Satan himself transforms himself
into an angel of light.*
—————————————2 CORINTHIANS 11:14 NKJV

*D*eception. The sound of this word brings images of shrouded beings that are up to no good. Deception clothes itself in many ways. It can appeal to our senses and better judgment, and always sound so true. Deception can be anything it wants to be—beautiful, logical, prosperous. Too often, however, this multipronged fork pokes, prods, and finally embeds itself into a heart.

Every day we are confronted by immorality, clouded ethics, greed, and violence. Most of these are blatant, but others knock on our doors subtly. As our mind opens its door, it may only see the surface of an inviting presence, never knowing what lies below or behind. Many times it happens quickly and without warning. But the deceiver has thought it out well. He has a plan. Taken in by a flash. No pain, no outward scars. Upon realizing our dilemma, we feel the internal bleeding and then feel the pain. *Deceived.*

There is help, however. The believer who incorporates God's truth in his life has the weapon necessary to protect himself.

Take Root!

And in His law he meditates day and night.
He shall be like a tree
Planted by the rivers of water.
_____**PSALM 1:2–3** NKJV

*D*avid wrote in Psalm 1 about the benefits of setting our mind on God's Word. God's Word gives us clear direction to become like the tree David describes in this verse. We need a set standard to guide us down our path and God's Word can provide that for us.

David says if we meditate on and delight in God's Word, we are like a strong tree firmly planted by a stream of water. Just as the tree remains stable, we become stable and solid in our faith. We draw spiritual nourishment from trusting in God's unconditional love, realizing that He is faithful and accepting His forgiveness of our past.

A tree planted and growing in a healthy environment produces fruit. The fruit for us will be a closer spiritual relationship with God, a healthier view of our own value, and the ability to encourage others with our experiences.

THOUGHT FOR THE DAY _____
Drench the searching roots of your heart in the nourishing water of promises.

FRANK MINIRTH, M.D.

One Step at a Time

Sticks, Stones, and Words Hurt

We made a list of all persons we had harmed and became willing to make amends to them all.

The Ten Commandments have a lot of relevance to each of us in our daily lives. They're not just for murderers and thieves. They're for all of us, and they are easily violated in many different ways. You can kill people in more ways than one. You can ruin their reputation or gossip about them.

Imagine throwing a handful of confetti into the air on a windy day and then trying to recover it all. That's how impossible it is to take back words spoken in jealousy, hatred, lust, or lies. Harsh words are like daggers that tear the flesh.

Are your family members and friends wearing bandages right now? Don't hurt others whom Christ died to help. Use your tongue to help people feel better. Love manifests itself in encouraging others, not in tearing them apart.

THOUGHT FOR THE DAY _____
My tongue can bring life or death to someone. I want to give life— encouragement and love.

God Never Wastes Anything

Though outwardly we are wasting away, yet inwardly we are being renewed day by day. For our light and momentary troubles are achieving for us an eternal glory that far outweighs them all.

2 CORINTHIANS 4:16–17 NIV

The call came without warning. Leighton Ford's twenty-one-year-old son, Sandy, was in the hospital with a heart problem. The surgery began at 7:15 A.M. The morning gave way to afternoon as the hours ticked slowly away. Finally, at 6:50 P.M. the doctor came to tell this dear family that the surgery had been successful, but they could not get their son off the heart-lung machine. His heart wouldn't start. The doctors frantically kept working. Sometime after 8:00 P.M. the doors opened and the doctor solemnly walked into the waiting room. "We never got him off the table."

Just days later a newspaper headline asked, "When a good man dies; what a waste, who can explain it?" Among the many loving expressions of sympathy which came, one stood out. It came from a missionary with whom Sandy Ford had worked one summer in France. Among the other things said in his letter, he wrote, "God never wastes anything."

I believe this is the true meaning of Romans 8:28: "And we know that in all things God works for the good of those who love him, who have been called according to his purpose" (NIV). In other words, in supernatural ways we do not know of or understand, God sovereignly engineers our circumstances for our good—even when they seem bad —because He never wastes anything.

One day at L'Abri a young girl was to make some cakes but ended up, instead, with a big bowl of goo. It seemed the only thing to do was throw it out but, since money was so scarce, Edith Schaeffer sat down and figured out all the ingredients the girl had dumped into the bowl to end up with this goo. By adding another ingredient she was able to turn the goo into what Francis Schaeffer described as some of the most marvelous noodles you ever tasted.

This is how God works. What the nonbeliever thinks is "scrap" to be thrown on the pile of human waste, God sees as the "ingredients" of His recipe to make us whole. He takes the goo we are in, then adds the necessary ingredients to work it for good. He never wastes anything.

Christians have no inoculation against suffering. Crushing blows are felt by the believer and nonbeliever alike. That is because the radical effect of the Fall touches the same points of humanity in the believer as the nonbeliever. We all ache from the flu, bleed when we are cut, and sneeze when we catch a cold. Christians have financial catastrophes, broken relationships, die from cancer, and live with multiple sclerosis.

But there are differences at the spiritual level. Several times I have heard Steve Brown pastorally encourage believers, "I believe that every time a non-Christian gets cancer God allows a Christian to get cancer, too, just so that the world can see the difference." In other words, God uses calamities for higher purposes—He makes them work for good; they are not scrap; God never wastes anything.

THOUGHT FOR THE DAY _____
Don't panic at the struggles you or another person is going through. You never know what God is doing.

God sovereignly engineers our circumstances for our good—even when they seem bad—because God never wastes anything.

Patrick M. Morley
The Rest of Your Life

Learn to Assess

Satan wants to see perfection. God wants to see improvement.
—————————————————————————————CHRIS THURMAN

All of us have picked up negative messages from the past. Some of us were so good at hearing negative messages that we began to see the Bible as a book of legalism and conditional love.

God gave us helpful guidelines for life, but He also gave realistic passages about human weakness, our need for rest, and how to have peace of mind. The rules were intended to motivate the lazy. The verses of peace, rest, and comfort were given to ease the burden of the perfectionist and the overachiever. To read only one message will give us an extreme view of God.

Our church recently featured a motivational speaker who enthusiastically told us what we "need," "should," and "ought" to do to have success and spiritual growth. There was a time when I would have felt guilty for not living up to such lofty expectations. Today, I am learning to assess where I am already performing adequately, where I need improvement, and where I choose not to compete at all. Since no amount of performance can generate love from others anyway, I can lift the pressures and just be myself.

THOUGHT FOR THE DAY ————————————————
Thank You, God, for Your unconditional love and grace.

Good Things Take Time

Recognizing that something needs to be changed is the first step toward changing it.

—DONNA TILLINGHAST

*O*ne of the reasons God does not allow us to change instantly is because we would not learn anything. Things that come to us easily seem not to hold much value. Self-improvement makes a lasting impression when we put forth effort and hard work. The journey of improvement involves walking, stumbling, sometimes falling down, getting up, and continuing to move forward. Fortunately, we do not have to walk through this process alone.

God promises to provide us with the wisdom and strength we need when we are willing to be humble and ask for His guidance. We can also get encouragement from other people who have experienced the journey. The insight and support they provide for us offers a great blessing.

Instead of feeling frustrated when we recognize a defect in our character, we should be encouraged that we are gaining insight and moving toward improvement.

THOUGHT FOR THE DAY _____

Own the negative aspects of yourself and begin working with the power provided by God.

Let Go

Therefore do not cast away your confidence, which has great reward. For you have need of endurance, so that after you have done the will of God, you may receive the promise.

———————————————————**HEBREWS 10:35–36** NKJV

*A*nger is expressed in many ways. We may be angry that we can't change circumstances from being so painful or abusive. We may even be mad at God for allowing things to happen to us.

Some of us are angry at our own behavior. Maybe we spend money we don't have or become so absorbed in work that we shut others out. Maybe we express our anger in an abusive way and then become angry with ourselves. A low self-image causes us to constantly seek approval from others. It backfires on us when we take casual comments as criticism or rejection. The pain we feel causes us to withdraw or to lash out at someone close to us.

God is patient and kind. He loves us no matter what we think or do. He is gentle and He tolerates our immaturity, always guiding us toward self-control.

THOUGHT FOR THE DAY ———————————————————
Help me to internalize the outward laws that have protected me but now can be made wholly my own.

Translating the Night

"(If) Thou hast delivered my soul from death: wilt not thou deliver my feet from falling, that I may walk before God in the light of the living?"

——PSALM 56:13 KJV

I invite you to join me on a journey through night toward a distant horizon where light always beckons. I offer you the stuff of my own personal discoveries as well as what others have found. During the period that I was making many of these discoveries, I found myself being awakened night after night at two or three o'clock. There were days I felt that lack of sleep would be my demise.

When volcanic eruptions in the soul are breaking forth, they seem to wait for the darkest times of night. In times of catastrophic change, we often don't get the full backwash until we close our eyes.

Whether the problem is death, divorce, devastation, personal failure, we can't solve our problems simply by picking up new rational explanations for them. We have to live through the emotional consequences. That's the hardest part. Generally other people not only don't understand, frequently they misunderstand and misinterpret. So we may feel paranoid and alienated. I found this isolation made it even harder to face the loneliest hours.

During one of those nights, I got up and started reading the Bible. Picking up a pencil, I began translating Psalm 56 into personal terms. My personal paraphrase helped me so I kept my scribblings in my Bible for a long time. When I began writing these pages, I found those lines helped me recall many discoveries that I had made in the dark. Here's my personalized version:

O Lord, don't abandon me. For heaven's sake, don't do what "they" have done to me!

I have been stepped on, oppressed, and arrogantly attacked. I even have former friends who now only wait to hurt me.

No matter where I turn, they are watching to see how they can damage my reputation. These enemies of my soul are always distorting my best intentions.

I don't want to be paranoid, but if I were unable to trust in You and Your Word, I would be without hope!

Nevertheless, in my darkest nights, I am comforted because I know that You are keeping count of every time I turn in my sleep. Not even a single tear has been in vain, but You are keeping them all stored in Your bottle.

I am so thankful that Your bookkeeping includes a record of my pain.

Since I can trust You so completely, I remind myself that I can quit worrying about my detractors. If I will discipline my mind, I won't even have to think about all of the confusion around me and the uncertainty within.

Rather, I want to concentrate on thanking You for this time in my life.

Because You have already delivered me from the finality of the effects of death (which is the worst that could happen), everything else can be handled.

So, I know that You won't let me make a fool of myself.

Even when I don't see it, Your light is certainly always there!

So be it!

THOUGHT FOR THE DAY _____
Take the times that God comes to you and answer Him.

A
Deeper
Walk

. . . in the
Light

A just man falleth seven times, and riseth up again: but the wicked shall fall into mischief Proverbs 24:16 (KJV).

Human beings make mistakes. Along life's path everybody stumbles. But the success of your personal journey doesn't depend on how frequently you fall, but rather, how often you get up again. As long as you can get to your feet, you'll *never* have to accept defeat. To put it another way, a step is a stumble forward, which is prevented from becoming a fall, by *another step.*

The divergent lives of Simon Peter and Judas Iscariot are vivid illustrations of this truth. This historic pair once traveled the same path. But when they both stumbled on the very same night, their individual reactions propelled them in two different directions.

Iscariot, tripped by greed, traded his friend Jesus for a bag of empty promises and shiny silver. When Judas finally came to himself and realized how far he had fallen off the path, he simply gave up and continued to fall, with a rope of condemnation about his neck.

That same Passover night, Peter also stumbled; toppling over his impulsive words of defiance, fear, and denial. Like his counterpart, Simon's slip was painful, remorseful, and full of regret. Yet in the midst of his agony, his mind happened across another set of words, spoken to him just a few hours earlier: *"Simon, I have prayed for thee, that thy faith fail not: and when thou art converted, strengthen thy brethren."**

Peter knew that his own words condemned him, but he also knew that Christ's words outweighed his own. They were full of hope, forgiveness, and faith. Their meaning was more valuable than any bag of silver, and as genuine as the very promises of God. Therefore, Simon, in the midst of his stumble, decided to put his foot down. He took a bold step and righted himself on the faith that God, through Christ, *forgives!* Regaining his footing, Simon Peter then continued down the

* (Luke 22:31, 32 KJV)

path, having obtained *A Closer Walk* with the very One he had denied.

Two men stumbled on the same night; one man faulted himself for doing so, the other mustered the faith to keep walking.

A step is a stumble forward, which is prevented from becoming a fall, by *another step*.

—Barton Green

Let There Be Light!

"I have come as a light into the world, that whoever believes in Me should not abide in darkness."

—JOHN 12:46 NKJV

*D*uring a thunderstorm one night the lights went off in Michal's home. For years she had kept a flashlight in a drawer of her bedside table to use in emergencies. Michal found the flashlight and switched it on, but nothing happened. Over the years the batteries had lost their power. All of the components of the flashlight were operable, but because there was no energy in the batteries, the flashlight could not produce light.

Before we have a personal relationship with Jesus Christ, we are like a flashlight with no batteries. We have no light within and are unable to see the path toward God.

When we receive Christ in our hearts, He becomes the energy source that produces light in us. Our purpose is to shine, but we can only do that with God as the source of power in our lives. His light will illumine the path ahead of us and guide us to truth.

THOUGHT FOR THE DAY _____
We no longer need to fear the darkness when we walk in God's light.

We are either fashioning our lives by pressure from without, or we are transforming our lives by power from within. The difference is worship.

Warren W. Wiersbe
Real Worship

Read the Owner's Manual

When all else fails, read the instructions.
———————————————ANONYMOUS

*W*hen the car breaks down, we take it to the mechanic. If the plumbing gets clogged, we call the plumber. For most of the problems we encounter, there is a specialist we turn to for assistance. Why then, when we are confronted with a need that is beyond the capabilities of another human being to fix, do we turn to ourselves instead of to God?

The owner's manual for our complete care was written long ago by God himself. The Bible is full of Scripture exhorting us to lean on God for our well-being. Psalm 55:22 says, "Cast your burden on the LORD, and He shall sustain you." Proverbs 3:5 tells us, "Trust in the LORD with all your heart."

What can we expect once we make the decision to trust God with our will and our care? Philippians 4:6–7 tells us not to worry about things, but instead to pray about our problems. God will answer our prayers and provide us with the instructions to perform the most impossible of repairs.

God's Love Must Be Earned, Right?

Know therefore that God exacteth of thee less than thine iniquity deserveth.

—JOB 11:6 KJV

"Diane," I said, "why do you think you've never enjoyed your Christianity?"

"Would you enjoy it if you always felt you were trying to measure up and never making it?" she challenged me.

"No, I wouldn't. You know, what you are describing is something a lot of Christians seem to struggle with, and it seems to stem from their view of God. How do you view God?" I inquired.

"I see God as a harsh judge who damns people to hell," she shot back.

"Where do you think that view came from?"

"My preacher back home. All he seemed to preach on was hellfire and damnation. I think my image of God comes largely from that."

"Was *grace* ever mentioned by your pastor?" I asked.

She laughed, a bit sardonically. "If it was, I can't remember. I just remember being very scared."

"Any other pictures pop into mind?"

"Well, yes," she said. "Of me as a kid, getting punished. My father was strict. He yelled and screamed at us a lot. He showed little, if any, compassion."

"And do you see God and Christianity the same way?"

"Well, yes. Isn't that what Christianity and God are all about? To keep us good, on the straight and narrow path?"

THOUGHT FOR THE DAY ⸻⸻⸻⸻⸻⸻⸻
Jesus + nothing = Everything. I don't have to be good for God. He loves me as I am.

Why Did God Make Me?

"Beloved, let us love one another."
————————1 JOHN 4:7 NKJV

$\mathscr{I}$ was sitting with a young woman in therapy when she looked at me piercingly, wanting and needing an answer, and asked, "Why did God make me, anyway?" She caught me off guard, and I found myself repeating the question to regain some balance. It seemed I had surely answered that question for it sounded familiar. Yet as I repeated it, I was impressed by its depth and significance. I looked at her and honestly responded, "I'm not sure I've ever answered that question for myself. I'm not certain I know why God made me." She immediately, without a second's hesitation, looked at me and replied, "I know why God made you. He made you for me. I'd be dead today if it weren't for you."

As I reached out and took her hand, I reminded her that she needed me, but so did I need her. She was one of the reasons my life has meaning and purpose. "God made us for each other," I concluded.

William Glasser, the creator of Reality Therapy, claims that in order for a person to be healthy he must gain some worth and recognition.

Basically, what he's saying is, *I must believe my life on this earth is worth something—has a purpose. If my life were to be wiped away—what would be missing on this earth?*

I truly believe God made each of you to be used by Him to touch and alter and inspire and detour me to where He needs me to be. There I can touch and help and be used to help others get to where they need to be. Then we can all find more of Him and prepare for eternity.

I honestly feel that what I have to give you is so insignificant and trite. There's my honesty. The touch of my hand to yours. My listening heart that is not judgmental. My deep belief in your uniqueness and power as an individual. My openness to hear what you have to say. But I extend them all to you. If in some quiet moment I can touch your life and make a difference, then my living will not be in vain. And please keep giving away what you have. No one can replace you or give what you alone can give.

THOUGHT FOR THE DAY ⎯⎯⎯⎯⎯⎯⎯⎯⎯⎯⎯⎯⎯⎯
We can stand in this world for each other.

1¹/₂ *Hours with God*

Give, and it shall be given unto you . . . for with the same
measure that ye mete withal it shall be measured to you again.

————————————————————————————LUKE 6:38 KJV

𝒯ime is one of the greatest assets God has given you. When you were born, you were given a bag of gold coins, one for each day of your life. These coins are time, and they disappear one by one, day by day, from the day of your birth.

How will you use your coins? For eternity, I hope. God wants each of us to use part of each day's time for work, for play, for study, for family, for friends, for Him. In the past you haven't given much thought to using your time for God. It's easy to spend time (or sometimes waste it) on the affairs of this earth.

Just as your money all belongs to God, so does your time. How does He want you to use it? If you take 10 percent—a tithe of your day—that means 10 percent of the fifteen hours you are awake each day; that is, one-and-a-half hours for God. Prayer, Bible reading, and study time are an important part of your time tithe. What are some other ways to give God your time? Here are a few:

- Visit patients in the hospital.
- Participate in a prison ministry.
- Invite friends and acquaintances for a meal at your home, where God will be honored.
- Offer your time to the church, whether to lead or to help paint, count the offering, be an usher, teach a Sunday school class, or change diapers in the nursery. Do whatever your talents lead you to do.
- Read books that will broaden your understanding of God and His world.
- Help widows or elderly singles who need lawns cut, or take them to church meetings, or just be their friend. If you are a college student, perhaps someone down the hall is in need of a friend; a friendly act will make his or her day. Use your God-given imagination to its fullest.
- Consider teaching or inviting neighbors and friends to a home Bible study or being a host or hostess for these occasions.

Giving to God out of your resources of money, time, and talent is at once an obligation and an opportunity.

THOUGHT FOR THE DAY ⸻⸻⸻⸻⸻⸻⸻
It is a wonderfully strange paradox that the more we give, the more we receive.

Overcome by Doing the Opposite

"That you may distinguish between holy and unholy, and between unclean and clean."
————————————————LEVITICUS 10:10 NKJV

*I*n a documentary, sociologist Tony Campolo shared a scene he saw on a bridge in Selma, Alabama. The sheriff told some civil rights demonstrators to leave the bridge, but they knelt down instead. They would not leave. The sheriff warned them that, if they didn't leave, they would be attacked with clubs and by dogs. Shots were finally fired. But the demonstrators began chanting: "We have overcome! We have overcome!" At the sheriff's command, his men charged into that group of mostly Afro-American demonstrators and began beating them with clubs and having their dogs attack them.

While watching the replay of this confrontation on TV, Campolo made an interesting statement: "They won! They won! At that point they won!"

How did they win? By responding with the opposite spirit. *Nonviolence had overcome violence.* Commitment to honesty and human rights overcame abuse and threats. The response of those demonstrators, and others like them, has helped to shift our entire country toward the positive side of today's racial issues.

As radical and unfair as it may seem, when God doesn't take us out of an unjust situation, He doesn't give us problem avoidance as well. I wish He would, but He isn't going to. He said instead: "I'm rootin' for you—and, by the way, there is healing available."

THOUGHT FOR THE DAY _____

If you will determine in your heart to respond to this hostile world in a Christlike "opposite" spirit, He will give you the grace and the ability to pull off His masterful plan.

PATRICK M. MORLEY
Walking with Christ in the Details of Life

When God Disciplines, Be Thankful

But if ye be without chastisement, whereof all are partakers,
then are ye bastards, and not sons [of God].

———————————————————HEBREWS 12:8 KJV

*D*o not be alarmed if God shakes up your world. Though at first you may naturally disagree, it is a blessing. It is not a sign that you are unworthy—every one of us is unworthy. It is not a sign of hatred, but love. If He did not love you, He would let you completely self-destruct. As it is, He cleanses your life from sin. "Some of the wise will stumble, so that they may be refined, purified and made spotless until the time of the end, for it will still come at the appointed time" (Dan. 11:35 NIV).

When God disciplines you by removing created things, by shaking up your temporal kingdom, rejoice and be glad. Created things divide our affections from God and become competition to our devotion. They lure us into the wrong race. They consume our creativity and deflect our thoughts away from the Lord Jesus.

When I slipped into "cultural" Christianity, created things became idols and divided me from complete devotion to our Lord. As a result God removed most of the created things I accumulated. I had built a shakable kingdom, and God shook it. Words are inadequate to express the joy and gratitude I feel toward God for the wounds He faithfully inflicted. It may be the single greatest blessing of my spiritual pilgrimage.

The removal of the shakable gave me a deep respect and awe for the character of God, especially His holiness. Gone was the folly that I could outmaneuver God. "Be thankful, and so worship God acceptably with reverence and awe, for our 'God is a consuming fire' " (Heb. 12:28–29 NIV). He is jealous to the point of removing created things.

When my children refuse me when I speak, my tendency is to overreact. If my daughter deserves to be sent to her room for one hour, I tend to send her for two. I overdiscipline. God never overdisciplines. You can trust God.

When He shakes the shakable, when He removes the removable, He is perfect in His discipline of us. In fact, because of His great mercy we can often join Ezra and say, "You have punished us less than our sins have deserved" (Ezra 9:13 NIV). Sometimes God underdisciplines.

THOUGHT FOR THE DAY _____

When God lovingly inflicts pain and removes the shakable, know that you are blessed. He is purging the cultural Christianity from your life. He is making you holy even as He is holy. "Endure hardship as discipline" (Heb. 12:7 NIV).

No question about it, God wants to mature His people; and the way He does that is by bringing us into difficult circumstances.

Everett L. Fullam
How to Walk with God

This Too Shall Pass

I am Alpha and Omega, the beginning and the ending, saith the Lord, which is, and which was, and which is to come, the Almighty.

REVELATION 1:8 KJV

*S*everal years ago, Barry McGuire, the famous Christian folksinger, performed for our congregation. On this occasion, he shared not only his testimony, but a fascinating story as well.

One afternoon Barry told us, when he was reflecting about sin, death, and eternity, he asked Jesus: "Lord, why did You make time?"

Though the Lord didn't reply in a booming voice from heaven, Barry did hear a quiet voice inside him answer: "I made time so sin wouldn't fill eternity."

Time is a limiting factor to all that is outside of God's will. Yet, eternal life has invaded the realm of time and space with the living reality of Jesus Christ.

I thought that was a fascinating revelation the Lord shared with Barry. Pain and suffering have been incarcerated within time and space. The troubles of this earth are not eternal. Heartache, disease, and disappointment; these too shall pass. Christians understand this, for our faith in Christ has freed us from the limitations of this temporal world. We have been given an eternal viewpoint.

Therefore, take heart! If you will simply trust in the eternal power of Christ, you have the assurance of outlasting every heartache, every problem, and every disease of this earthly existence, for you are going to outlast time itself!

THOUGHT FOR THE DAY ⎯⎯⎯⎯⎯⎯⎯⎯⎯⎯⎯
Time can't capture the soul; you are free to enjoy Christ forever.

Your soul is the best gift you will ever possess.

Ronald W. Cadmus
God's Loving Embrace

RONALD W. CADMUS
God's Loving Embrace

Can We Talk?

And they heard the voice of the LORD God walking in the garden in the cool of the day.

GENESIS 3:8 KJV

*C*omedienne Joan Rivers has a trademark one-liner in her comic monologue, a statement that draws thunderous applause: "Can we talk?"

In three words Ms. Rivers moves from comic monologue to a brief glimpse of serious dialogue with her audience.

Prayer is our ability to *get serious* with life, with ourselves, and with God. Not briefly. Unceasingly. We need to approach God simply by saying, "God, can we talk?" and move into life's most creative dialogue and faith's most endearing relationship.

We encounter God in many ways. He is most real in our prayer life. We hear Him more clearly when we are alone with Him in prayer. In this intense encounter we are made aware of His constant care.

We are not the only ones who ask of Him, "Can we talk?" It is God's desire to be open and available to us. From the Creator we hear the same question. His desire is to be close. Be still and know Him as

God. You will hear Him say: *"Can We Talk?"* God wants to be intimate with us. He yearns to embrace us with His love.

The encounter with God in prayer gives us strength for living. Without prayer we are not in touch nor in tune with His will. Engaging our lives in prayerful dialogue with God will provide us with limitless power for creative living.

Without prayer, life is spiritually shallow. With prayer, God can profoundly change us and help us grow. Prayer is an intense encounter that absorbs us in the presence of God, a complete encounter with Him. Without it there can never be abundant life.

THOUGHT FOR THE DAY —————————————————
Help us meet with You in the light and in the night of each day, God.

Jesus is not the end of your problems,
but the beginning of your solutions.

Florence Littauer
I've Found My Keys, Now Where's My Car?

Into Capable Hands

"Vengeance is Mine, I will repay," says the Lord.
—————————ROMANS 12:19 NKJV

This verse used to be quite a consolation to me. I thought that forgiveness meant giving up my need to get even with my enemies. Instead, I would tell God, "Okay, I'll let go of it. I'll let *You* get even for me!"

The truth is that although God does expect us to give vengeance over to Him, His way of getting even is not at all what we expect. He may leave your enemy to reap the consequences of his actions. He may also allow him to hit bottom. Then again He may do nothing for now. That's why David laments in the Psalms, "Why, Lord, do You let the wicked prosper?"

No, forgiveness is not praying for God to get even *for* you. It is totally turning the other person over to God's loving and capable hands and focusing on your need for forgiveness.

THOUGHT FOR THE DAY ————————————————
God, help me let go and let You deal with my enemies. Help me forgive them.

Speak Up!

Men shall speak of the might of Your awesome acts,
And I will declare Your greatness.

—————————————————————**PSALM 145:6** NKJV

$\mathcal{I}$ don't usually chance sharing with people my relationship with God. It's a very personal topic, and perhaps I have feared rejection. I grew up with the idea that it was easier to hold my feelings inside than to risk rejection.

During dinner with two friends, we began talking about religion and faith. I learned one of my friends was agnostic and the other was an atheist. I remember feeling startled. All my life I had operated with the knowledge there was a God who was far more powerful than I. We discussed how they felt and their justifications. Then they asked me why I believed in God. No one had ever asked me that point-blank.

What followed next came as a surprise. I began to talk, but I found myself saying things I had never said to anyone before. Thirty minutes passed, and my companions still listened. They didn't interrupt. The odd thing is, I don't remember what was said.

My friend who was agnostic has since become a Christian. I have no doubt God was with us that night, and I'm sure He remembers what was said.

THOUGHT FOR THE DAY ———————————————
God, I want to boldly talk about my faith, but I'm afraid. Give me courage.

No Grave Doubts

For every hour and every moment thousands of men leave life on this earth, and their souls appear before God. And how many of them depart in solitude, unknown, sad, dejected, that no one mourns for them or even knows whether they have lived or not.

————————————————————FYORDOR DOSTOYEVSKY,
THE BROTHERS KARAMAZOV

*W*hile the graveside mourners walked solemnly back to their cars, the immediate family members remained in quiet solitude and grief beside the bronze casket, which shimmered as it reflected the rays of sunlight dancing through the leaves overhead. Silent hugs were filled with caring love. The remains of a loved one lay isolated in the empty space where moments earlier 150 people offered their final respects to a beloved man of my congregation.

The cars edged their way along the small winding path, leaving the cemetery. The union workers, in their dirt encrusted work clothes, seemed callously disengaged from the broken hearts which only seconds before had gathered in a circle of love.

The waving hands of a funeral director summoned me from across the grounds. Walking toward the other gravesite, I found myself standing before a gray, compressed cardboard casket. The unknown person in this casket was a state case, no family, unnoticed while alive and alienated even in death. I was asked to say a brief prayer.

This person was one of the thousands who "depart in solitude, unknown, sad, dejected, that no one mourns for them or even knows whether they have lived or not."

But to God, this magnified moment of dejection was filled with the truth that He would never leave any of us desolate. We need have no doubts about the fact that God's loving embrace was wrapped around this moment of loneliness. Such a thought made this moment a bit more humane and shed a spirit of light and promise on this soul now appearing before God.

To the believer in Jesus Christ, God made a wonderful promise regarding His loving embrace. Whoever believes in Him, whether living or dead, will have eternal life. No grave! A hole in the ground, earth's last cold embrace, would gain no possessive claim or rights over any of God's faithful children.

THOUGHT FOR THE DAY _____

Have no grave doubts. God intends for you to have, not a grave, but the warm, loving embrace of His kingdom. This is the power of the cross. It is the promise of Easter. Such a truth God yearns for each of us to embrace.

Empty-Handed

As he came from his mother's womb, naked shall he return,
To go as he came;
And he shall take nothing from his labor
Which he may carry away in his hand.

ECCLESIASTES 5:15 NKJV

*S*omeone once pointed out that we never see a U-Haul℗ behind a hearse. Solomon reflects on this truth as he states that when we enter this world we bring nothing but our bodies and that it will be the same when we leave.

Two things will last eternally. They are the souls of men and the Word of God.

Many men have committed themselves to the purposes of God. A friend of mine, Ken Canfield, executive director of the National Center for Fathering, has committed himself to strengthening the role of the father. He sees the need to support and encourage fathers in their important role. The work he does, influencing their lives, is an eternal investment.

What eternal impact are you having in your world? You may be making million-dollar deals in your business or constructing beautiful homes for others. Although the job you do is essential to your survival, none of it will last forever, except your influence on the souls of other people and the time you spend learning the Word of God.

THOUGHT FOR THE DAY ———————————————
God, help me live a life fraught with meaning and purpose.

Keep Your Faith in Balance

Beloved, believe not every spirit, but try the spirits whether they are of God: because many false prophets are gone out into the world.

—1 JOHN 4:1 KJV

If you accept prophetic utterances as valid for today, I would encourage you to test them in the following ways.

First, is the person giving the prophetic utterance living a balanced and righteous lifestyle?

Second, is the person committed to building God's kingdom or his own; is Christ being lifted up or is the person?

Third, does the prophetic utterance establish confidence in the Word of God and is it consistent with a balanced presentation of it? Are people going to have a greater dependency upon God's revelation or man's inspiration? Are prophetic utterances a substitute for the serious, personal study of God's Word?

Fourth, does the use of the spiritual gift bring unity and build up one another? Be careful in this test, because those who hold to a form of godliness but deny its power are not in balance either. They will quench the Spirit through censorship and very little will be accomplished in the church. They can cause disunity as well.

Last, do the spiritual manifestations bypass the mind? God operates through our mind; Satan bypasses it. If a person takes on a medium-like trance, beware. God renews our mind and brings back to our mind all that He has taught us. We are to think so as to have sound judgment.

All of us receive input from a myriad of sources today. With Satan still using false prophets in his battle for our minds.

THOUGHT FOR THE DAY _____
Have faith, but keep it balanced.

Learning Wisdom

The fear of the LORD is the beginning of wisdom.
————————————**PSALM 111:10** NKJV

I grew up with a misshapen view of God. To me He was a cosmic killjoy, wanting me always to be a good little boy and behave. I can't blame the church I went to or even my parents, but somehow it just came to me that God was to be feared. Verses like the one above supported that viewpoint. In short, God was out to get me!

Today, I understand the verse differently. Fear has more to do with *respecting* God's perfect law, His perfect plan for me, and His provision for me in Jesus Christ. Understanding what God wants me to do and say and taking that as a goal toward which I strive is what fear of the Lord is for me. And that is the beginning of wisdom.

I doubt if I will ever be truly wise in God's sight, but it is my goal to get as close as I can, day by day, to the knowledge and assurance of His plan for my life.

THOUGHT FOR THE DAY ————————————
God, help me to understand Your plan for me and grow in wisdom today.

The truth we all need to see is that we don't have to do anything. That's how free we are. Seeing this leads to more acceptance of personal responsibility for what we choose to do in life.

Dr. Chris Thurman
The 12 Best Kept Secrets for Living an Emotionally Healthy Life

Check Your Daily Account

"Who shall give account to him that is ready to judge the quick and the dead."

1 PETER 4:5 KJV

*A*ccountability is not a popular word today. However, we will all give an accounting. Whether Christian or non-Christian, we will all stand before the Lord Jesus to give an account for that which He has entrusted to us.

The other day we received two notices from our bank regarding overdrawn checks. We were terribly embarrassed.

I rushed to the bank, and the bank clerk and I went over each item and each deposit. To my chagrin, we found I'd deposited the $300 into savings instead of into checking. Our bank balance had come up short because I put our investment in the wrong account.

This incident brings to mind a verse from 1 Peter: "Who shall give account to him that is ready to judge the quick and the dead' (4:5 KJV). The term Peter used for *accounting* is not unlike the accounting I went through at the bank that day. We will all, ultimately, at the end of time, give an accounting for how we've invested and how we've deposited the time God has allotted to each of us.

As an example of His accounting, Jesus used the illustration of a rich man who gave one servant one talent, another servant five talents and another ten talents. Those who received larger amounts aggressively invested theirs at some risk and reaped good returns. The servant who had been given one talent literally buried it in the ground for safekeeping, gaining no return whatsoever. When the rich man returned to collect on his investments, he was delighted to learn that those with the larger sums had invested theirs with great returns, but he was very upset with the man who played it safe by doing nothing with his.

Jesus summed up the parable with this lesson: "To him who has, more will be given; but to him who has not, what he has will be taken away" (Matt. 25:29, paraphrased). Another lesson this parable brings home is the same point Peter tried to endorse here: We will all give an accounting to the Lord.

Jesus' message here is that life is to be lived to the fullest.

- What would you try right now if you knew you couldn't fail?
- Is there anything you have left unattempted in your life?
- Why don't you attempt it? What is stopping you?

THOUGHT FOR THE DAY _____

Remember: Life is what happens to you while you're waiting for life to start. Don't get caught putting your life investment in the wrong place!

Know His Purpose

Open my eyes
To see Thy face
Let me rejoice
In Your embrace.

M.W.H. 1992

I have a little dog who is a real character. Captain has learned that if he comes near me in the morning when I'm having breakfast, every once in a while I might drop a little crumb for him. Well, instead of just hoping he finds one on the floor, or hoping he happens to be there at the right time, the minute he smells the toast in the toaster, he is next to me. He follows me to the table. He sits right in front of me, following my every move . . . just waiting. His eyes never leave my hand. If I move my hand up, his eyes go up. If I move my hand to the left, his eyes follow my hand. He is watching because I have food for him, and he does not want to miss even one crumb.

That's the way I think we should be with our heavenly Father. Our eyes should be on Him constantly, and we should be eagerly awaiting every morsel. We should let Him see that we are excited about what He might give us and that we understand our food, our joy, our confidence, and our peace all come from Him.

God's purpose for prayer first of all is for all of those He created to glorify Him. He desires for us to love Him, worship Him, and have fellowship with Him. His purpose is also that He might become known to all men and we might be drawn closer to Him. He wants our eyes to be constantly fixed on Him, eagerly expecting things from Him.

Each time I pray, I create a setting or picture in my mind. Jesus and I may be sitting in my office or some other place in my home, or I may see myself entering His throne room and bowing before Him. Whatever the setting, I focus on His face. I do not see an image I could draw for you, and generally not even an image I could describe in words, but I concentrate on the image He gives me of Himself. First Chronicles says we are to "seek His face evermore!" (16:11).

THOUGHT FOR THE DAY _____

I often pray, *Dear Jesus, let me see Your face. Let me sense the response of Your eyes as I talk with You. Keep me sensitive to Your responses that we may always be in tune with each other. In Jesus' Name, Amen.*

Embrace Faith

Hold fast that which is good.
———1 THESSALONIANS
5:21 KJV

$\mathcal{F}$or forty years he sat at the roadside just outside the entrance of the city, at a gate called Beautiful. He was a pathetic, lame man longing to capture the essence of meaning for life. For four decades his supplication was for wholeness.

His hope was never affirmed until the disciples Peter and John intersected his life with the gift needed to heal his wounded spirit and life. This ideal spirit suddenly made the once-distant healing within touch and thought.

As it was his practice to beg for alms, Peter and John heard his solicitations as they crossed the threshold of Beautiful Gate. The surprising miracle for the lame man was to be the discovery of the cross at the threshold of Beautiful Gate. For something beautiful was going to adorn his life with grace.

Expecting a handout from Peter and John, he stretched his hands out urgently. In his begging for forty years, he had squatted in valueless human despair. But this day he was to be embraced by new life.

Instead of alms placed within his hands he hears these words from Peter: "Silver and gold I do not have, but what I do have I give you" (Acts 3:6).

What was this, "What I do have"? The lame man reached out and received Jesus' healing touch. Peter and John were the love of Christ, embracing all those who needed wholeness.

Peter and John embodied the life-changing love of Jesus. When the lame man touched Peter and John he grasped faith! He was embraced by God's love. They had no silver and gold. The greatest love in life was their only possession. They embraced the man with this gift of life at Beautiful Gate. They shared with him Jesus Christ's love.

To the amazement of all who knew him, he began leaping, walking, and he entered the temple praising God.

The disciples said, "And His name, through faith in His name, has made this man strong" (Acts 3:16).

After this miraculous recovery we observe the lame man restored to complete agility, walking along the road with Peter and John. His hand is tightly grasping their shoulder. For strength? For support? To stabilize his unsteady walk?

Why did he need the support of their shoulders since in the previous verses we have witnessed him becoming a man, who through the power of God, was able to stand firm on his two feet, to leap in joy, suspended in the midair of ecstasy? Running into the temple to praise God! He was literally a man transformed from lameness to dancing with joy!

What security did Peter and John provide?

Was he holding on to them because he needed stability? Was he uncertain and untrusting of the miracle performed within his life? Was there a chance that this was merely a fleeting, short-lived experience, a dream from which he was soon to awaken?

No!

He found the secret. He discovered the answer of power for living. The power came in the encounter with the embracing love of God. It was an embraceable love manifested in the love of two men, Peter and John. If he could continue to grasp on to them, on to the Jesus within them, he would possess a faith that would make him strong.

"I want them to continue in good heart and in the unity of love and to come to the full wealth of conviction which understanding brings, and grasp [embrace] God's secret" (Col. 2:2 NEB). The lame man found the secret of his new life. He "grasped" and embraced that secret and brought Jesus into his life. At Beautiful Gate, the beautiful love of God became real for him.

THOUGHT FOR THE DAY _____

Every one of us, at some point in our lives, will find ourselves standing at Beautiful Gate, asking for a better quality of life. All you need to do is reach out and embrace it. Yes, it's that simple.

Prayer Can Be Lethal

Fear not, Daniel: for from the first day that thou didst set thine heart to understand, and to chasten thyself before thy God, thy words were heard, and I am come for thy words.

————————————————————DANIEL 10:12 KJV

In the garden of Gethsemane, the night before Jesus was crucified, Jesus said to His disciples, "Pray, lest you fall into temptation." Prayer has a power over evil. It is lethal.

C. S. Lewis's *Screwtape Letters* introduces us to Screwtape, a devil who is training young Wormwood, his novice nephew. Screwtape is to provide the young, inexperienced destroyer of good with the techniques necessary to undermine the influence of faith in Christians.

Wormwood, however diligently he tries, continues to botch up his efforts. He cannot seem to defuse the power of these lovers of God.

A disgruntled Screwtape, in giving young Wormwood a few keys to certain success says, "The best thing, where it is possible, is to keep the patient from the serious intention of praying altogether. It is funny how mortals always picture us as putting things into their minds: in reality our best work is done by keeping things out."

Screwtape affirms that prayer is lethal to evil's cause.

"At all costs, do not let these people pray to their God. For prayer is lethal to our cause."

Evil has no power over prayer.

Temptation will always attempt to break down the power of God within your life. A life without prayer is "open season" for the Screwtapes and Wormwoods that lurk over our shoulders and gently whisper in our ears.

THOUGHT FOR THE DAY _____
Our greatest battles are fought and won on our knees.

*Prayer doesn't change God;
it changes us. The value of prayer
is that it helps us discover and
get in tune with God's will.*

Patrick M. Morley
The Rest of Your Life

Don't Let Your Foot Get Caught in the Door

Don't get your foot caught in the doorway of God's will, for what's on the other side is your destiny.

*I*magine, if you would, a door in the path ahead of us. God's will is on the other side of that door. We crave to know what it is. Will God show us what's on the other side of that door? No. Why not? Because we have to resolve an issue on this side of the door first. If He is Lord, He has the right to determine what's on the other side of the door. If we don't afford Him that right, then we are not acknowledging Him as Lord.

Why do we want to know what's on the other side of that door? Isn't it because we want to reserve the right to determine whether or not we will go through it? Some boldly walk halfway through, but keep their foot in the door just in case they don't like what they see and want to go back. It's going to be awfully hard to continue walking with God if your foot is stuck in the door. Jesus said, "No one, having put his hand to the plow, and looking back, is fit for the kingdom of God" (Luke 9:62).

One man probably spoke for many when he said, "I'm so used to running my own life. I'm not sure I even can or want to trust someone else. Besides, God would probably haul me off to perform some task I couldn't tolerate." What we need to realize is that if we give our heart to the Lord, and God did call us to some special task, by the time we got into it we wouldn't want to be doing anything else.

Do you believe that the will of God is good, acceptable, and perfect for you? That's the heart of the issue. In the Lord's Prayer we are taught to approach God with the intent that *His* will be accomplished on earth. It makes no sense to petition God if we are not predisposed to do His will.

In the last half of the nineteenth century, George Mueller founded the Bristol Orphan Home which would become known all over the world as one of the most remarkable monuments of human faith and divine guidance in history. Year after year, without a single advertisement to the public or appeal to Christian friends, hundreds of children were fed, clothed, and educated. The home was maintained simply through prayer and faith. George Mueller epitomizes the essential prerequisite to divine guidance in these thoughts:

> I seek in the beginning to get my heart in such a state that it has no will of its own in regard to a given matter. Nine-tenths of the trouble with people is just here. Nine-tenths of the difficulties are overcome when our hearts are ready to do the Lord's will. When one is truly in this state, it is usually but a little way to the knowledge of what His will is.

THOUGHT FOR THE DAY _____
Knowing that "what's on the other side of the door" is something planned by our loving, omnipotent heavenly Father, would you pray this prayer with me?

Do Unto Others . . .

If any of you lacks wisdom, let him ask of God, who gives to all liberally and without reproach.

JAMES 1:5 NKJV

*W*hen you pray and ask for acceptance, what are you struggling to accept? Is it the behavior of your spouse? Do you feel criticized when what you need is love and affirmation? Why do you feel a lack of peace and serenity?

Let's say you have had a busy day with the housework, three preschoolers, and errands to run, and your spouse comes in tired and ready for dinner. Do you both take time to greet each other with a smile, a hug, and a warm hello, or are you only concerned with yourselves?

If you give love and praise to others who struggle with their problems, then your problems won't grow so big by your constant dwelling on them. Your heart may feel empty without words of praise from others, but when you treat others as you would like to be treated, you receive a gift in return: the gift of acceptance.

THOUGHT FOR THE DAY _____

I need wisdom to communicate well with those You have placed in my path.

Trouble Transformed

[Look] carefully lest anyone fall short of the grace of God; lest any root of bitterness springing up cause trouble, and by this many become defiled.

HEBREWS 12:15 NKJV

Last summer I learned about roots. I was trying to get rid of some particularly pesky weeds that were becoming troublesome in our yard. Many times I had cut the weeds to the ground, but they grew back. Then I decided to pull them out by the roots. The roots were amazingly long in comparison to the plants. It was hard work to get them out of the ground.

The roots of bitterness also go deep within our souls and cause us great trouble. If we allow ourselves to become embittered by life's disappointments and injustices, the roots will grow and grow.

The solution to bitterness is the grace of God. God is able to take the terrible experiences of life and turn them into growing and learning experiences by His grace.

THOUGHT FOR THE DAY
There is a great evil in the world, but there is also great compassion, because God is a God of grace.

Know the Disposition of Your Heart

For the LORD searcheth all hearts, and understandeth all the imaginations of the thoughts: if thou seek him, he will be found of thee.

———————————————1 CHRONICLES 28:9 KJV

Is there a litmus test you can take to know yourself? In one sense, you cannot ever fully know yourself. "Who can discern his errors?" (Ps. 19:12 NIV). Our natural hearts always have the capacity to deceive us at any moment. Tiny pinholes in our character leak under too much pressure. And our hidden (or unknown) needs motivate us in ways we know virtually nothing about.

In another sense, though, we can walk in the power of the Holy Spirit and not gratify the desires of the sinful nature. Though dark, secret caverns dot the landscape of our minds, the blood of our Savior covers, cleanses, and sanctifies the secrets of our sinful nature. "Forgive my hidden faults" (Ps. 19:12 NIV).

The biblical Christian walks in the Spirit, while the cultural Christian gratifies the desires of the sinful nature. How can we know with certainty whether we live in the Spirit to please God, or in the flesh to please self?

Jesus knows that we are filled with a mountain of motives, an avalanche of ambitions, and a den of desires. He knows myriad thoughts roam our minds when we make decisions. He knows that our hidden needs for approval, respect, love, and survival compel us in ways we know virtually nothing about. That's why the Scriptures indicate that deceit can so easily seep in through the pinholes of our weak character.

Even so, the question is easy to answer. The first disposition of our heart reveals whether we are a biblical or a cultural Christian. How can we discover the first disposition of our heart?

Jesus said, "For where your treasure is, there your heart will be also." Jesus says how we spend our money reveals what we love, our true affections. Look at where your money went—it reveals the first disposition of your heart. Where you have stored your treasure is the record of where you have walked, either as a biblical Christian or a cultural Christian. Follow the money.

When the government or a business suspects fraud, the auditors always follow the money. The money trail—not the verbal trail—proves what motivated the man, what the first disposition of his heart was. Although good, evil, and ambiguous motives may commingle together, where the money goes settles the record. It precisely indicates where the heart went.

If you want to know the first disposition of your heart, Jesus provides the foolproof test. He asks, "Where is your treasure?"

Where does the money trail lead in your life? Does it please God? Have you been storing treasure as a biblical Christian or a cultural Christian?

The cultural Christian lets "the worries of this life and the deceitfulness of wealth choke [the Word], making it unfruitful" (Matt. 13:22 NIV). The root of cultural Christianity is worry and deceit—worry over the temporary world and deceit over what money can accomplish.

If you find it difficult to segregate the multiple motives of your heart, if you find it difficult to know if you are pleasing God, then examine the record of where your treasure is. If you suspect you have lived the life of a cultural Christian, you are probably right. If you desire to please God, to be a biblical Christian, to pass the treasure test, then redirect the trail of your money.

THOUGHT FOR THE DAY ————————————————

" 'For where your treasure is, there your heart will be also' " (*Luke 12:34* NKJV).

God Doesn't Grade on the Curve

"And what does the LORD require of you
But to do justly,
To love mercy,
And to walk humbly with your God?"
—————————MICAH 6:8 NKJV

*M*any people compare themselves to others and come away saying, "I don't sin like that guy," or "I'm doing at least as good as she is."

God doesn't grade on the curve. He doesn't compare us to others. He also doesn't judge us according to a sliding scale of righteousness.

Christians frequently say to me—and to other pastors and counselors—such things as these:

"I know I'm not praying as much as I should."

"I know I'm not giving enough."

"I know I'm not reading my Bible as much as I ought."

My comment to them is, "How much is enough?" People need to pray, give, and read the Bible as much as they are able and then trust God that what they have done is sufficient in His hands. If God desires for you to pray more, give more, or read more, He'll direct you to pray about specific things, give a specific amount, read a particular passage, or study a particular subject. God doesn't say, "Do more." He says,

"Do this. Do that. Do the other." God deals with us in specifics, not generalities.

If God has called you to do a certain thing and you aren't doing it, you should get busy and obey Him.

If your feelings, however, are ones of inadequacy and of guilt for not being perfect or of not achieving something for God, you need to reappraise and to rethink your position.

God doesn't ask you to perform for Him. He doesn't ask you to try harder. God will never speak from the heavens to you and say, "You aren't doing enough for Me."

God's direction to us is always very specific. He will say, "I want you to teach this Sunday school class," or "I want you to remind that person of My promise in the Word," or "I want you to give this amount to that project." God speaks to us about what He wants us to do *in the present tense* of our lives.

When we have an overwhelming sense that we should do this, ought to do that, or must do the other, we experience false guilt. It's not of God. It's something we require of ourselves or something others have taught us that we are required to do.

THOUGHT FOR THE DAY ———————————————
Obey the leading of the Lord and follow His footsteps into the success He has planned for you.

RANDY PETERSEN

Flying Solo

Heart of the Issue

"Teacher, which is the great commandment in the law?" Jesus said to him, " 'You shall love the LORD your God with all your heart, with all your soul, and with all your mind.' . . . And the second is like it: 'You shall love your neighbor as yourself.' "

——————————————————MATTHEW 22:36–39 NKJV

It was a trick question posed by Jesus' enemies. Surely, the pretender would offend somebody as He made His nomination for the greatest commandment. If He said, "Keeping the Sabbath," the antiadultery crusade would scorn Him. If He said, "False testimony," the "no other God before Me" faction would have a field day.

Jesus grabbed two teachings from Deuteronomy that throw a blanket over all those commandments. Love God and your neighbor. And that's exactly what the rulemongers had forgotten.

That's still the heart of the issue today. Christians may crow about morality, but we must always, always be driven by love.

THOUGHT FOR THE DAY ————————————————

May the law of Your love rule in my heart.

*Love is the glue that holds us together
and the oil that keeps us from
rubbing each other the wrong way.*

Patrick M. Morley
The Rest of Your Life

TOM WHITEMAN
Flying Solo

Who's Got the Power?

Direct my steps by Your word,
And let no iniquity have dominion over me.

PSALM 119:133 NKJV

*O*ther people's sins can have power over us—if we let them, that is. I can remember how upset I was at the attitudes of other Christians when I was facing trouble. There was no question that many of them treated me unjustly.

As I sat at home harboring bad feelings and thoughts toward them, I found that I could work myself into a very foul mood. Who was I hurting? Myself!

Do you feel that others have power over your life? Perhaps they haven't done anything to you in months; yet, they still have the power to ruin your day. You are giving them that power.

Accept the injustice that others inflict on you, and give it over to God. He can surely handle it better than you can.

THOUGHT FOR THE DAY
Whom have I given power to hurt me? God, take that power and set me free.

Strength Enough

I can do all things through Christ who strengthens me.
————————————**PHILIPPIANS 4:13** NKJV

*E*very culture has had its superheroes. Odysseus, Wotan, Roland, Pecos Bill, Paul Bunyan, Superman—on goes the list. Unlimited by ordinary limits, these mythical characters overcome all and emerge victorious from every struggle.

Paul's statement sounds mythical too. How can faith in Christ enable me (ordinary me) to do everything? Will I now leap over tall buildings in a single bound and be faster than a speeding bullet?

No, Paul is not teaching us to believe in magic. Instead, he is encouraging us to believe that God has sufficient strength to bear us up and carry us through any hardship that we may have to face. Paul was in prison as he wrote. Because Christ was strengthening him, he was able to be content with his circumstances.

If God has placed you in some particularly difficult circumstances, remember that His strength is great enough to protect you and guide you through anything that you have to do.

*Do what can be done, and God will
do the rest.*

Tony Campolo
How to Rescue the Earth Without Worshiping Nature

Take a Closer Look

Who can understand his errors?
Cleanse me from secret faults.
————————PSALM 19:12 NKJV

*W*e seldom want to admit that we have secret sins. We act like the little boy who hated to take a bath. He especially disliked it when his mother used soap and a washcloth to clean those hard-to-get spots on his face. During one episode, the mother tried to reason with him and asked, "Don't you want to be clean?" "Yes," he responded, "but couldn't you just dust my face?"

As with all of our defects of character, the hidden areas need to be cleansed. God desires for us to learn the daily discipline of allowing Him to show us areas that need to be cleansed. As we spend time in God's Word the light of His truth becomes brighter, and we can more clearly see the flaws in our hearts.

Each of us needs to humbly ask God to reveal the secret sins that we have locked away.

THOUGHT FOR THE DAY ————————————————
Thank You, God, for Your grace as You reveal to us our secret sins.

Tell Him Today

Therefore by Him let us continually offer the sacrifice of praise to God, that is, the fruit of our lips, giving thanks to His name.

————————————————————————HEBREWS 13:15 NKJV

*I*n *Fiddler on the Roof,* Tevye asks his wife a simple question: "Do you love me?" In response, she details all the things she has done for him over their thirty years of marriage. She has scrubbed the floors and cooked the food and raised the kids—how ridiculous to speak of love!

But Tevye persists with his question. He needs for her to say the words.

We show love for others by doing things for them—but also by telling them. That's true of God too. He wants our obedience. He wants our good deeds. But He also wants the "sacrifice of praise" from our lips. He wants us to tell Him—and everyone else—how much He means to us.

When was the last time you told God how much you love Him?

THOUGHT FOR THE DAY ————————————————
I do love You, God. Help me to tell others of my love for You.

W. MATTHEW REED, JR.

Flying Solo

Actions Overturned

> *But now, do not therefore be grieved or angry with yourselves*
> *because you sold me here; for God sent me before you*
> *to preserve life.*

GENESIS 45:5 NKJV

After twenty years of separation, Joseph was finally reunited with his brothers. It is almost unbelievable.

One would expect Joseph to be bitter. Their actions had caused him great suffering. But he was able to avoid that trap because of his proper view of trials. He was able to see suffering's source and purpose. He saw his brothers as God's agents, accomplishing His will. Their intent was bad, but God's was good. The Lord overturned their actions and brought about a good result for Joseph and then glory for Himself.

Who has wronged you? Your spouse? Your children? Your friends or church? No matter who or what it is, God will overturn the actions to bring about your good and His glory.

Trust Him without panic, and when it happens, thank Him without pride. Have patience. He will act for you in His time.

Had I been Joseph, I may have been bitter. Help me believe as he did that there is purpose in my pain and that good will somehow result from it.

Consider the Cross

*And whosoever doth not bear his cross, and come after me,
cannot be my disciple.*

LUKE 15:27 KJV

There it is on the communion table: the shiny brass crucifix. And there it is again on the lapel of the businessman, who wants his customers to know that he is a Christian. And again, hanging from the ear of a heavy metal singer. And in the corner of the business card of the Agape Plumbing Service. And on the steeple of a church, and on the bumper of a car, and in the hotel lobby, next to the Star of David, to show lodgers where they might worship if they care to. I went to school with a boy who had a cross tattooed under his eye. I was never sure what that meant. Sometimes I'm not so sure what the cross means in any of those other places either.

The pop singer, Madonna, says, "It's sexy to wear a crucifix because there is a naked man on it." Her statement reflects a sick movement in secular rock music to empty the cross of its meaning. It is a movement, unfortunately, that started in the American Christian church years ago. The cross used to stand for Jesus, and more precisely, the suffering of Jesus. Now it stands for an institution that most often doesn't really stand for anything other than the advancement of its own institutionality, its buildings and programs.

I have a small plastic replica of a panel from an ivory box in the British Museum, which dates around A.D. 200. This panel depicts Jesus on the cross in one corner and Judas, hanging himself, in the other. The craftsmanship is rather crude but the significance of the piece derives from something other than the artistic detail. It is the first known representation of Jesus on the cross in Christian art, or any art for that matter. A.D. 200! More than one-hundred-and-fifty years after the crucifixion. It took the early Christians that long to finally get around to portraying Jesus on the cross.

The early Christians had other symbols, the fish or icthus. They sometimes even used the star of David, since most of them were Jewish.

Why didn't they utilize the symbol of the cross? Were they ashamed of it? Or were they merely embarrassed by it? Who can tell. My guess is that they shied away from representing the cross because it meant too much, not because it meant too little (as it does today). They cherished the cross in their hearts. Maybe they desired that it become a vivid reality, which could only be kept alive in their hearts, instead of a symbol around their necks or below their eyes.

THOUGHT FOR THE DAY _____

The Cross is not a symbol. It is the center of the universe, the nexus of history, the most meaningful event that ever took place.

TOM JONES
Flying Solo

His Promise

*For our light affliction, which is but for a moment, is working
for us a far more exceeding and eternal weight of glory.*
—2 CORINTHIANS 4:17 NKJV

The world is full of trouble. We all have our share. But Christ has promised that when we go through times of trouble, something wonderful will be accomplished. An eternal glory will be achieved! In some way our hardships and sorrows will accomplish an everlasting reward.

We do not know how this works, but we can be sure that it does, for it is His promise. When life is over, when we have entered into His glory in the kingdom of heaven, we will not look backward at our earthly troubles and complain. Instead, we will rejoice, for all the pieces of the puzzle will fit.

THOUGHT FOR THE DAY
Trust Him today no matter what trouble you face. The glory is coming!

Reconsider God

"You are worthy, our Lord and God, to receive glory and honor and power, for you created all things, and by your will they were created and have their being."

—REVELATION 4:11 NIV

*N*early everyone has had the experience of meeting someone particularly dignified, but in a quiet, unassuming way. That person doesn't say much about himself; yet, he projects an incandescent, warm self-confidence. He seems so genuinely interested in you that you speak freely and openly with him in the casual, familiar everyday talk you use at home or with close friends—the kind you would never use around your boss or pastor.

Only later, you learn the person with whom you spoke is an important industrialist, a distinguished diplomat, or a celebrated speaker. When the breadth of his accomplishments becomes known to you, your attitude changes sharply. You would never again speak to that person with such casually chosen words, expressing such capricious thoughts. The next time, if there would ever be a next time, you would rehearse every word carefully before you spoke. You would carefully frame each thought to show the respect due such an important person.

Why is it, then, that we display such a casual, even capricious, attitude when speaking to Him who "created all things," and through whom all things have their being?

Our family once attended a tawdry, gimmicky religious meeting. As the minutes painfully ticked away, I slumped deeper and deeper into my chair. The meeting organizers created a freakish, carnival-like atmosphere, like a sideshow off the midway. The barker hawked religious souvenirs with Brother Love's zeal. I couldn't help but wonder, *Would they be a little bit embarrassed if they learned Jesus had sat on the front row?*

If we ponder who God really is before we carelessly utter any remark before or about Him, surely we will render a more considered, respectful utterance. This is no different from the respect we would show the distinguished stranger if we knew his true identity. When once we see Him as He really is, the trite or casual remark no longer seems appropriate.

In fact, when we know the God who is, our first reaction is to hide from the awfulness of His presence. We want to see the face of God, until the presence of His glory draws near. Then, we want Him to hide us in the cleft of a rock. His presence is like peals of thunder and the fierce winds of a violent storm, and we reconsider the foolishness of our whim to see Him. He is a holy God. Not only holy—but holy, holy, holy. " 'Holy, holy, holy is the Lord God Almighty, who was, and is, and is to come' " (Rev. 4:8 NIV).

In heaven one hundred million loyal angels will encircle the throne of God and sing in a loud voice, " 'Worthy is the Lamb, who was slain, to receive power and wealth and wisdom and strength and honor and glory and praise!' " (Rev. 5:12 NIV). The four living creatures, those beings allowed closest to His throne say, "Holy, holy, holy." The elders who sit on the twenty-four thrones which surround the throne cry out, "You are worthy."

After that "every creature in heaven and on earth and under the earth and on the sea, and all that is in them" will sing, " 'To him who sits on the throne and to the Lamb be praise and honor and glory and power, for ever and ever!' " (Rev. 5:13 NIV). You and I will be "every creature."

Reconsider who God is—His power, His wealth, His wisdom, His glory, His honor, His praise. Let us take our cue from the living creatures, the elders, and the angels. Let us not approach the God who is holy, holy, holy with caprice or unthinking casualness.

Let us come into His presence with praise and thanksgiving, but also in sober recognition that we are in the presence of the Holy. "Let us then approach the throne of grace with confidence" (Heb. 4:16 NIV), but with the bearing and respect we would show to the One whose identity we have learned: the God who is, who created all things, in whom we have our being.

When you come apart to meet with God, consider these statements as you begin your time in His presence. Pause and meditate upon them:

- Father, I come to meet with You. Meet with me.
- Lord Jesus, I come to meet with You. Meet with me.
- Holy Spirit, I come to meet with You. Meet with me.

THOUGHT FOR THE DAY _____
Enter into the presence of the God who is with the respect and honor and praise He is due. Do it as you would when you learn the identity of the dignified stranger.

The greatest use of life is to spend it for something that will outlast it.

Anne and Ray Ortlund
You Don't Have to Quit

Lord, Be My . . .

And God said to Moses, "I AM WHO I AM." And He said,
"Thus you shall say to the children of Israel, 'I AM has sent me
to you.' "

EXODUS 3:14 NKJV

*W*hen God called Moses to lead the children of Israel out of slavery in Egypt, Moses had several questions. He asked God who he should say had sent him as the leader. God responded that Moses should tell the people that "I AM" had sent him.

When we are discouraged, we can remember that God is still the great "I AM." We can fill in the blank of what we need for God to be for us. "I AM" your comforter, encourager, strength, friend, confidant, healer, guide, heavenly Father, or support. God has the awesome ability to be what we need, when we need it. He shows concern for all of our feelings and knows us intimately.

God is perfect, and His abilities are limitless and multifaceted. People have let us down in the past, but God remains trustworthy and will never fail us. We can place our confidence in His ability and desire to take care of us.

THOUGHT FOR THE DAY
God is with us at all times. And in Him, we have everything we need.

The Good and Bad of Life (God's Providence)

Now therefore be not grieved, nor angry with yourselves, that ye sold me hither: for God did send me before you to preserve life.
———————————————————GENESIS 45:5 KJV

Let God handle the "bad" in your life. His providence has a way of accomplishing more than you could ever dream. Providence is all things working together.

Providence comes from two words: *pro,* meaning "before," and *video,* meaning "to see." To see before—that's providence. The providence of God means that God sees beforehand and plans accordingly. A great picture of providence is found in the Old Testament life of Joseph:

One day, wearing the new brightly-colored sport coat his father had given him, Joseph was sent to check up on his brothers. When they saw him coming, they said, "Here comes that dreamer. Let's kill him! Then let's see what becomes of his dreams!"

But Reuben (the eldest) persuaded them not to kill the boy but to throw him in a pit in the wilderness and let him die.

After throwing Joseph in the pit, the brothers had lunch. As they were eating, they saw a caravan of Ishmaelites heading their way. They said, "We can make some money off this deal. Let's pull Joseph out of the pit and sell him to those guys."

That's bad. Well, not so bad, because before they reached the pit, some Midianite traders happened by, saw Joseph in the pit, and pulled him out.

That's good. Well, not so good, because they sold him to the Ishmaelites who dragged him to Egypt where Jews weren't appreciated and sold him as a slave.

That's bad. Well, not so bad, because they sold him to Potiphar, one of Pharaoh's officers who did not hate the Jews.

That's good. Well, not so good, because Potiphar's wife began to hit on Joseph and tried to seduce him.

That's bad. Well, not so bad, because Joseph refused her advances.

That's good. Well, not so good, because she lied and said that Joseph tried to rape her and he was thrown in prison.

That's bad. Well, not so bad, because in prison he met a chief cupbearer and a chief baker who, because Joseph was able to interpret their dreams, vowed they would remember him when they were released.

That's good. Well, not so good, because they forgot about him. At least the cupbearer did; the baker was hanged.

But then Pharaoh himself began to be troubled by his dreams and could find no one to tell him what they meant. Suddenly the cupbearer remembered his former cellmate's ability to explain dreams.

Joseph was brought before Pharaoh and interpreted the monarch's dreams, which said that there were going to be seven years of fatness, then seven years of famine.

On the spot, Pharaoh appointed Joseph as food administrator, gave him the king's signet ring, dressed him in fine clothes, and placed a gold chain around his neck. He put Joseph in charge of the palace and the entire household was told to submit to Joseph's orders.

And if that wasn't enough, listen to what the king said: "I am

Pharaoh, but without your word no one will lift hand or foot in all Egypt."

Providence: God's purpose accomplished. Let God handle things; He's already seen them coming. That's good!

Safe in His Hands

Yet I will not forget you.
See, I have inscribed you on the palms of My hands.
————————————————ISAIAH 49:15–16 NKJV

*H*ave you ever seen a baby who was born prematurely? These tiny infants may weigh as little as one or two pounds and can fit in the palm of a father's hand. Underdeveloped, they depend for their survival on powers out of their control. Qualified professionals assure that these infants have the proper life support, nutrition, protective environment, and the comfort of human touch.

Picture yourself as a child being held in God's hands. Like the premature infant, you are in need of a power greater than yourself for survival. The only true provider is God almighty, who not only promises to be the caretaker providing for the needs of His child but promises never to forget you by impressing your image into the palms of His hands.

THOUGHT FOR THE DAY ————————————————
Thank You, God, for bearing the pain of the Cross for me. Thank You for caring for me.

The Renewing Source

> *Those who wait on the LORD*
> *Shall renew their strength;*
> *They shall mount up with wings like eagles,*
> *They shall run and not be weary,*
> *They shall walk and not faint.*
>
> —————————————ISAIAH 40:31 NKJV

*G*od, I'm busy again. I'm cleaning out my closets and packing in a frenzy. I'm determined to make this move to a new city in a fresh way. I want to break my old defeating habits and begin new clean ones. But I'm having a problem, Lord. All my willpower seems to be poured out on the earth as if it had never been. When my will is aligned with Yours, it becomes mighty; but today I feel tired, weak, and in despair.

How tragic that we trust our own strength, when what we crave is the chance to begin again, knowing from the wisdom of all our scars what not to do. God, serenity is simple when I take time to allow You to reveal Yourself, to perceive Your will, and then to flow with it.

Help me remember that You are the source of all new life. You give me not one or three or seven new chances, but as many as I need, drawing me ever nearer to You.

THOUGHT FOR THE DAY ————————————————

Jesus gives us living water to refresh ourselves. All we have to do to receive it is draw near to Him.

The Approval That Secures

The Spirit himself testifies with our spirit that we are God's children.

ROMANS 8:16 NIV

*O*ne of Florida's senior statesmen, a distinguished gentleman in his sixties, exhorted me to spend time with my father. "When he is gone, you will really miss him," he said.

His father had recently died, and I could literally feel his heartache as he mourned the loss of his natural father.

"Fathers are imperfect," he continued, "but they are so important to us. My dad, for example, was not much for showing affection. He never once gave me his approval when I was growing up. This caused me to strive to measure up—to get a nod from my dad. It didn't come. So I redoubled my efforts and worked to get better grades. Nothing. Then I worked on my career and became extremely successful. Still no approval.

"It was not until I was elected as an elder in my church that my father ever gave me his approval. He had been an elder in the same church for decades. As I knelt to be accepted, my father reached over, finally, after all those years, put his hand on my shoulder and said, 'I'm proud of you, son.' I burst into tears. That was one of the sweetest moments of my entire life. Fathers are not perfect, but when he is gone, you will really miss him."

Did your father ever give you his approval? Or do you still long for your dad to say, "I'm proud of you"?

The need for approval is the unintended, hidden motivator behind so much of what we do. Whether from our father, our mother, our spouse, our children, our peers, our friends, or our boss—the need for approval is a silent, inescapable influence upon our lives. We need the nod from our dad, the embrace from our mother, respect from our spouse, appreciation from the boss for a job well done. Most of us, if we will be honest, are starving for human dignity. Nothing reduces us to loneliness and indignity faster than withheld approval.

Our eternal Father and God loves us with an unconditional, everlasting love. He does not love us because we have done anything to win His approval, anything to deserve it. Rather, He loves you because He made you. Have you grasped the magnitude of that love yet?

When once we have placed our faith and trust in Christ and His atoning work for us on the cross, then nothing can separate us from the approval of the Father. " 'My sheep listen to my voice; I know them, and they follow me. I give them eternal life, and they shall never perish; no one can snatch them out of my hand' " (John 10:27–28 NIV). The approval of God secures salvation. Your earthly father may never say, "I'm proud of you," but your heavenly Father will personally wipe away every tear of yours someday. You have His Word on it. Approved, and secure forever.

THOUGHT FOR THE DAY _____

Have you accepted the approval of the Father? Do you have the assurance of your salvation? Do you have confidence that your faith has saved you? Or does the drone of doubt still whisper its menacing monologue to your mind?

If you don't believe in yourself, how do you expect God to work through you?

Ronald W. Cadmus
God's Loving Embrace

Keep in Touch

Seek [wisdom] as silver,
And search for [wisdom] as for hidden treasures . . .
_____PROVERBS 2:4 NASB

*S*ometimes we lose contact with people for one reason or another, and the next time we see them we notice how much they've changed. Sadly, the same thing can happen to the relationship between us and our heavenly Father.

Because we can't see God, we tend to forget His presence. Frequently, we only think of Him when we are in desperate need in a crisis.

The important difference between our earthly relationships and the one we have with God is that He doesn't change every time we talk with Him. He is always the same and will always be there when we seek Him. Proverbs 2 speaks volumes of the importance of a daily walk and talk with God. It tells how we must search for His knowledge and understanding as we would for something very precious.

THOUGHT FOR THE DAY _____
Talking to God daily is the only way to let Him become our best friend. More importantly, it is the only way we will know His will and recognize His voice when He speaks to us in times of peace or crisis.

A Box of Broken Dreams

"Time stays, we go."
HENRY AUSTIN DOBSON
THE PARADOX OF TIME

*D*uring Christmas vacation of my senior year in college, my father took me into the den one afternoon and told me how proud he was of my achievements in speech and English. He reached in behind the piano and brought out a box of clippings he had kept hidden from the family. They were articles and letters he had written and sent to newspapers. There was even a response from Senator Henry Cabot Lodge to some advice Father had sent him. I asked him why he hadn't shown me these before. He responded that Mother had told him since he didn't have any education he shouldn't try to write. If he tried and failed, we'd all be humiliated.

At that moment I realized, in spite of all my father had taught me, I had never given him much credit for knowing anything. Like my mother, I had always felt that he didn't have the education necessary to be a success. In the past I had downgraded his ability and he had wisely waited until I was mature enough to share his hidden hobby.

Warmly, we discussed our mutual love of English and for the first time he shared that he had always wanted to be a politician. We laughed over how, when I was a child, he had made me sit and listen to political speeches on the radio.

As we discussed these and other subjects, Father brought the conversation back to his secret writing and he told me in confidence that he had sent an article to the editor of *Advance* magazine a few months before concerning the methods used in selecting delegates to our denominational conventions. He had looked each time the issue had come to see if his article had been published.

So far it had not been included and he said, "I guess I tried for something too big this time. Your mother is right. I don't have any talent."

The next day we three children decided to manage the store and let my father and mother take the first day off they had had together in twenty years. We felt we were old enough to handle everything and we joyfully sent them off to Boston. Besides, after working a seventeen-hour day, seven days a week, Father deserved a rest.

About supper time we looked out the window and saw Mother get off the bus alone. When she came in we asked where Father was. "Your father is dead," she said simply. She didn't cry. She just told us the story as we stood by in shock.

They had spent a beautiful day together and as they were walking through Park Street subway station, Father suddenly grabbed his heart and dropped to the cement. She said a nurse had been in the crowd of pushing people and knelt down to check him. She looked up at Mother and said, "He's dead," then slipped into a subway car and was gone. Mother told us how she just stood there in disbelief as busy commuters stepped over Father's form and went their way. A priest came by as a lone good Samaritan and said, "I'll call the police," and disappeared. For over an hour Mother kept watch over the body of her husband as indifferent people pushed and tripped around him.

She then told us how she had sat beside him in the ambulance, stayed with him in the emergency room where he was officially pronounced dead, and then had to take another lonesome ride to the city morgue where the man on duty had her go through Father's pockets and remove his belongings. After all this trauma, Mother took a bus from the morgue to North Station, the train to Haverhill, and then another bus home. She had faced the tragedy bravely and alone. As Mother told the tale, customers came in and listened, and soon we were all crying together.

The morning of the funeral, as I was going through the mail and reading the day's sympathy cards, I noticed the new issue of *Advance*, January 1949. As I glanced over it I discovered to my surprise that my father's article entitled "For More Democracy" was in print. It had come too late for him to see, and had he not chosen to share his secret ambition a few days before, I would never have looked in that issue of *Advance*.

We would have missed this fulfillment of Father's humble dream.

Have you ever suffered the loss of a loved one? How did you react? Have you been able to use something from this person's life to encourage others? Have you ever felt guilty over what you wished you'd done? I've been sorry that I didn't realize my father's talent sooner so that I could have given him encouraging words, but I am grateful he chose that day to show me his box. One more day would have been too late.

THOUGHT FOR THE DAY ————————————————
Take time today to be with those you love; discover something new about them.

Only Believe

"Your daughter is dead. Why trouble the Teacher any further?"
As soon as Jesus heard the word that was spoken, He said to the
ruler of the synagogue, "Do not be afraid; only believe."

——————————————————————————————MARK 5:35–36 NKJV

$\mathscr{I}$ have heard this story of Jesus restoring the little girl to life many times in church. Maybe you have too. If so, I'm sure you were told how the story illustrated Jesus' power over death, how clearly Jesus' humility and lovingkindness show through. Perhaps I wasn't listening, but I don't remember hearing about what my part should be: "Do not be afraid; only believe."

That little word *only* may mean one of two things:

1. Begin with your entry level faith.
2. Trusting Jesus is all we need to do. It's enough!

I believe that both are true. So when I'm afraid, rather than whistling a happy tune, I try instead to remember Jesus' instruction. I try to believe—*only* believe. As I try, the image of Jesus, loving and kind, powerful even over death, comes to my mind. And guess what? I'm not so afraid anymore.

THOUGHT FOR THE DAY ——————————————————————
Faith chases away fear. Believe.

Jesus: Victorious Through Surrender

God hath chosen the weak things of the world to confound the things which are mighty.

—1 CORINTHIANS 1:27 KJV

*A*nyone who has suffered through high school Latin is familiar with the phrase, "*Veni, vidi, vici.*" It means, "I came, I saw, I conquered." It is found in a letter Julius Caesar wrote to Amautius describing his victory at Zela in 47 B.C. It was Caesar's motto. But his empire finally crumbled, and he who was the conqueror became the conquered.

Jesus, who possessed infinitely greater power, lived His life by a strange and unexpected twist of Caesar's saying. Jesus lived by the motto, "I came, I saw, I surrendered." By living out this unorthodox pronouncement Jesus demonstrated that what the world regards as power is really impotence. True victory is only possible through surrender.

Jesus' primary surrender was to the taking on of human flesh, the Incarnation. It was this surrender that made possible the Cross. Although He might have grasped equality with God, He nonetheless surrendered to becoming human out of obedience to the Father. And so His human life began as it would end, based on the paradox of victory through surrender.

Jesus' total embrace of humanity, His becoming like us, is the basis of our hope to someday be like Him. His identification with our frailty provides our confidence that someday we will cast aside our fragile, fallen humanity and see Him as He is.

So we are caught up in a dilemma. We follow a Savior who conquers by allowing Himself to be conquered, who saves us by not allowing Himself to be saved. He bids us follow in the same way.

THOUGHT FOR THE DAY _____
God, help us live the paradox of surrendering to win.

Wise Counsel

Do you not know that friendship with the world is enmity with God? Whoever therefore wants to be a friend of the world makes himself an enemy of God.

——————————————————————————JAMES 4:4 NKJV

*A*s a young man, I was a conformist. It was very important that people like me. If people liked me, I knew I had value as a person. If they didn't, I was certain I was worthless. Most people I met in those days were, unfortunately, just like me. They valued themselves and others on externals, liking and disliking themselves and others because of appearances.

People who make judgments like that are fools. And I was the companion of fools. Eventually, through a number of painful experiences, I came into the company of wise people. Who were these wise people?

Wise people loved God and others unconditionally. They loved me for who I was. They told me the truth in love. They became God's instrument to help me change.

The wise people warmed me up with their wise counsel. Most importantly, by loving me for who I was at the time and by convincing me that they would love me no matter what, they allowed me to learn about the love of God.

Going against the tide requires strength and courage. Don't try to go it alone. Seek the support of wise, loving friends.

Fun in the Simple Things

"A merry heart makes a cheerful countenance."
_____PROVERBS 15:13 NKJV

"Honey, why are we stopping at this sporting goods store," i
asked with a frown.

"because tomorrow i am taking you fishing!"

FISHING! i had tried to like fishing. we had fished on our honey-
moon & various places. with people who came to visit us in idaho.
either i was too cold or too hot. the worms were so fat & wiggly &
slimy & disgusting. my line always seemed to tangle with someone
else's. worst of all, it seemed so boring. waiting, it seemed forever, for a
fish to bite. tomorrow we had to go fishing AGAIN?

for will, it was fun. his favorite childhood memories were of his dad
taking him to wild & wonderful wildernesses to fish.

the next day was warm & sunny. my mother-in-law came to watch
the babies. another couple joined us. a new fishing pole was in the
trunk, that will said he bought just for me. for hours, i had been praying God would help me to learn to like fishing.

it took an hour to arrive at a certain part of the snake river. parking the car in the shade, i crawled out with 5 layers of clothes on. will convinced me i could get cold, & nothing spoils my fun quicker. the men informed me we had a hike before arriving at the choice spot.

"see, honey, i thought of you. some exercises. a little workout. i knew you would like that."

the "hike" was a 1,000 foot drop, almost straight down, to the river below that looked miles away. i could not imagine staying vertical on such a drop-off. this *was* fun. i was happier by the minute. anything that involved challenge & muscles, & was outdoors . . . well, i liked that.

the hike down was not nearly as hard as the steep, vertical hike back up in pouring rain & claps of thunder & lightning over our heads. we had crawled through brush to fishing holes. will was my hero & guide. salmon flies crawled on my neck & i screamed. worms wiggled off the hooks & we lost a few. i would try to cast right out to the spot will showed me. tammy caught the biggest trout of the day.

we laughed. we screamed to each other above the roar of the river. we shared worms. bob & tammy kept trying to pull my line free from places it continually snagged in the river. we cheered each other on. no airplanes. no campers. no noises but rushing water & exotic birds & a coyote way off in the distance. the smell of pine & unmarred earth. a crisp, clean breeze. pulling each other up the incredible incline, sliding in the mud as it began to rush down the cliff. driving through a tiny town en route home & passing a little baptist church, & will saying, "let's stop & see if the minister lives next door, & encourage him."

hot tea & cookies in the little trailer where the elderly couple pastor this tiny church. often only one or two others besides themselves worship there.

now THAT is what i call fun!

i am learning to have fun with the little obscure moments. in the most simple ways. even on on blue days. in tough situations. when i am not sure where my value is, & will has had a bad potato season. without humor & a little laughter, the complexities of life would wash over me & drain all my joy & hope in an abyss of despair.

"honey, let's just pick up the babies, & get into the car, & go find someone to visit."

i suggested that one frustrating sunday afternoon, & we ended up having so much fun that now it is ritual. tradition. every sunday evening, with babies in our arms, we take ice cream or cake somewhere, & surprise people. we begin to laugh & share. our children play together. suddenly we forget all the problems facing us. the seemingly impossible dilemmas. we are not alone. there is fellowship.

THOUGHT FOR THE DAY ————————————————
with laughter, there is hope for anything.

Simply Believe

That whosoever believeth in him should not perish, but have eternal life.

JOHN 3:15 KJV

$\mathcal{I}$ used to think that mysteries existed only to be solved, like a Dorothy Sayers' novel. It may have been the result of living in a scientific age. Or more likely it was the presumption of my own fallenness. Like so many others today, I actually believed I had the ability to understand it all, given enough time to figure things out. When I heard someone refer to the "mystery" of Christ, I assumed that Christ was only a mystery to nonbelievers. Yet the Mystery of Christ is reserved only for those who do believe. To "know" the Mystery of Christ is to realize that it is indeed just that, a mystery.

To represent faith in Jesus merely as something we come to understand and accept is to rob it of the mystery of being in relationship with something that is infinitely bigger and wiser than we are. His ways are not our ways, the prophet Isaiah tells us, and that hasn't changed. He is still the Creator and we, His creatures. Like the birds, we receive our daily bread from His hand and each breath of life as His gracious gift. Is that not itself a mystery?

Mystery is not a category only for the spiritually elite, secret knowledge reserved for the members of the "deeper life club." The mysteries of faith in Christ are for everyone who claims to be in relationship with Him. The basic truths of Christianity are mysteries, not understandable, not "our ways": the virgin birth of Jesus, the Trinity, grace, prayer, the union of the believer with Christ, the Cross, and perhaps most mysterious, and key to them all, the Incarnation.

A simple man, a carpenter from obscure Galilee, was not merely the representative of, but was God incarnate and man deified, "very God of very God," as the creed says. The Infinite contained in the ridiculously finite. Is *anyone* willing to raise his/her hand and say, "I understand"?

So what is our condition, then? Are we irrationalists, left to stumble about, blind, in the dark? Is that the purpose of mystery? Nothing could be farther from the truth. The purpose of the mystery of Christ is not to blind our eyes but to open them to belief in Him. The purpose is not to separate us into the "spiritual" and the "worldly," but to make us one as we try to live the mystery. In fact it is the substance of the mystery that makes possible the only true "knowing."

We are not irrationalists, we are believers. Only by believing do we "know." We do not claim to fully understand the mystery. Not in the least, or else it would be no mystery. It is because of the mystery, and not in spite of it, that we know. The mystery calls forth faith, giving us the ability to "know" with the heart as well as the mind. Even the knowing is a mystery.

THOUGHT FOR THE DAY _____
Understanding God is not as important as simply believing in Him.

Refocus Daily

And whatever you do in word or deed, do all in the name of the Lord Jesus.

COLOSSIANS 3:17 NKJV

*D*uring the Korean conflict several soldiers had a young Korean houseboy. They played endless jokes on him, such as nailing his shoes to the floor and setting water above doorways to fall on him. At Christmas the soldiers felt guilty and decided to stop the practical jokes. They explained to the houseboy that there would be no more nailed-down shoes and no more water poured on him. He responded that he would "no more spit in soup."

We all despise injustice, and we hate the thought of being ripped off or overlooked, especially at our jobs. Many of us find a passive way to get even by "spitting in the soup." We may leave work early or call in sick when we feel fine. This passive-aggressive way of expressing our anger does not solve the problem. God has a healthy plan for us in unfair situations. He wants us to take the focus off what those around us aren't giving us and turn our eyes toward Him.

THOUGHT FOR THE DAY
God, help me honestly admit my anger, and allow You to bring about justice.

If we find ourselves huffing and puffing our way through life, maybe we're not walking with God.

Dr. Neil T. Anderson
Walking in the Light

Set Yourself Aside

"Not my will, but thine be done."
———————————LUKE 22:42 KJV

*I*t's hard for us to know God's will because of our obsession with our own desires. We talk a better story than we live. The obstacles stumbled over along the way often force us to become lucid about our mixed and confused motives. We need opposition to make us look at the many aspects of our own denial and self-deception. Every delusion is a hidden but considerable roadblock in our pursuit of fulfillment. Our lack of clarity only prolongs the recovery of the soul, concealing God's intentions for us.

Dante had penetrating insight for us in *The Divine Comedy*. He wrote about why we lose sight of both God's best intentions and personal satisfaction. As he traveled through the place of purging, he met three groups of people who had failed to truly fulfill the will of the heavenly Father. As a result, their earthly experiences went uncompleted and their lives unsatisfied.

The first group were not bad people, but they did not really struggle with what God wanted. Avoiding evil, they had little interest in fully embracing the good. While they did not capitulate to the pressures of life, they were not completely faithful to their vows. They compromised.

Next was the company of people of leadership and integrity who fought for good causes. However, their motives were misused with selfishness and vanity. They took too much pride in their own achievements.

The last group had natural gifts of love and were gracious and kind people. Unfortunately, they overindulged themselves, letting their love become sentimental and soft. They were not willing to hold to the hard things that had to be done in the name of love.

From our point of view there is much to be commended in each group. Yet, they all grew weary and fainthearted. They came short in the race set before them. Their failure to struggle fully with the cross set before them robbed them of their joy.

What would have made the difference?

When Dante inquired about their deliverance, he received an extraordinary answer, "*E sua voluntade e nostra pace.*" "His will is our peace." Both the vast ocean in which we all fare as well as the wind that moves us across the waters, His will is also the harbor that we seek. We cannot anchor our lives anywhere else but in completely embracing God's will. Sanctuary awaits our decision to will only one will. His will and our peace are one thing. Beyond knowing, beyond doing, serenity is found only in fully wanting what He wants.

Such singleness of vision and mind can't be found without a personal emptying of ego that isn't possible without considerable pain. It is accessible only when the designs and manipulations of the ego are pushed aside in order that unity with God's will can settle into the soul. One of the great assets of our brokenness is that it brings us to the place of total self-surrender as nothing else can. Once we have gotten past anger and are simply abiding in the place of our hurt, we are at the threshold of that awesome inner chapel when we can truly and fully pray, "Nothing in heaven and earth do I desire but Thee, O Lord." These moments of consecration are the most profitable times in our lives.

Nothing demonstrates this principle as does the agony and cruelty of the Cross, which was the ultimate means by which Jesus demonstrated the joy of embracing the Father's will. Our traveling companion, Paul, again paints the picture for us:

> Have this mind among yourselves, which you have in Christ Jesus, who, though he was in the form of God, did not count equality with God a thing to be grasped, but emptied himself, taking the form of a servant, being born in the likeness of men. And being found in human form he humbled himself and became obedient unto death, even death on a cross. Therefore God has highly exalted him and bestowed on him the name which is above every name (Phil. 2:5–9 RSV).

Sooner or later we all find ourselves on a cross of some variety. The critical issue will be our ability to pray, "Father, forgive, for they know not." The very act of embracing His will at that moment is the first step toward serenity.

For the joy set before Him, Christ Jesus pursued the will of the Father without variance. Praying, "Not my will, but thine, be done," in the Garden of Gethsemane, Jesus was staring the final despair in the face. Without blinking He saw the cost. But seeing beyond, He also comprehended the final satisfaction found by all who set themselves aside. Our full recovery of joy requires a similar response.

THOUGHT FOR THE DAY _____
God, help me embrace Your will. Forgive my offenders.

To learn the Bible is to learn the mind of God. To be willfully ignorant of the Bible is to invite disaster.

Patrick M. Morley
The Rest of Your Life

Calling God by Name

"The name of the LORD is a strong tower;
The righteous run to it and are safe."
——————————**PROVERBS 18:10** NKJV

If you have a poor relationship with your parents, or if you have been victimized by the father-figure in your life, you may have difficulty relating to God as Father. If you have not had a human model you can comfortably equate to a heavenly father, I would like to suggest that you look over some of the names of God that are listed below:

Names of God (NASB)*

Names	Characteristics	Key Passage
Advocate	Helper, divine lawyer who pleads our case	1 John 2:1–2
Almighty	All-powerful	Revelation 1:8
Anointed	Messiah	Psalm 2:2
Beloved	Perfectly and uniquely loved by God the Father	Matthew 12:18
Bright Morning Star	Brilliant, awesome	Revelation 22:16
Chosen One	Special to God, anointed	Luke 23:35
Creator	Maker of all	Ecclesiastes 12:1
Deliverer	Rescues, compassionate	Psalm 18:2
Door	Entrance to a relationship with God	John 10:7–9
Eternal Spirit	Equal with the Father and Christ	Hebrews 9:14

Father of Lights	Giver of perfect gifts	James 1:17
Father of Mercies	Kind, sensitive	2 Corinthians 1:3
God Almighty	All-powerful, keeps promises	Genesis 17:1
God of my Salvation	Redeems, rescues	Micah 7:7
God of Recompense	Rewards good or evil	Jeremiah 51:56
God of Vengeance	Just judge, punishes evil	Psalm 94:1
Heavenly Father	Perfect, holy, personal, generous	Luke 11:13
Holy Spirit of God	Righteous third person of the Godhead	Ephesians 4:30
I AM	Eternal LORD	Exodus 3:14
Immanuel	God with us	Matthew 1:23
Jesus Christ	Fully man, fully God	Romans 3:22
Jealous	Righteous zeal	Exodus 34:14
Judge of All	Divine determiner	Hebrews 12:23
King of Glory	Awesome majesty	Psalm 24:7–10
King of Kings	Above all rulers	Revelation 19:16
Lamb of God	God's provision for our sins	John 1:36
Master	Leader, teacher, Lord	2 Peter 2:1
Mediator	Reconciler of God and man	1 Timothy 2:5
Only Begotten Son	Unique, only one of His kind	John 3:16
Only One	Unique relationship with God the Father	Zechariah 14:9
Physician	Divine healer	Luke 4:23
Prince of Life	Author and founder of life	Acts 3:15
Refuge	Gives security, peace	Psalm 46:1
Rock	Security, stable, faithful	Deuteronomy 32:4
Shepherd	Compassionate leader	John 10:11
Spirit of Promise	Seals, gives hope	Ephesians 1:13–14
Teacher	Instructor, communicates truth	Matthew 19:16
Truth	Accurate, reliable, trustworthy	John 14:6
Vine	Source of life and goodness	John 15:1
Vinedresser	Prunes His people to make them bear more fruit	John 15:1
Wonderful Counselor	Totally understands us	Isaiah 9:6
Word of Life	Jesus is God, God's living message	1 John 1:1

* Dick Purnell, *A 31-Day Experiment: Knowing God by His Names* (Nashville: Thomas Nelson, 1993). Used by permission.

On a journal page, start your prayer with a different name for God than you have ever used before and build a setting around that name. One of the names I have enjoyed using is "O King, O Sovereign King." In Scripture David said many times, "My King and my Lord." In Deuteronomy He is referred to as "Our Sovereign Lord." When I think "king," I think of myself entering the royal palace, walking in, and bowing before my king. Then I see myself able to tell Him the things that I need because He has summoned me to come into His presence.

This kind of exercise can refresh our prayer life and add some excitement to it that maybe we haven't had in quite a while. Choose a name or names that appeal to you which will cause you to worship and glorify God. Write your prayer to God using these new names. Picture yourself in each new setting and share your thoughts with God.

THOUGHT FOR THE DAY _____
God, help me to know You by all of Your names.

Unconditional, Irrevocable

Jesus Christ is the same yesterday, today, and forever.
———————————————————**HEBREWS 13:8** NKJV

*U*nderstanding the concept of God's unconditional love for us is often difficult. Many of us feel unworthy of such overwhelming acceptance from God. We often feel guilty for our past failures, so we compose a mental list of all the things we have done wrong and then decide that God could never love someone as "lousy" as we are. Others of us who feel unworthy try to gain God's love through performance. We believe that if we work hard enough, that will make us good enough to receive the love of God.

The truth is that God's love does not have anything to do with us, but it has *everything* to do with God. He loves us because it is an attribute of His character to express unconditional love toward us.

The Bible assures us that the love of God will never change. God will never love us any more or any less than He does at this very moment! What will change is our love and dedication for God. As we seek to know Him and spend time learning the truths that the Bible has to offer, we will grow into a richer, fuller, and more intimate relationship with God.

THOUGHT FOR THE DAY ———————————
We can do nothing to change God's love for us.

Life's Breath

You will seek Me and find Me, when you search for Me with all your heart.

JEREMIAH 29:13 NKJV

*A*n inquirer went to a wise hermit who was known as a man of God. "Tell me the way of salvation," he asked. The hermit led him to the river. There he grabbed the inquirer and held his head under the water. The man fought desperately to get free, but the hermit was strong and held him under. Finally, when he thought his lungs would burst and he had nearly lost all strength, the hermit released him. As the man coughed and gasped for breath, the hermit said, "When you want salvation as much as you wanted air, you will find it."

God knows that we will not truly come to Him until we realize that our lives depend on it. When we recognize that we need God more than anything, we will seek Him desperately.

THOUGHT FOR THE DAY
What do I want most?

In Search of Identity

"And this is eternal life, that they may know You, the only true God, and Jesus Christ whom You have sent."

——————————————————————**JOHN 17:3** NKJV

*W*ith Campus Crusade for Christ staff in approximately 150 countries, my husband and I do a great deal of traveling. Our ministry responsibilities usually require us to visit each continent every year where we meet with staff, other Christian leaders, and government officials all over the world.

Around the globe, I have encountered the poor and the rich, the illiterate and the highly educated, the discouraged and the greatly motivated. I have met people of all ages in many different cultures and stations in life. I have observed their lifestyles and the way they express themselves and relate to each other. All this has taught me that people around the world are much alike, separated only by language and culture.

Modern travel and communication have shown us that, though our cultures are different, there is a thread of commonality in all of us: We have similar needs for fulfillment; we have unanswered questions in our quest for identity.

In my lifetime I have seen major changes in our value system which have had a dramatic effect upon what people believe will provide maximum fulfillment. As a college student in the late 1940s, when family was still important, I was encouraged to prepare for a career—in case I needed it, and for the pleasure of culture, knowledge, and understanding.

At that time, women in large numbers had experienced the liberty of working outside the home in defense plants to aid the war effort. As the postwar years rolled by, they were taught that fulfillment came in achievement and that their maximum potential was to be found in the marketplace where they would have visible leadership and identity. As a result, even more women sought careers, only to discover frustration and disillusionment.

In recent years I have seen the mood of women in the United States come full circle from an era when the family was most important, through the disillusionment of the '60s and '70s, then through the 1980s when marriage and family once again became of greater value, though coupled with the woman's career. The mother of the 1990s, according to the December 4, 1989, issue of *TIME* Magazine, is returning home to care for her family if it is at all economically possible.

Often, in the very moment of achievement, there is no satisfaction. Have you ever felt empty or unfulfilled at the point of accomplishment as though something inside were saying, "So what? Big deal"? The rewards of achievement and visible leadership are rarely enough.

The road to achievement often is a struggle for power—all the power you can get. But the Word of God—and even secular psychologists—tell us there is much greater fulfillment in giving than receiving. Thus the steps we often take toward achievement are leading us in the opposite direction of fulfillment.

In many countries and cultures, today's woman is trying to stretch herself into a number of roles at one time. Perhaps for economic necessity or personal achievement, she may have her own identity; a career; she must be a perfect lover and companion; a good mother; devoted to social causes with perfect calmness and composure; and she must *achieve* in each area. The result, doctors tell us, is that more women are suffering from heart attacks and stress-related illnesses than ever before.

I have learned that lasting happiness is found in relationships, not achievements. What happens if the function or circumstances in which a woman places her identity changes? If identity is in *career* and that fails, where is her identity? If identity is in *marriage* and that fails, then what? If identity is in *children*, where is her identity when they leave home? We need to place our identity in that which will not change.

The great French physicist and philosopher, Pascal, is well known for having said, "There is a God-shaped vacuum in the heart of every person which cannot be satisfied by any created thing, but only by God, the Creator, made known through Jesus Christ." People think they can find identity in circumstances or functions, but these can change. I believe a rewarding, sustaining lifestyle is that which is found in a personal faith and trust in Jesus Christ and in being obedient to that which He desires us to do. We must place our identity in the One who will not change.

Identity in Jesus Christ is the glue that has held my life together. Although I grew up in the church and appreciate my religious background, God was not a reality in my life. Life was routine, and happiness depended upon circumstances. Into my confusion walked Bill Bright, handsome, moral, and successful. We had a whirlwind romance, but waited three years to be married.

During that time, Bill was growing in his faith. I was getting farther away from mine. I decided he had become a religious fanatic, and he detected that I was not a Christian. Since we were idealistic enough to seek agreement on every major issue, we questioned our coming marriage.

To make a long story short, I was very much impressed with Bill's friends at Hollywood Presbyterian Church. He introduced me to Dr. Henrietta Mears, director of Christian education, who compared the reality of knowing God personally to performing a chemistry lab experiment. Since I minored in chemistry in college, it made sense to me to add the person of Jesus Christ to the ingredients of faith I already knew. I received Jesus Christ as my personal Savior. As a result, God has become a vital reality in my life giving me identity and direction.

Early in our marriage, Bill and I committed ourselves totally to Christ as a couple. God blessed us with achievement.

My teaching career was successful, and a course of study written for my master's project was selected to be taught in the Los Angeles public schools and syndicated throughout the United States. God gave Bill the idea for a Christian movement that would help reach the world for Christ and help bring our nation back to the fundamentals on which it was established.

I chose to work with him so we could build and achieve God's purpose for our lives together.

I used my experience in teaching to help write our staff training manuals. Together we have influenced two human beings—our sons Zac and Brad—to become accountable, responsible, godly young men who are both now in Christian ministry. Through them and our thousands of full-time and associate Campus Crusade staff, we are touching tens of millions of lives around the world with the life-changing message of Christ's love and forgiveness.

There were times of adjustments, hard work, great concern, and many joys that have given me a message to share and enable me to minister to the lives of others today.

In examining my life and analyzing my identity, I realize that God has given me role models in women whom I have admired and sought to emulate. Some of these are mentioned in Scripture. My favorite among Bible women is Esther, the queen of the Persian Empire who risked her life to save her people, the Jews.

Another model is Catherine Booth, wife of William Booth, founder of the Salvation Army. She was the mother of eight children, whom she left in the care of others when she traveled from her home in England by boat to the United States to minister to the "down and out" in New York City. No doubt some said, "Catherine, your children are going to go astray while you minister away from home." But she lived a godly life and was obedient to what God called her to do. And all eight children entered some phase of Christian ministry.

What about some present-day models? Mother Teresa, the Albanian nun who has received worldwide recognition (including the Nobel Prize) for her mission to the poor and dying in Calcutta, is an inspiring model today. When asked by someone how she dealt with so much failure, her reply was, "God has not called me to be successful. He has called me to be faithful."

Henrietta Mears, a single woman who invested her life in Christian education, is another. She influenced many in her lifetime, including Bill and me and more than four hundred young men who entered the ministry as pastors of many different denominations.

Let me tell you of a couple of "ordinary women" who, in addition to my mother, serve as role models to me.

Mrs. Louis H. Evans, Sr., the wife of one of America's most outstanding Presbyterian pastors, was the mother of four children. She totally devoted herself as a wife and mother to her family who are making their mark on the world.

The other woman was a beautiful and gifted school teacher who married a rancher. At age sixteen she had committed her life totally to Christ, telling Him she wanted only to do for the rest of her life that which would glorify God the most.

Her life on the 5,000-acre ranch in rural Oklahoma was hard. She gave birth to eight children, one of whom died shortly after birth. Her home was the rural entertainment center for the community, and at mealtimes she was never sure how many people she would be serving in addition to her family.

Her children recall how she spent time reading her Bible each morning and evening and sang hymns as she went about her work. The most Christlike person in the community anyone could recall, she lived thirty-five years with a non-Christian husband, then lived another thirty-five years with him after he received Christ.

She was extremely ill most of the nine months that she carried her seventh child. There was little hope from the doctor that she would live to give birth to the child. She prayed earnestly, promising the Lord that she would commit this child to Him and His service, if He would let her live to give birth.

This woman was truly a Proverbs 31 woman whose 109 members of her family, including children, grandchildren, great grandchildren and great-great grandchildren, made their way to her bedside to express their love and appreciation before her death at age ninety-three. All of them have risen up to call her "blessed." This woman continues to have a great influence, perhaps even in your life, for she was my husband's mother, Mary Lee Bright.

All of these women had one thing in common—their identity in Christ. Inspired by the models in my life, I decided to follow Christ. I learned to apply the Scriptures to daily living, not content to declare one thing and live another, or to export that which didn't work at home.

Each of us is a special person with unique skills, gifts, and capabilities. Each of us has a unique sphere of influence. Whoever we are and wherever we go, we are going to be a role model for someone. The question is, what kind?

The greatest lesson I have learned is that my significance, fulfillment, maximum potential, and identity come not from achievement, recognition, or position, but from a relationship with a Person—the most remarkable Person of all time—One whose life literally changed the course of history—our Lord Jesus Christ. I desire to have others know that lasting identity, too.

THOUGHT FOR THE DAY _____
Thank You, Lord, for loving me and making me Your child. Help me share that love with others.

Fervent Prayer Changes Things

Confess your trespasses to one another, and pray for one another,
that you may be healed. The effective, fervent prayer of a
righteous man avails much.

JAMES 5:16 NKJV

*D*oes God ever change His mind? I mean, does it really do any good to pray about something? Isn't God going to do exactly what He predestined anyway? So why pray?

One of my favorite phrases, found several places throughout the Scriptures, is "so God changed His mind." I love it so much because it proves that prayer *does* make a difference. When we confess our sins, God always hears the prayers and immediately forgives us. But we make other requests that are answered only after much fervent prayer.

There is strength in numbers, and when it comes to prayer, getting others involved in praying with us is even more effective.

THOUGHT FOR THE DAY
O Lord Jesus, help us to know that when we reach up to Thee, Thou art reaching down to us. **Peter Marshall**

Praying with others for God's intervention in any given situation creates excitement and incentive to keep agreeing in prayer! Lost wallets, potential job opportunities, hopeful marriage partners, finances, the mending of relationships, from details to dreams—agreeing prayer is a faith-building experience, not to be neglected or considered as powerless.

Becky Tirabassi
Let Prayer Change Your Life

Personality Plus

"Be kindly affectionate to one another with brotherly love, in honor giving preference to one another."

——————————————————————ROMANS 12:10 NKJV

*E*arly in life I developed a talent for straightening out other people. Innately I believed I could spot faults in others and improve them if they would only listen to me. My mother called this my Cinderella complex—always ready to transform any damsel in distress.

I had grown up as the oldest child in a family of three and felt I was a born leader. When my father died, I simply took control of my family. My grieving mother, who was weak and exhausted, allowed my strong will to reign, and no one questioned my authority. It was the same when I taught school. My pupils doted on my every word. Not until my marriage had anyone ever suggested I needed help.

Meanwhile, Fred had been brought up believing he was God's perfect child and there was no such thing as sin. His mother encouraged this belief and told him he was God's gift to women. Both of us entered marriage expecting the other to be grateful for receiving such a prize.

The result of this unreality was a constant battle of the wills. I thought everything should go my way, and Fred insisted it go his. I submitted on the surface, but underneath became more rebellious with each passing year.

By the time God reached down and picked up the imperfect pieces of our marriage and began putting them back together, we were almost too antagonistic and apathetic to care. We each hoped the other would recognize his faults and improve. When we both asked the Lord Jesus to come into our lives and make us what He wanted us to be, we were at the bottom. We knew we were failures, and wanted to improve, but we were not sure how to begin.

As we groped for direction in our new Christian life, a friend gave us the book *Spirit-Controlled Temperament* by Tim LaHaye. I found myself on page thirteen: "Sparky Sanguine, the warm, buoyant, lively, and 'enjoying' temperament. When he comes into a room of people, he has a tendency to lift the spirits of everyone present by his exuberant flow of conversation. He is a thrilling storyteller because his warm, emotional nature almost makes him relive the experience in the very telling of it."

Oh, how I loved to talk and oh, how I thought everyone but Fred enjoyed listening!

As I read more of Sparky and his "disarming effect on many of his listeners," I was more convinced than ever I had married a dullard who couldn't appreciate my sense of humor. Fred just liked the straight facts. Before we were married he used to think I was amusing, but after twelve years of my fun and games, he groaned every time I repeated a story.

There was a section in the book about the strengths of the Sanguine temperament. I could hardly wait to show Fred how much fun I really was. But then I read the chapter on Sanguine weaknesses, and it sounded as if Fred had written them about me.

"His life is spent running from one target to another, and, unless disciplined, is not lastingly productive." Fred often pointed out that I seemed to run in circles, make a big production out of every little thing, and accomplish nothing at the end of the day. I felt I was a super achiever and had perfectly good reasons why my days looked incomplete. I never really listened to Fred, and I certainly never thought I was wrong.

Tim LaHaye went on to point out that the Sanguine temperament "can go overboard and become obnoxious by dominating, not just the major part of the conversation, but all of it." While Fred never called me obnoxious, he had for years told me I talked too much. "God hasn't appointed you official gap-filler in every flagging conversation," Fred said frequently. At dinner parties Fred often kicked me under the table when he thought I was too domineering. He also waved negatively from across the room if he heard my voice above the crowd. I barely tolerated his judgmental attitude and constant interruptions, and in twelve years it never once struck me I might possibly be obnoxious.

As I continued to read, I began to wonder if these verbal gifts I'd been so proud of may have a negative side. Did Fred have reason to be disturbed about me?

Fred also began to read the book and identified himself as a Melancholy. "Mr. Melancholy has strong perfectionist tendencies. His standard of excellence exceeds others." Fred began to realize that it was a positive trait to have high standards, but his wife couldn't live up to them, and his well-meaning instruction only made our marriage worse.

"He does not waste words like the Sanguine, but is usually very precise in stating exactly what he means." How true! Fred could say in ten words what took me a half hour! He opened his mouth only when he had something to say. I'd never thought of this as a strength, but the book said it was.

"Mr. Melancholy will be found to be very gloomy, depressed." Fred never seemed to be genuinely happy. No matter what I did, he would find something wrong with it. This attitude made me feel our marriage was hopeless. I gave up trying, and when I gave up, Fred became depressed. In retrospect, I see that living with me, a perpetual comedy act in search of an audience, was enough to send any serious man into a depression!

It was easy for an objective observer to see where each of us was wrong, but it took a miracle for us to begin to see ourselves as others saw us. We prayed for the ability to examine ourselves and began taking steps to break the judgmental patterns we had established in our lives. One day it dawned on me that just because Fred didn't see things as I did, he wasn't wrong; he was just different.

We each started to pray, as the book suggested, that God would help us to accentuate our strengths and eliminate our weaknesses. When we did, God began a mighty miracle in our lives that resulted years later in my actually falling in love with my husband and giving him the genuine affection he'd been craving.

Why had no one ever told us to look at ourselves first? Or perhaps someone had told us and we hadn't listened. Gratefully, God began to show both of us that we would never know true joy until we began to put our own interests aside and aim to please each other. We had so much to learn and so far to go.

THOUGHT FOR THE DAY _____
God, help us focus on pleasing our spouse before ourselves.

Are You Anchored?

For he who doubts is like a wave of the sea driven and tossed by the wind.

JAMES 1:6 NKJV

Growing up in Houston, Texas, brings an appreciation of severe weather, especially during hurricane season. As a teenager I had a friend whose family owned a boat that they kept anchored down on the Gulf Coast. One season a hurricane was developing, and everyone was taking precautions in Galveston and in the bays. There was no time for my friend and his family to check on their boat. They just had to trust that they had secured and anchored it well.

The storm came through and did considerable damage. I was asked to join my friend when he went to assess the damage to his boat. We saw boats tossed and mangled like so much litter, but to our surprise and joy my friend's boat had weathered the storm. By securing the boat effectively and firmly anchoring it, he had averted disaster.

Our lives are like that boat. Life's storms rock us and toss us about, but we have a safe harbor and refuge in Christ and in God's Word.

THOUGHT FOR THE DAY
God is not only our anchor in rough times; He also calms the seas.

God Pursues

What do you think? If a man has a hundred sheep, and one of them goes astray, does he not leave the ninety-nine and go to the mountains to seek the one that is straying? And if he should find it, assuredly, I say to you, he rejoices more over that sheep than over the ninety-nine that did not go astray.

————————————————————MATTHEW 18:12–13 NKJV

*J*ust like the prodigal son, we've all had our moments of straying. I've had a few times that I wouldn't want to share with you. When it happens, the last thing I want to do is go to God and ask for help or guidance. No, I'm usually headed full-steam in the opposite direction. But notice in the verses above that the shepherd goes after the sheep; the sheep perhaps made no effort to find his way back home.

When I have gone astray, there's no question that God has pursued me. I eventually am convicted and willingly return to the fold. But I take no credit for making wise choices. I only rejoice that I am a child of God and that He will never let me stray too far.

THOUGHT FOR THE DAY —————————————————————
Thank You, God, for pursuing me and not letting me go.

Jesus: The Lamb of God

> *And Abraham said, "My son, God will provide himself a lamb."*
> —GENESIS 22:8 KJV

It was John the Baptist who first recognized Jesus as the "Lamb of God." "Behold! The Lamb of God who takes away the sin of the world!" he shouted as Jesus approached. The sacrificial "seal of approval" had already been placed on Jesus.

The Old Testament says a lot about sacrificial lambs. The children of Israel sacrificed them and painted the doorposts of their houses in Egypt with the blood so the angel of death would "Passover" their houses. In the New Testament Jesus is our Passover Lamb. We mark the doorposts of our hearts, as it were, with His blood so the angel that is the second death will "Passover" us.

One of the details of the offering of the Passover lamb was that none of its bones were to be broken. It was permitted to pull the carcass apart at the joint, but the bones were to be kept intact. When Jesus is crucified the apostle John is moved by the fact that His bones were kept from being broken. The Jews did not want the bodies of the three crucified men left on the crosses during their Passover. They were afraid it might dampen the celebration! They went to Pilate with an almost unbelievably gruesome request. Because the prisoners had to be dead before they were taken down, and there was a good chance that all three were still alive, (crucifixion usually took days to kill a victim), the priests asked that the legs of the three crucified men be broken so that their deaths might be hurried along.

The Romans used a heavy wooden mallet to break the two lower leg bones, causing the full weight of the body to be brought to bear on the chest, causing a quicker death by suffocation. As horrible a death as crucifixion was, it is hard to think of how it might have been made worse. But the breaking of the legs, though bringing about a more immediate death, must have been excruciating. (The Latin root for *excruciating* is the word for *cross*.)

The two thieves on either side of Jesus were apparently still alive. Like most other victims of crucifixion, they would probably have lasted for days. The soldiers broke the legs of both men. When they came to Jesus, however, they discovered that He was already dead. He had "dismissed" His spirit with the words of Psalm 31:5, "Into Your hand I commit my spirit." (He had earlier quoted Psalm 22:1.) Since He was already dead, there was no need for the soldiers to break His legs. The prophecy of Psalm 34:20 (NIV), "He protects all his bones, not one of them will be broken," was perfectly fulfilled. To make sure Jesus was dead, the soldiers pierced His side with a spear, causing blood and water from the broken sack around His heart to flow.

Three years earlier in that uncluttered countryside, when John had shouted across the Jordan, "Behold the Lamb of God," who would have ever thought it would mean this?

THOUGHT FOR THE DAY _____
Thank You, God, for the sacrifice of the Lamb.

Only a Father's Eyes

Whom I shall see for myself,
And my eyes shall behold, and not another.
How my heart yearns within me!
———————————————JOB 19:27 NKJV

In 1968, as the Vietnam war was at its peak, my father went off to that faraway land to serve his country. The good-bye was painful and the adjustment difficult, but there was nothing to do but let go. I loved my father very much, and I missed being with him. Months went by, and finally we got word that he was coming home. Joy filled my heart as I thought of his return. I would see him again! When the day came, my body ached from excitement. Finally, there he was. I could hardly believe it, and I wouldn't have had I not seen it with my own eyes. To see his eyes looking at me again as my father, oh, how I yearned for that.

As great a feeling as this was for me, it cannot compare with seeing the heavenly Father face-to-face. This is every believer's desire. The day my father got off that plane, he was not alone, but he was all I could see. When we are in heaven, there will be nothing greater than to see God, for there is no one greater.

THOUGHT FOR THE DAY ——————————————
Increase my desire to see You, God.

Test Results

*And I thank Christ Jesus our Lord,
who hath enabled me.*
——————1 TIMOTHY 1:12 KJV

*L*ife tries us and tests us.

Reginald was a high-school classmate of mine. It had been many years since I saw him. He was told by many people that he would not amount to anything. In the ghettos of Newark such unsupportive attitudes could have resulted in an unproductive life, in underachievement, if Reg had succumbed to the world's opinion of himself. But he did not.

I remember having my own dreams challenged on the vocational aptitude tests. My high-school results placed me in the category of professional opportunities that excluded ministry.

It was at this point that I knew that the Holy Spirit's ability to "call one to the ministry," did not exist through any test results. On the opposite page from my qualifying choices, standing out in blaring letters was the word *ministry*. Committed to that dream and calling, I checked the box for ministry regardless of my tabulated score.

A few weeks later my test evaluator, reviewing my results, called me into his office, explaining to me my apparent error in vocational choice and my misunderstanding of the test results.

I told him it was a selection intentionally made. "I want to be a minister," I said.

He informed me that I did not "rate" in that category and that my test results would be invalid if I did not change my selection.

For my counselor I changed it.

But I left his office knowing my intention to pursue a calling to the ministry, confident this was what I wanted to do and what God was calling me to do.

Fourteen years later, when my wife was in the hospital recuperating from a miscarriage, I came into her room while the resident intern was examining her.

He looked familiar. Glancing at his name tag I made the connection through his name. "Reg Jenkins!" I said. "Art's High School in Newark!"

He associated his patient's last name with mine and said, "Ron Cadmus!"

We shook hands. Fourteen years later he was a medical doctor and I an ordained minister. He was told he would not amount to anything. Here he stood before me a young doctor in a prestigious hospital. And I was one of the ministers of the Collegiate Churches of New York City.

When we stand strong in the Lord and are confident in the power of His might, we have a partner who will enable us to pursue and fulfill our dreams and whose design for our lives will embrace us and lead us to that fulfillment.

Life might threaten you with obstacles. Have confidence in yourself —and in Him, the author and finisher of faith. This faith will make you confident.

THOUGHT FOR THE DAY _____
God knows "the you that could be"!

One Step at a Time

I sought the LORD, and He heard me,
And delivered me from all my fears.
——————————————PSALM 34:4 NKJV

$\mathcal{A}$ lot of things in our lives today pull us down, like television, movies, and bars. Have you ever felt so low that you thought God didn't care about you and wasn't listening to your prayers? You might have been thinking like Sharon. She felt that she was not worthy of God's blessings and that He had done all He was going to do for her. Sharon just did not know how to make things better.

If you feel low and in despair, do the one thing that you probably want to do least: pray! Yes, you've tried it before in many ways: pleading, bargaining, discussing, reasoning, threatening, standing, and kneeling. God loves for us to talk with Him, no matter what mood we're in and no matter what is on our minds. We're His children, and He wants us to be open and share our feelings, joys, and fears. He is always there to listen, and His love is unconditional. Just think of your own children. Aren't you committed to them no matter what their moods or actions are?

"When you are in the dark, listen, and God will give you a very precious message for someone else when you get into the light."

Oswald Chambers

The Power of a Flower

> *"Hope deferred makes the heart sick,*
> *But when the desire comes, it is a tree of life."*
> —————————————**PROVERBS 13:12** NKJV

In front of the three cement steps outside our family store was a blacktop sidewalk leading to the gas pump—an orange Gulf monster that spewed gas into the cars that honked for service. Behind the pump was a patch of weeds that belonged to the drugstore next door and next to our building was a strip of dirt.

I'd tried to plant some flowers there, but like the seeds in the Bible, they fell on hard soil and never took root. Some up close to the store forced their way up but died for lack of water. A few hardy seedlings popped up through the cracks in the blacktop sidewalk, but they were quickly trampled down by the feet of those who didn't know I cared. I'd sit on those steps in the evening and wonder, *Will I ever have any flowers?*

Across the street from our store was the local church. It was the only social center we had and we were there every time it opened. Once a year we had Children's Sunday, a special day in June when we got our awards for perfect attendance and were given recognition for any honor we might have received throughout the year. It was a dress-up day when we happily put on the best we had because we knew we would be called up front by name. I remember the excitement as we met in our Sunday school rooms and were given our instructions on how to behave in "big church."

We marched in a quiet, awe-struck army and dutifully took our assigned seats. Helen Badashaw, our perpetual Sunday school superintendent, stood at the appointed time and walked to the platform. I always wondered why her legs puffed out over her shoes. Did it hurt to walk with legs like that? She would read off the winners' names and we'd walk forward with dignity. No one ran or giggled. This was church.

The most exciting part came at the end of the service: the giving out of the geraniums. The platform was ringed with little pots of bright red geraniums and we knew from the start we would each get one. The toddlers went first and I can still see my brother Ron's big eyes as he brought his first geranium up the aisle to his seat. My other brother Jim gave me a proud grin as he passed by and then it was my turn. I always wished I had a prettier dress or curly hair, but at least I was going to get a geranium. Miss Badashaw handed me the little clay pot with one lonely geranium at the top of a long stalk. I had a flower of my own.

I'd take my little pot home and each year I'd vow to make my geranium last forever. One year it fell off the porch railing where I'd put it for decoration. Once it shriveled up and died in the dark kitchen. Another time I planted it outside in the hard dirt and a hurried customer stepped on it. "Sorry," he called back to me as he hastened on, unaware that he had trampled the only flower I'd have for another year. I sat on the steps and wondered, *Will I ever have a geranium that will last?*

I realize now why my favorite hymn was always "In the Garden." The words expressed my childhood dream, that I might trade the blacktop and the gas pump for a garden. I wanted to find an Eden full of geraniums. I wanted to "come to the garden alone while the dew is still on the roses." I wanted to walk with Him and talk with Him and have Him tell me "I am His own."

When I chose this hymn for my baptism back in 1966, I didn't realize that my choice sprouted from that inner childhood longing for a garden full of fresh flowers—or at least one little lonely geranium.

How about you? Is it possible you had a childhood without flowers? Did you long to touch a tulip or reach out for a rose? You don't need to live another day without the smell of a gardenia, the smiling face of a pansy, or the bright color of a geranium. Find some fresh flowers at your florist or purchase a potted plant in your supermarket. Hang silk flowers in a basket from your ceiling. Paper the walls with bouquets of lilacs and nosegays of violets.

THOUGHT FOR THE DAY ————————————————
Make up for what you missed out on as a child. You don't have to be without flowers ever again.

RONALD W. CADMUS
God's Loving Embrace

You're Always in His Sight

For the ways of man are before the eyes of the LORD, and he pondereth all his goings.

————————————————————**PROVERBS 5:21** KJV

"*If* looks could kill . . ." This common phrase is used often to convey our attitudes and perceptions about outward appearance. Perhaps you have used this statement or have even suffered its cruel criticism.

Looks! Appearances! We can feel warmly embraced by them or kept at a distance through their cold indifference or hateful glare.

In the gospel of Mark, a man ran up to Jesus, fell on his knees and said, "Good teacher, what shall I do that I may inherit eternal life?" Jesus said, "You know the commandments: 'Do not commit adultery,' 'Do not murder,' 'Do not steal,' 'Do not bear false witness,' 'Do not defraud,' 'Honor your father and your mother.' "

"Teacher," the man declared, "all these I have observed from my youth."

"*Jesus, looking at him, loved him. . . .* 'One thing you lack: Go your way, sell whatever you have and give to the poor, and you will have treasure in heaven; and come, take up the cross, and follow Me.' "

The man's face fell. His look turned away from Jesus. He went away sad because he had great wealth.

Jesus was trying to bring this man to a certain condition and position in life. Through His look, He did more than embrace this man with abundant life. He simply stated how he could find it. "Follow Me!"

But the man's face fell. The embraceable look of love was separated. The man could not tell Jesus how he felt about Him, nor was he willing to respond to the promise that Jesus was readily providing him. By choice he looked away from Jesus. In walking away from Jesus, he discovered sadness.

Jesus Christ wants you to walk toward Life! By following Him! He is the provider of everything we need. Yet in the one who asked Jesus how to inherit eternal life and the one to whom the answer was given reflects our frequent inability to convey to God, through the expression of our feelings, our love for Him.

Jesus looked on him and loved him. But the man's eyes fell away. He went away sad.

Jesus' look always embraces us with love. God perceives goodness in all people. His embraceable look of love provides us with the way to a fulfilled life. The man in the story from Mark simply could not return that look. And thus the potential of life's greatest love affair was denied.

The important affirmation to remember, however, is that while we might take our eyes off God, Jesus will always look upon us with that embraceable look of love. The man's eyes fell *away* from Jesus. Jesus' eyes fell *upon* him!

THOUGHT FOR THE DAY _____

If you ever turn from Jesus and then come back, you will discover that He never leaves you out of His sight.

Solomon's Confusion

Let us hear the conclusion of the whole matter:
"Fear God, and keep his commandments:
for this is the whole duty of man."
——————————ECCLESIASTES 12:13 KJV

*W*ho had the highest IQ? According to the Bible, Solomon was the wisest man who ever lived. Of course, that he had the highest IQ could never be validated. However, it is worth heeding the wisdom of a man who asked God to give him wisdom. Ecclesiastes is a record of his search for happiness. He concluded his search with the words of today's Scriptures. Fear God and keep His commandments.

God has given us a simple plan to make this life work. First, we need to respect God. This means giving Him the honor and glory He so justly deserves. Second, we are to obey God's Word.

One of my friends who was a theologian studied God's Word all of his adult life. Shortly before he died, I spent some time with him. He shared how the Lord had been preparing him for his own death. He talked about the deep conversations he had with his loving Father. He truly practiced the suggestion made by Solomon. It didn't make him the richest man, nor even the best-known theologian. It made him a friend of God.

THOUGHT FOR THE DAY ⸺⸺⸺⸺⸺⸺⸺⸺
God, I want to be Your friend.

In Plenty and In Want

> *"I know what it is to be in need, and I know what it is to have plenty. I have learned the secret of being content in any and every situation, whether well fed or hungry, whether living in plenty or in want."*
>
> —PHILIPPIANS 4:12 NIV

*H*e always had a big job. The Lord had occupied his heart and mind with gladness. He rarely reflected on the days of his life. Then, after twenty-two years, he was caught in the corporate "downsizing" (or as some euphemistically say, "right-sizing") craze.

Middle-aged. Never without a job before. Difficult job market. Down economy. Unemployed.

Week after week passed. Nothing. Weeks turned into months. His predicament clung to him like a bad case of flu. Sometimes he was overwhelmed by the agony of it all. In his quiet times he would call out to God in groans, he could not put his thoughts or feelings into words. After six months without employment, he forgot who he was. He lost his identity.

A man finds much of his identity in his work. Perhaps it should not be so, but it is true.

His wife could not understand why he couldn't find work. She knew he was putting in the hours and going to some interviews, but she openly wondered if there was something wrong with him. "Why can't you convert an interview into a job?" she asked. "Are you expecting too much? Maybe you're acting too anxious. Maybe you should read a book on interviewing. We are running out of money. How will we pay the kids' tuition? I was able to find work in two weeks; I can't understand why after eight months you still haven't found something."

Each question, each insinuation, each doubt, each worry pierced his heart like a razor-edged, white-hot saber. His self-esteem began to flutter. On those occasions when his wife would doubt him, he would slip below the line which separates positive from negative. Each time it was harder to come back. By the end of the eighth month, his confidence was gone. He had lost his self-esteem.

A man's *identity* usually comes from his work, while a major chunk of his *self-esteem* comes from his wife. If a man loses both his work and the support of his wife at the same time, he trembles on the brink of destruction.

When a man and woman tie the nuptial knot, they make a pledge to be there for each other in joy and in sorrow, in plenty and in want, in sickness and in health, for better or for worse, till death do they part. Unfortunately, none of us really understands ahead of time all that this will entail. Some of us find it more difficult than we ever imagined.

The apostle Paul, our brother, said, "I know what it is to be in need, and I know what it is to have plenty. I have learned the secret of being content in any and every situation, whether well fed or hungry, whether living in plenty or in want." What was Paul's secret?

The secret of being content in any and every situation is to completely surrender every desire of your heart to the Lord Jesus, so that whatever happens, the peace of God remains with you.

- "Be content with your pay" (Luke 3:14 NIV).
- "But if we have food and clothing, we will be content with that" (1 Tim. 6:8 NIV).
- "Keep your lives free from the love of money and be content with what you have" (Heb. 13:5 NIV).

Husbands and wives need to be there for each other in daylight and darkness. When the dark hour comes, remember your vow. Keep the faith. Finish the race.

THOUGHT FOR THE DAY _____

Lord Jesus, I confess that sometimes I let my desires for security or luxuries tear at our marriage. Help me to be like Paul, content in any and every situation, whether well-fed or hungry, whether living in plenty or in want. May my mate know that I am always for him/her. Amen.

Jesus: The Resurrected

*Justified by His grace we should become heirs according to the
hope of eternal life.*

TITUS 3:7 NKJV

When I was in high school, I worked for a while for an ambulance company, which was owned, oddly enough, by a funeral home. I worked from midnight until eight in the morning. That meant a lot of waiting around and listening to police radios to see if we could beat the other ambulances to accident sites. (A pretty ghoulish thing to do as I look back on it.) From time to time I was asked to help clean up in the "front," or funeral parlor section of the building. This meant that I had many chances to view bodies that either were in caskets or lying on tables in the "prep" room, waiting to be put out for "viewing." (I have since decided to be cremated!) Usually, this was in the middle of the night, a time when the imagination is somewhat more active, alone in a room with a dead body.

Over and over, when looking at a deceased body, one thought kept repeating itself in my mind: "There is no way in the world this person is ever going to get up again!" It is one thing to talk about resurrection in a seminary classroom or Bible study. It's another to stand before prospective "resurrectees" and claim that they will rise again. Yet Jesus Christ did just that. He rose from the dead!

The simple details in John's account of the contents of Jesus' tomb are fascinating and cause me to imagine what the moment of the Resurrection might have been like. A picture that repeatedly comes to mind is that of Jesus' heart, which had been still since Friday, beginning to beat again. His chest expands, and begins steadily to rise and fall. His eyes slowly open beneath the facial cloth. Jesus is alive again!

The fact of Jesus' resurrection is the reason for our hope that we will rise again as well. I wonder if there will be the same absence of haste when my own eyes, though dust and ashes, slowly open to finally see His face.

THOUGHT FOR THE DAY _____

Jesus, thank You for submerging Yourself into the water of death so that we would know Death Has Been Conquered.

Max Lucado (para.)

His Touch Is Forever

I know that whatever God does,
It shall be forever.
—ECCLESIASTES 3:14 NKJV

The giant redwoods of our national parks are a testimony to strength and longevity. Spiraling skyward, reaching heavenly heights, these trees are admired for their beauty and their history. Men consider these trees masterpieces and treasures of nature. We could never manufacture something comparable. As we come to appreciate them even more, we are confident that they will stand forever.

Man's structures and machines are as he is—temporary. Buildings fall every day and machinery gives out. Money is invested daily to improve, to study, and to attempt to construct "eternal" structures. Meanwhile the trees grow freely, seedlings sprouting up by God's design, God's nurture, and God's hand. This tree will transcend generations, not from man's toil, but instead from an eternal God.

The God of eternity has touched our lives as well. As we grow, we can be assured that as a result we will "last forever." We can do nothing to separate us from the love of God. Truly, what God does is forever.

THOUGHT FOR THE DAY _____
Help me to invest my life in what is eternal—people and You.

Learn from nature that everything has to take its course and that when life is rushed, nothing is really gained.

Tony Campolo
How to Rescue the Earth Without Worshiping Nature

Mine the Nuggets of Truth

The ear that hears the rebukes of life
Will abide among the wise.
——————**PROVERBS 15:31** NKJV

*N*o one likes to be confronted. We don't want to hear about our shortcomings or mistakes. Usually we become defensive or even hostile toward the person who is pointing them out.

It has been said that in any criticism or confrontation there lies the potential for at least a nugget of truth. I once worked for a very demanding employer. He was often critical of the work his employees did. The employees felt a lot of anger and hostility toward him. One day, it was my turn. As he was commenting in a very angry way about the job that I had been doing, I remember practicing this truth. While most of what he said was out of proportion and untrue, I did find a small nugget of truth that actually helped me improve the job that I was performing.

Wisdom comes from being open to hearing the rebukes that may come in our lives. While anger may be our initial reaction, it is important to evaluate the confrontation and heed any wisdom that might be included in the message.

THOUGHT FOR THE DAY ————————————————
Help me to hear the nugget of truth in any criticism I may receive.

BOB DYER
The Man Within

God and God Alone

Let us come before His presence with thanksgiving;
Let us shout joyfully to Him with psalms.

—————————————————PSALM 95:2 NKJV

"*M*ad? You think I'm mad? I'm livid! Not a 'thank-you,' a 'good job,' or even a 'not bad.' Nothing. I deserve better!"

How many times have you heard this chorus or even felt it yourself?

It's always nice to be appreciated, to have a sense that our work and who we are are noticed. It seems, though, the only time we are noticed is when something goes wrong. Imagine being the Creator of the universe, the giver of life, and the loving, sovereign God that gave His only Son for mankind. Continue to consider what it must feel like to have done all of this and rarely be given a word of thanks, be spoken to only when your beloveds need something or question why.

Although we cannot suppose to feel as God does, we do know that we have been given everything by a loving, unconditionally accepting Father, God.

God is many things to us all. He alone is worthy of our praise. Are you praising Him daily?

THOUGHT FOR THE DAY _____

You alone are worthy of praise, God. Thank You for all You have done for me.

Multiple Joy in Obeying God's Will

Give, and it will be given to you: good measure, pressed down, shaken together, and running over will be put into your bosom.

LUKE 6:38 NKJV

*O*beying God's will in your life will eventually include some form of giving. Sometimes that giving may hurt.

We were receiving money one Sunday in 1980 toward our new church property, and people were coming forward to give all kinds of things—cars, houses, property. A woman walked forward and took off a large gold bracelet and put it in my hand. She said to me, "This is the most valuable thing I own." (The bracelet was, indeed, valuable. It sold for $17,000 when we turned it in for the church building fund.)

Up to that moment, I thought our family had given everything we could possibly give—we had sold a car and our travel trailer and given the money to the building fund. When the woman dropped that gold bracelet into my hand, however, the Lord spoke in my heart and said, *You've never given Me anything but money.*

My thoughts turned immediately to my cameras. Now, I love to take photographs. That's my hobby. I'd rather be off on a trip taking photographs than doing just about anything else but preaching and being with God's people. Down through the years, I had acquired quite a bit of camera gear. And I thought, *Oh, no, Lord, that's asking too much*. But I knew instantly that selling my cameras was what I had to do.

The next day, I got all my camera equipment together and took it down to a friend who bought and sold used camera equipment. I said to him, "I'm here to sell my equipment."

He said, "Why are you doing that?"

I said, "Well, we are buying this property for the church, and the Lord has laid a certain amount on my heart to give. I've sold a car and my travel trailer and given that money, but I still need to give more. What can you give me for my cameras? I know you'll treat me right."

I had felt strongly impressed that we were to give at least $5,000 more than we had given. I had saved about $1,600. The camera store owner went into the back and figured up what he could give me on my cameras, and he came back and said, "How does $3,420 sound?" I said, "That's perfect."

I gave the $5,000 the next service. For about two or three weeks afterward, however, I was feeling some sense of loss. I had given my cameras, but emotionally, I was still holding on to them. The day came when the Lord reminded me of the verse in the Bible that says, "Where your treasure is, there your heart will be also" (Matt. 6:21). I had to ask myself, "Is my heart tied up in my cameras, or is my heart tied up in what the Lord is doing?" And I decided that I would choose, by my will, to link my heart to what God was doing in our midst rather than to a collection of shutters and lenses and film holders.

In that moment, I truly gave those cameras to the Lord. I turned them over to Him in my heart, and I became a cheerful giver before the Lord.

Several months later, a woman rang the doorbell of my house. When I answered the door, she said, "Are you Charles Stanley?"

I said, "Yes, ma'am."

She said, "Here!" and she handed me a suitcase and a paper bag. Then she walked away. I started to ask her, "What is this? Why are you giving me this?" But she left before I could get the questions out of my mouth.

I brought the suitcase and paper bag inside, and I found in them every single item of the camera gear that I had sold and given to the Lord. Every camera body, every lens, and every filter was there.

I went down to the store, and the owner looked at me and said, "Don't ask me." He had promised never to reveal the identity of the person who bought my equipment and gave it back to me.

I've had a *triple* joy from that experience of giving my cameras. The single joy was the genuine joy of giving those cameras to the Lord—of truly giving them out of my heart as sacrificial giving of treasure to the house of God. That joy would have stayed with me all my life, even if I had never seen those cameras again. But that isn't the way God works. His Word says, "Give, and it will be given to you: good measure, pressed down, shaken together, and running over will be put into your bosom" (Luke 6:38). The Lord could have chosen to give me back anything He wanted. He had no obligation to give me back those cameras. And yet, that was His pleasure, and I had the double joy of receiving back my camera gear.

The triple joy has come in recent years as the Lord has allowed me to publish several books that include photos I've taken.

I couldn't help being reminded of Simon Peter lending his fishing boat to Jesus. He, too, experienced a multiple joy. Peter had the joy of giving his boat to Jesus so that Jesus could use it as an offshore pulpit and teach the multitudes from it. Then Jesus gave the boat back to Peter but with the command, "Launch out into the deep and let down your nets for a catch" (Luke 5:4). After protesting, Peter did what Jesus said, and he and his partners caught such a load of fish that their nets began to break and their boats nearly capsized.

Out of that experience, Jesus called Peter to come and follow Him. He said to Peter, "From now on you will catch men" (Luke 5:10).

We don't know how Peter felt about giving his boat to Jesus, but we do know that Peter certainly didn't feel like launching out into the deep for that catch of fish. He had said grudgingly, "Master, we have toiled all night and caught nothing; nevertheless at Your word I will let down the net" (Luke 5:5). We also know that Peter's response to the miracle catch of fish was one of astonishment and fear. Peter fell at

Jesus' knees, saying, "Depart from me, for I am a sinful man, O Lord!" (Luke 5:8).

The point is, however, that Peter obeyed Jesus in both cases. He launched his boat. He followed Jesus. And in so doing, the Lord led him into an entirely new path—one that was to last Peter's entire lifetime.

THOUGHT FOR THE DAY _____

Ultimately, we must do as Peter did. We are called to obey, no matter how much God's plan signals a change in our lives. We are called to give. When we do, the Lord multiplies our joy and gives us a sense of fulfillment.

PATRICK M. MORLEY

Walking with Christ in the Details of Life

Spiritual Malnutrition

Like newborn babies, crave pure spiritual milk, so that by it you may grow up in your salvation, now that you have tasted that the Lord is good.

1 PETER 2:2–3 NIV

My dad was my hero. I remember his strong muscular physique, and how I wanted to grow up to be exactly like him in every way.

I was puny—the classic ninety-seven-pound weakling. So as a young ten-year-old boy, I fell hook, line, and sinker for the "Charles Atlas" ads that promised all us little boys that we could be titans of toughness, gain those precious pounds, and never again have big-mouthed bullies kick sand on us. They could help make me strong, just like Dad!

If someone wants to gain five pounds, he doesn't eat five pounds of food and instantly register five pounds at the scales. Instead, he eats five pounds of food and incrementally gains an ounce or two. Then he eats another five pounds of food and gains another few ounces, and so on. Obviously, the energy needed for the daily press burns up most of our daily food intake.

When someone wants to gain spiritual weight, he doesn't read five pounds of Bible and gain five pounds of spiritual weight. Rather, he studies the Scriptures for an hour or so and is fortunate to gain one or two spiritual insights to add to his spiritual weight.

Most of the five pounds of Bible we might devour during our personal devotions gets burned up on that day's challenges or quickly forgotten, and we add only an ounce or two of new spiritual bulk.

The Scriptures are similar to the most delicious, well-balanced meal you have ever eaten, one you will often remember and hope to repeat—"now that you have tasted that the Lord is good." What brings us back to the Lord's table? We want to add to our spiritual weight. We want food that lasts, that adds precious ounces of spiritual wisdom and truth. We must consume much to retain little, so we come again and again each day. Do not fast from the Scriptures, or you will grow weak. Nourish your soul daily. Drink of the Word of God. Eat of it, and add weight to your beliefs.

We live in a Christianized age, but an age of spiritual malnutrition. We are heavyweights when it comes to spiritual talk, but desperately lightweight in our behavior. Have you unwittingly been on a spiritual fast? Are you weak from abstaining from "pure spiritual milk"? Have you made the error of thinking five pounds of Bible will add five pounds of spiritual weight?

If anything is true, it is that for our spirit and soul to grow we must drink daily from His cup and eat daily of His body. We must be regular —daily—in our intake of spiritual food. We need a balanced spiritual diet. Too much of one and too little of another will lead to spiritual malnutrition.

Do you want to be spiritually healthy? Do you want to "grow up in your salvation"? Then crave pure spiritual food; eat and drink of it. Desire the Word to nourish your soul more than food and drink for your body. " 'Do not worry about your life, what you will eat or drink. . . . Is not life more important than food?' " (Matt. 6:25 NIV).

To gain an ounce of spiritual weight, you must take on five pounds of spiritual food. Most of what you consume will be burned up as spiritual energy for that day. Linger at the table, feasting on His pure food, consuming more than a day's supply, and add an ounce or two to your spiritual weight. This is the prerequisite step to growing up in your salvation. Insufficient intake means insufficient growth.

THOUGHT FOR THE DAY

Do you want to grow up to be like your Father? If you partake daily at His table, you will grow up to be like Him.

God's Loving Embrace

We know that all things work together for good to those who love God, to those who are the called according to His purpose. . . . whom He predestined, these He also called; whom He called, these He also justified; and whom He justified, these He also glorified.

—————————————————————ROMANS 8:28-30 NKJV

$\mathscr{T}$his affirmation is necessary for you to begin an exciting life-fulfilling partnership and adventure with God. When we place our life in His will and keeping, we will gain a faith that will make us confident.

Only under this affirmation can we do all things through Christ who strengthens us. We are given power for living by living in the powerful embrace of God's love. Anything short of this absolute faith will result in unfulfilled living.

Without faith it is possible to lack confidence within yourself. It is difficult to comprehend, then, why people, with faith, still often lack confidence in themselves. Why?

As I realistically look at life I am truthfully aware that I am qualified to do some things because of special talents and that I had best leave some other things alone. Math, for instance, was one of my worst subjects. In fact, I still count on my fingers to balance a checkbook. Perhaps this is a reason why I seem never to be able to balance monthly statements.

No matter how qualified we might be, a lack of confidence will immobilize us with fear. We will then never be swift in going after the position, never soar to attain our goals, never be strengthened in the courage that we can achieve life's successes.

But a sense of confidence, a deep faith in God, can do far more within us than we ever thought or imagined.

While standing at a McDonald's counter waiting for my order, I glanced over to an employment opportunity poster. Under the great golden arches it said: "Golden Opportunity! Help wanted: No experience necessary. Just an enthusiastic and inspired spirit."

Now, that job was for me. I knew I could be hired for it on the spot. I was certain I was an enthusiastic person with an inspired personality. I was confident of that!

Christ has a golden opportunity for you and your life under the arch of His loving embrace. The only requirement is that you are filled with an enthusiastic, spirit-filled faith.

God works for good with those who love Him with such an attitude of faith in everything they do. He will enable you to develop your fullest potential. If you lack the confidence, you will never achieve even that for which you are qualified.

THOUGHT FOR THE DAY _____
When discouraged, I will take heart in the knowledge that I am called, justified, *and* glorified!

Be willing to go where the Lord directs you to go. Be willing to do what He asks you to do. He will not lead you into failure; rather, He will lead you into success —as the Lord defines success.

Charles Stanley
The Source of My Strength

Learn to Have Fun

"A merry heart does good, like medicine."
—————————**PROVERBS 17:22** NKJV

$\mathcal{I}$ remember the wintry day I was going to be alone, so I went to the closest bookstore and bought a biography I had been wanting to read. I came home, baked a batch of cookies, and sat for hours curled up on my sofa with an afghan wrapped around me, munched cookies, and escaped into someone else's life. Sometimes fun is doing exactly what is easy and without any challenge.

When I think of having fun I think it means getting involved doing something that will bring me peace and a sense of well-being. I am actually meeting a personal need of some kind when I engage in something that is fun for me. Are you sometimes surprised by the reality that in everything we do we meet some deep need inside ourselves? Even when we do something we resent and resist doing, we are at least meeting the need to please or keep someone's approval.

When I run, I meet the need of feeling good about my body.

When I read, I feel stimulated and confirmed that I am surely smarter than what my fifth-grade experience told me I was.

When I spend an evening reading books and playing games with my children, I feel like I'm a good mother, being true to the needs of those in my care.

I can get so caught up in living and working and keeping deadlines and worrying about how I'm ever going to be good and smart and strong enough, that I fail to understand the significance of having fun. It's these great fun moments that get us through all the awful, grim, discouraging situations of life. It's the moments we really throw back our heads and laugh together uncontrollably that make us able to survive any relationship. If there is no fun between us, our bonding will disintegrate and die.

Elisabeth Kubler-Ross, M.D., believes that people have the greatest difficulty dying if they have never really experienced life. Regardless of whether you are single or married, young or old—there are uncountable opportunities today everywhere around you that can bring you moments of joy, laughter, exhilaration, and stimulation. It is in these moments we find strength to face all the rest that life can deal out.

Tom, from the day I married him, has been creating what he calls "cheap fun." Recently we met some great people, Nathan, Marie, and Natalie Price, in California and spent a few days together. We reserved four dormitory rooms at a college there right on the Pacific to conserve funds. We were each handed the thinnest washcloth, hand, and bath towels you ever touched and were directed to four of the grimmest, sparsest rooms I've ever seen. No wonder college kids get depressed! We had to share a common bath and every time we flushed a toilet, the sewer backed up in the shower. The odor was almost intolerable. Every morning early, Nathan would go out and bring in hot coffee and donuts, and we would sit and laugh and solve the world's problems (our own, that is!). Tom is right—there's plenty of cheap fun for everyone to enjoy. One night the baby was asleep and Tom took one boy and I the other. We read, played games, and then Nash and I went to the kitchen and created banana splits for everyone and brought them up on a tray. Cheap, wonderful fun. Connecting with people you enjoy and adding just a touch of sparkle.

THOUGHT FOR THE DAY ⎯⎯⎯⎯⎯⎯⎯⎯⎯⎯⎯⎯⎯
A happy memory is a joy forever!

PATRICK M. MORLEY

Walking with Christ in the Details of Life

God Owns Everything

Moreover, when God gives any man wealth and possessions, and enables him to enjoy them, to accept his lot and be happy in his work—this is a gift of God.

ECCLESIASTES 5:19 NIV

The meeting broke up, and the three of us made our way toward the parking lot. The other two men unlocked expensive luxury cars and slipped inside onto soft, handcrafted leather seats. As their engines cranked, rows of luminous dials and gauges blinked and sputtered to life in the cockpits.

One of these men is a believer; the other is not. For the one who is not, his automobile represented the apex of his achievements. It symbolized his human potential; it discreetly certified his prosperity to the world around him. His car was the icon of his identity. It represented the end to which he aspired.

The believer appreciated the quality of the car he drove. God had blessed his life with prosperity, yet a sense of guilt lingered about the abundance of his life—especially when compared to many of the struggling saints in his church.

He ran the company he owned on Christian principles—not as a "Christian" company with a big Bible positioned pretentiously on the reception table, but one which held integrity and ethical behavior as its highest values. He employed several people, enabling them to support their families. His own behavior influenced many employees to trust Christ as their own Savior and Lord.

He shared regularly with the poor and spread good works throughout his community. He was leaving the world a better place, a more spiritual place. His life was a testimony to Christ. Still, guilt over his prosperity lingered, haunting his thoughts. He had never been able to accept his lot in life and, as a consequence, he didn't enjoy his possessions. He missed the gift of God.

What is the purpose of prosperity? God owns everything. He searches for men and women to whom He can entrust the material world He owns. Pagans cut throats as they compete for their slice of the prosperity pie. But the hand of God bestows prosperity on certain of His children without trouble. He does so exclusively to extend the kingdom of God in the temporal world. He hides no secret reason.

What happens to the one—believer or unbeliever—who misses the purpose of prosperity, who ignores the mandate to extend the kingdom of God? He does not please the Lord, and the blessing will be taken away. "To the man who pleases him, God gives wisdom, knowledge and happiness, but to the sinner he gives the task of gathering and storing up wealth to hand it over to the one who pleases God" (Ecclesiastes 2:26 NIV). Has God blessed you materially?

THOUGHT FOR THE DAY _____
Don't lose the gift of God. Please Him. Don't miss the purpose of your prosperity. Prosperity is from God, not for you only, but as a means to other ends—the ends of God. Undo the guilt you have felt, and do the work of God. Determine your personal financial needs, then devote the balance to kingdom work. Please God with your prosperity.

Walk So You Leave Behind Good Footprints

> *"Therefore let us go forth to Him, . . . For here we have no continuing city, . . . But do not forget to do good and to share, for with such sacrifices God is well pleased."*
> ———————————————————————HEBREWS 13:13–16 NKJV

*L*ive each day so that later on you'll look back with satisfaction.

You can do that! You can't manage your circumstances, but you can manage *how you react* to your circumstances. Remember, living is between your ears!

So from this moment on, God helping you, if you choose, you can do two things to leave behind good footprints.

1. *Start building for yourself the memories you want when you look back tomorrow.*

Two women sat next to us recently in a restaurant. When our conversation lulled, we realized they were discussing handling their teenage sons.

"Well," said one, "it's not always easy. But my husband is so wise. He says, 'Trina, say or do in such a way that you'll feel good about it later on, when you look back.' "

We said this to a couple at a conference recently. They hadn't been married too long, and they had "his" children and "her" children under one roof, and they were going so crazy that they were thinking about splitting.

"Look," we said, "think about down the road. Don't just get a little temporary relief by divorcing and then have years of regret forever after.

"So it's bad now. But when the children are gone, you'll be so glad you hung in together. The children cause temporary stress, but you have the great privilege of a permanent marriage. Outlast them!"

Build now the memories you want when you look back tomorrow.

At another conference a while back at a really wonderful church, the assistant pastor's wife took us aside for a little confidential chat.

"Pray with us," she said, "that Charles [the senior pastor] will move on. There are a lot of people in this church, including us, who feel the church has outgrown him, and we need a fresh start."

Now, the senior pastor of that church was a godly, humble, beautiful man who had come ten years earlier when the church was nothing and had brought it to its current strong, basically healthy condition (although in the last year there had been a ground swell of criticism and opposition).

With all the fervor in our bones we said, "Look, dear April, we don't know all the details of your situation, and neither do we know Charles deeply and well.

"But we believe whether you stay in this church or move on elsewhere, or whether Charles stays here or moves on—if you've been utterly loving and loyal to Charles, praying for him, encouraging him, maximizing his good points to others and quietly covering and filling in, where you can, for his weaknesses—if you've been that kind of assistant pastor and wife, you'll always feel good about it later on. You'll be glad you did. You won't lose.

"But if you murmur against him and join sides with others and let them murmur against him; or if you even simply 'damn him with faint praise' when he's on trial needing your defense and protection—in the long haul you could be terribly sorry. You could get caught in a mess that could damage your whole ministry career.

"Look down the road! Conduct yourselves each day in the light of the future—in the way you want your career to give you the greatest pleasure as you look back."

April began to cry! She knew we were right. She and her husband are two wonderful people who, in fatigue, had lost perspective. We loved them too much not to stop them short.

Build now the memories you want when you look back tomorrow. We could make it into a proverb: "Eat only what will leave a good taste in your mouth!"

2. *Start building, as well, other people's memories of you.* For instance, *speak your negative words, but write your positive ones.*

Don't put your negative feelings on paper! If you're distressed over people's actions, don't "write a letter." Pray first, perhaps take a wise third party, and go see them. When you're face to face, your touches and your tone of voice can soften what you say, and you can hear their side of it and maybe even reach an understanding.

(Incidentally, never, never write an anonymous letter. That's definitely shaky and flaky, and only shaky and flaky people in this world take them seriously.)

On the other hand, as often as possible write notes and letters of commendation and encouragement. Say them, yes—but also write them. Our friend Dr. Ted Engstrom does that, and he's much loved for it.

Think future! When you're dead and gone, you want to leave behind in this world not one bad piece of paper for people to find—but hundreds of good ones for them to remember you by.

And in everything you do, *live so they'll cry at your funeral.* Wouldn't you like some day to be really missed? Then "reach out and touch." Each smile of yours, each hug, each encouraging word could become a specific little memory in someone's mind later on. Why not?

Say it now, do it now while you can, to every person you can—and build those memories. Stack 'em up for a great funeral!

Get perspective.

Says Amy Carmichael, "We have all eternity to enjoy our rewards, but only a few short years to win them."

And God wants to do more than bring His sons to glory; He wants to bring glory to His sons! He wants to do more than bring your soul to heaven; He wants to bring heaven to your soul!

When you spend your life with future rewards in mind, your present life becomes rewarding as well. Build your own future memories, and build other people's future memories of you.

THOUGHT FOR THE DAY ⸻
Walk so you leave behind good footprints.

RANDY PETERSEN
Flying Solo

The Father's Lesson

For whom the LORD loves He chastens, / And scourges every son whom He receives.

—HEBREWS 12:6 NKJV

For many kids, time spent with grandparents is wonderful. Grandparents take you to fun places and buy you all the toys and candy you want. Do something wrong and they'll smile and turn the other way.

Then you come home to Mom and/or Dad. Parents take you to the dentist. They spend money on you, but it's for broccoli and school clothes. Do something wrong and you're in trouble.

Who loves the kid more? They both do, of course, but the parents have a more intimate stake in the kid's life.

We keep wanting God to be a grandparent to us, and He insists on being a parent. We want the candy, the carnivals, and a free ride with our behavior. But He is interested in caring for our needs and helping us develop into mature souls.

THOUGHT FOR THE DAY _____
Thank You, God, for parenting and loving me.

DR. CHRIS THURMAN
*The 12 Best Kept Secrets for Living
an Emotionally Healthy Life*

The Difficult Path to Truth

"*Ponder the path of thy feet, and let all thy ways be established.
Turn not to the right hand nor to the left: remove thy foot from
evil.*

PROVERBS 4:26-27 KJV

*W*hen poet Robert Frost wrote of a road that split into two different paths, he was warning us that the more traveled path might be easier to traverse but ultimately less satisfying and growth producing and that the less traveled path, though more difficult, ends up being the one that is more worthwhile. Each day in life we find ourselves facing this same Frostian dilemma of whether or not to follow the more difficult but healthier path of truth that few people follow or the easier but unhealthier path of lies that most people choose. Our choice each day concerning this "fork in the road" makes all the difference in how our lives turn out.

In the book *Alice's Adventures in Wonderland,* Alice came to a crossroads and asked the Cheshire cat which road she should take. "Where are you going?" asked the cat. "I don't know," answered Alice. "Oh, well," said the cat, "in that case, either road will take you there." If "there" is health and happiness, then either road won't take you there. Truth is the only road to a balanced life. There is no other path.

If you are interested in taking the difficult path of truth through life, there is good news, though. The good news is that truth is available to anyone who wants it, which also means that hope, health, and happiness is possible for everyone. It doesn't matter if you are male or female, black or white (or any other color), young or old, American or Russian, rich or poor, educated or uneducated, from a functional or dysfunctional family. Truth does not discriminate. The further good news is that truth, when understood and applied, produces life in full, liberty from unnecessary suffering and pain, and happiness in the form of peace and contentment no matter how your life may be going. In other words, the hard work of being a person dedicated to the truth pays off handsomely.

So we don't ever need to ask, "Can I be an emotionally healthy, mature, content, self-controlled, happy, and stable person?" The answer is a resounding, "Yes!" The more honest and difficult question we need to ask ourselves is, "Do I really want to be a well-balanced person badly enough to pay the price for it?"

If you want to be better than you are, you have quite a challenge in front of you. The effort to be a person of truth will demand more of you than anything else you will ever try to do. Anything! That is why most of us want emotional health but give up along the way in our pursuit of it. It is tough work.

Whether you realize it or not, truth is the most important issue in your life. It is more important than what you do for a living, who you are married to, or what you earn. I am convinced that truth is the bottom line of life. You cannot have "real life" without truth. A life without truth (or with only partial truth) is not much of a life at all. It contains little of the emotional health, maturity, or completeness that most of us want.

THOUGHT FOR THE DAY _____

If you have reached the fork in the road where you must decide between truth and lies, consider your choice carefully. Despite which path you take, somewhere along the way you will ultimately meet the truth. You can either choose the straight and narrow path, where you and the truth can travel as companions. Or you can traverse a twisting trail of lies; which will one day, without warning, intersect the straight and narrow and lead you into an unavoidable collision with the truth.

Memorable Souvenir

Then Jesus said to His disciples, "If anyone desires to come after Me, let him deny himself, and take up his cross, and follow Me."
————————————————————MATTHEW 16:24 NKJV

*S*everal years ago while on vacation in Santa Fe, I was looking for something to buy as a souvenir. I walked in front of the Governor's Palace where the local Native Americans sell their wares and I spotted a beautiful little silver cross. It had a design etched in the silver by one of the native craftspeople. I bought the cross, hung it on a silver chain, and have worn it around my neck every day since my trip.

This morning I was hurrying to get ready for work. Just as I put my dress on, the chain holding the cross came undone and both the chain and the cross fell on the floor. My first reaction was to pick both up, put them on the dresser, rush through dressing, and get going. But then I stopped and thought, *How often are we tempted to cast the cross aside because we are too busy or too rushed?* I stopped, picked up the cross, put it back on the chain, and hung it securely around my neck.

THOUGHT FOR THE DAY ————————————————
Following after Christ requires a daily, moment by moment commitment.

Have You Done Your Chores?

Then He said to His disciples, "The harvest truly is plentiful, but the laborers are few."

MATTHEW 9:37 NKJV

*T*here is the story of a city kid visiting his uncle's farm. Extremely early the first morning he was roused out of bed by a cousin and led around the farm doing everything from feeding the chickens to milking the cows—all before the sun was actually visible. Upon completing those tasks the city boy and his cousin went into the house for breakfast. After being satisfied by ham, eggs, and biscuits the city boy excused himself from the table and started back to bed. He had gotten only two steps away when his uncle asked what he was doing. After telling the uncle of his plan to slumber, he was rudely awakened. The uncle informed him that there was work to do. The boy wondered how this could be as he explained all that he had done. The uncle replied, "Those, my son, were chores. The real work is out in the fields."

And so it is in the Christian life. We too have chores. Reading Scripture, praying, tithing, and fellowshipping are just a few. These are the things that build up the church as well as ourselves. The work, however, is still in the fields. The work we are called to do, the work of the Great Commission, can be long and tedious, and it must be approached with care.

THOUGHT FOR THE DAY _____
There is joy in serving Jesus.

The Grace Apportioned to You

I urge you to live a life worthy of the calling you have received.
—————————————————————————EPHESIANS 4:1 NIV

A young man returned from the war in Vietnam. The destruction he witnessed left him disturbed, somehow unbalanced. He could not shake the aftermath of the depraved images he had observed firsthand. He had participated in the confusing ways of this broken world, and he despaired of the evil which men do to each other.

Not long after his return stateside, he received the calling to trust Christ for his salvation—a call to which he said yes. As he prayed "Lord Jesus, I need You," his body began to twitch and tremble uncontrollably. He had been born, and now he was born again. The instability of his disturbed world was replaced by the stability of the kingdom of God.

Over the next several years, he struggled to live a life worthy of the calling he had received, but he did not. The psychological trauma of Vietnam haunted him; people strained his edgy temperament. Eventually he became a commercial fisherman, finding solace in the lonely life of the sea.

Years later we saw each other again, and I asked him how things were going on his spiritual pilgrimage. "Well, I still believe," came his reply, "but it's really hard for me."

One morning three months later I received a phone call. After returning from two weeks at sea, this young man followed his weathered, crusty comrades to the local tavern. He soon passed out. His mates grabbed his arms and legs and carried his limp, languid body into the back room and flopped him like a frumpy, oversized rag doll onto the cold, bare floor. Even though he was turning blue, they turned and walked away. He never regained consciousness. Several hours later he was found dead from a drug and alcohol overdose. He was my younger brother.

Not everyone has the strength of courage and character to live a life worthy of the calling they have received. To live up to our calling is itself a gift from God. "But to each one of us grace has been given as Christ apportioned it" (Eph. 4:7 NIV). Some of us are impeded from living up to Christ. It may be a troubled childhood, a tough marriage, difficult children, or, like my brother, you may have seen too much evil.

If Christ has apportioned you with enough grace to live a life worthy of the calling you received, are you applying it? If not, should He let you keep it? Or should He take it away and give it to someone who will make full use of it? Many Christians under-apply their grace. It is such a waste.

If you are living a life worthy of the calling you received, how do you treat your weaker brother? Do you look in disgust at another who can't quite seem to get his act together? Does your mind get stuck thinking about how weak he is? Pray for him, that God's grace to him may increase. Fall to your face and implore God to have mercy on your weaker brother or sister with tears of remorse. Thank Him with tears of gratitude that He has mercifully given you so much grace. Why should it be the other person and not you that is weak? There is no reason except the grace Christ has apportioned to you at His sole discretion. "But for the grace of God, there go I."

"Be completely humble and gentle; be patient, bearing with one another in love" (Eph. 4:2 NIV). "Accept him whose faith is weak, without passing judgment on disputable matters" (Romans 14:1 NIV).

Every Christian is one for whom Christ died. If Jesus thought that person was worth dying for, why do you despise him? "You, then, why do you judge your brother? Or why do you look down on your brother? For we will all stand before God's judgment seat" (Rom. 14:10 NIV).

Let us, therefore, concentrate on living up to the calling we have received. Part of our calling is to bear with our weaker brothers, to not revel in the smug satisfaction that we overcome but they don't. If we overcome, it is because of the grace apportioned to us. And if we ourselves are not living a life worthy of our calling, then ask for more grace. Work out your salvation with fear and trembling, but know that the strength of courage and character to do so comes from the grace apportioned to you.

THOUGHT FOR THE DAY _____
Bolster my courage and character so that I may live up to the calling You have graciously given to me.

God gives people with gaps to other people with gaps to fill each other's gaps.

Patrick M. Morley
The Rest of Your Life

ABOUT THE
CONTRIBUTORS

Ann Kiemel Anderson is a former schoolteacher, youth director, college dean of women, and author of nine books, as well as coauthor of *Struggling for Wholeness.*

Dr. Neil T. Anderson holds five earned degrees and is an associate professor of practical theology at Talbot School of Theology. He is the president of Freedom in Christ Ministries and has written numerous books, including *Victory Over the Darkness, The Bondage Breaker, Walking Through the Darkness,* and *The Seduction of Our Children.*

Betty Lively Blaylock is a licensed professional counselor in Dallas, Texas, and a coauthor of *One Step at a Time,* a collection of daily devotionals for people in twelve-step recovery. She received her doctorate in guidance and counseling from Western Colorado University. As president of the Texas Association for Children of Alcoholics, a state agency that advocates for children of alcohol and other drug abuse, Dr. Blaylock has extensive experience counseling adult children of alcoholics.

Dr. Blaylock and her husband, Charles, are parents and grandparents and live in north Dallas.

Vonette Zachary Bright cofounded Campus Crusade for Christ with her husband, Bill, and has assisted him in ministry throughout their married life. Vonette has developed an international prayer ministry (which prompted the setting of a definite date for the National Day of Prayer by Congress and the President) and an International Prayer

Congress in Korea. She was one of the original members of the Lausanne Committee for World Evangelism, having served for fifteen years.

Ronald W. Cadmus has published articles in *Bride's* magazine and *Word and Witness*, a national homiletic and exegetical resource for sermon preparation. Ron is the forty-eighth minister in line of succession at the historic Collegiate Church of New York City, America's oldest congregation, founded in 1628. His church is situated in a community that speaks thirty-three different languages, which can make a clear presentation of the gospel a definite challenge. Through the ministry of the Collegiate Church, thousands of people are invited to discover life's greatest gift—God's loving embrace.

Michael Card is a well-known and well-loved singer/songwriter, described by *Moody Monthly* as an artist "who stands alone in biblical accuracy and integrity of lyrics." His compositions include "El Shaddai," which was rated the #1 song of the decade by Christian radio broadcasters, as well as the popular favorites, "Celebrate the Child," "Immanuel," and "That's What Faith Must Be."

Card's album *The Final Word*, the third part of *The Life* trilogy, was awarded the 1988 Dove Award for Praise and Worship Album. In addition to songwriting, Michael is a devoted student/teacher of the Bible with a master's degree in biblical studies from Western Kentucky University.

Ronald Dunn is an itinerant Baptist preacher, popular speaker, and the director of LifeStyle Ministries in Irving, Texas, where he lives with his wife, Kaye. Ron began preaching when he was fifteen and pastored his first church when he was seventeen. He later graduated from Oklahoma Baptist University and Southwestern Baptist Theological Seminary.

In 1975 Ron resigned his pastorate to become a full-time "traveling pastor," and his ministry has taken him all over the world. He is Minister-at-Large for MacArthur Boulevard Baptist Church in Irving.

Ron has written or cowritten nine books, including *Don't Just Stand There—Pray Something!* and *When Heaven is Silent*.

He is the speaker on the nationwide radio program, "New Life For You."

Bob Dyer is the director of clinical outreach at the Minirth-Meier/ New Life Clinic in Richardson, Texas. He holds a degree in psychology from Oklahoma Baptist University and a master's degree from Dallas Theological Seminary.

A licensed and ordained minister, Mr. Dyer was a counseling pastor in Dallas, Texas, before joining the MMNL Clinics staff. He also worked with Sportsworld ministries, a discipleship ministry for professional athletes.

Bob has spoken all over the country at family, marriage, and youth conferences, with key presentations on relationships, marriage, self-esteem, emotionally balanced living, and men's issues. Mr. Dyer is also a contributing writer for *Today's Better Life* magazine and coauthor of *The Man Within*.

Bob and his wife, Rebecca, have two children, Patrick and Kelsey.

Marilyn Willett Heavilin is a wife, mother, grandmother, former high-school counselor, and author of five books. She frequently teaches seminars, training people to become effective speakers and leaders, and has also spoken at several writers' conferences. Marilyn speaks at churches, Christian conference centers, and universities across the country. Her topics include developing a satisfying prayer life, marriage, parenting, and helping the hurting.

Marilyn is cochairman of the Southern California Women's Retreat, and the founder of her own ministry, LISTENING HEARTS.

Marilyn can be contacted at

LISTENING HEARTS
Box 1612
Redlands, CA 92373

Jeanne Hendricks is a wife, mother, author, gifted communicator, and a much-in-demand speaker at seminars and conferences. The wife of Dr. Howard Hendricks, chairman of the Center for Christian Leadership at Dallas Theological Seminary, Jeanne is an advisory board member of Pioneer Clubs and MOPS, International. She received her BA degree in journalism from Southern Methodist University in Dallas, Texas.

Cynthia Spell Humbert has a master of science degree in counseling psychology from Georgia State University and a master's in Christian counseling from Psychological Studies Institute in Atlanta, Georgia. She has led seminars on codependency, building self-esteem, post–abortion trauma, and incest recovery.

Cynthia lives with her husband, David, in Plano, Texas.

Florence Littauer is the president and founder of CLASS Speakers, Inc. A best-selling author of twenty books, she travels internationally as a Christian speaker and is a popular seminar and retreat leader, as well as speaker and talk show guest.

Paul Meier received an M.D. from the University of Arkansas College of Medicine and completed his psychiatry residency at Duke University Medical School. He also received an M. A. in biblical studies from Dallas Theological Seminary. Dr. Meier is cofounder of the national chain of Minirth-Meier/New Life Clinics, and has coauthored more than thirty books.

Frank Minirth, M.D., is the co-CEO of the Minirth-Meier/New Life Clinics, offering services in forty-nine cities nationwide. Dr. Minirth is a diplomate of the American Board of Psychiatry and Neurology and received an M.D. from the University of Arkansas College of Medicine. He also holds a graduate degree in theology from Dallas Theological Seminary.

Patrick Morley, best known as an author and speaker, began his career as a businessman. He founded Morley Properties, which was one of Florida's 100 largest privately held companies during the 1980s. Pat's vision is to help bring about a spiritual awakening in America. Through his ministry, he speaks at outreach events and citywide evangelistic missions throughout the U.S.

Morley graduated with honors from the University of Central Florida, which selected him as its Outstanding Alumnus in 1984. He is a graduate of the Harvard Business School Owner/President Management Program and holds a One-Year Certificate in Theology from Reformed Theological Seminary. He serves on the board of directors of

Campus Crusade for Christ and teaches a weekly Bible study to 125 businessmen.

Pat resides with his family in Orlando, Florida.

Doug Murren is senior pastor of Eastside Foursquare Church in Kirkland, Washington, and author of the bimonthly column "The Growing Church" in *Ministries Today* and *Worship Leader*. He is also host of the daily radio program "Growing Together." Murren is a graduate of Seattle Pacific University.

Dr. Brian Newman is clinical director of inpatient services at the Minirth-Meier/New Life Clinic in Richardson, Texas. He has coauthored *The Father Book*, *Passages of Marriage*, and *Love Is a Choice Workbook* and has written articles for *Today's Better Life*, *Christian Parenting*, and *Today's Christian Woman*. Dr. Newman is a frequent guest on the Minirth-Meier/New Life radio program.

Dr. Newman's wife, Deborah, is also a therapist with the Minirth-Meier/New Life Clinic in Richardson. They are the parents of two children, Rachel and Benjamin.

Anne Ortlund is an accomplished musician, as well as an author. Her books include the award-winning *Children Are Wet Cement* and the best-seller *The Disciplines of the Beautiful Woman*. She has ministered with her husband, Ray, in conferences around the world.

A graduate of Princeton Theological Seminary, **Ray Ortlund** is an ordained Presbyterian minister and the former pastor of Lake Avenue Congregational church in Pasadena, California. Ray has written four books including the best-seller *Lord, Make My Life a Miracle*.

Jan Kiemel Ream is a professional marriage and family therapist. She describes herself as a mother, wife, therapist, speaker, daughter, and friend.

Ted Scheuermann calls himself a professional layman. Author of *Men Like Us,* he is coordinator of MAN-TO-MAN, a program of Christian Service Brigade, and is a recovering alcoholic with fifteen years of sobriety. He has a ministry to the church through small groups and one-on-one discipleship and has written material for men's recovery groups, specifically those in twelve-step programs.

In 1993 Ted and his wife, author Jane Porter, founded Katargeo Ministries, a "fresh start" program for people of all ages who need job training, supplies, housing, and spiritual guidance.

Ted and Jane live in West Chicago, Illinois.

Barb Shurin is writer/researcher assistant for Doug Murren. They have collaborated on three books: *Is It Real When It Doesn't Work?*, *Iceman*, and *"Thirty-Something" in the Pew*. Barb has worked in twenty different languages, including Russian, Greek, Hebrew, Persian, Ottoman/Modern Turkish, phonetic Arabic, and phonetic Chinese.

Gary Smalley, president of Today's Family, is a doctoral candidate in marriage and family counseling and has a master's degree from Bethel Seminary in St. Paul, Minnesota. His previous best-selling books include *If Only He Knew; For Better or for Best; Joy That Lasts; The Key to Your Child's Heart*; and *The Blessing*. Gary is the father of three children and lives with his wife, Norma, in Branson, Missouri.

Charles Stanley is the senior minister of the 13,500-member First Baptist Church in Atlanta. He has written numerous books, and his popular program, "In Touch," is heard nationwide on TV and radio.

Twice-elected president of the Southern Baptist Convention, Stanley received his bachelor of arts degree from the University of Richmond, his bachelor of divinity degree from Southwestern Theological Seminary, and his master's and doctorate degrees of theology from Luther Rice Seminary.

Dr. Larry Stephens is a licensed professional counselor and a licensed marriage and family therapist with the Minirth-Meier/New Life Clinic in Richardson, Texas. For his Ed.D. dissertation, he conducted a survey of how Christians develop their image of God. Dr. Stephens is author of *Please, Let Me Know You, God* and coauthor of *The Man Within: Daily Devotions for Men in Recovery*.

Kenneth N. Taylor achieved renown as the translator of *The Living Bible*. In addition he has published twenty-three other books, including

What High School Students Should Know about Evolution and *Big Thoughts for Little People.* He received his bachelor's degree from Wheaton College, Illinois; studied at Dallas Theological Seminary; and received his Th.M. from Northern Baptist Theological Seminary. Wheaton College awarded him an honorary doctorate of literature. The recipient of numerous awards, Taylor is now chairman of the board of Tyndale House Publishers.

Dr. Chris Thurman is a licensed professional psychologist who maintains an active counseling practice in Austin, Texas. He is a highly sought after seminar speaker and the author of *The Lies We Believe, The Twelve Best Kept Secrets for Living an Emotionally Healthy Life,* and *If Christ Were Your Counselor.*

John Trent, president of his own ministry, Encouraging Words, has a Ph.D. in marriage and family counseling and holds a master's degree from Dallas Theological Seminary. In addition to the "Love Is a Decision" seminars he conducts with Gary Smalley, John Trent holds "Blessing" seminars across the country. He is coauthor with Gary Smalley, of the best-seller *The Blessing.*

Thomas A. Whiteman, Ph.D., is a licensed psychologist and president of Fresh Start Seminars, Inc., which conducts more than fifty divorce recovery seminars a year throughout the United States. He is also founder and president of Life Counseling Services, a Christian counseling center, in Paoli, Pennsylvania.

Dr. Whiteman and his wife, Lori, are the parents of two daughters, Elizabeth and Michelle, and one son, Kurt.

Warren W. Wiersbe focuses his energies on writing, teaching, and select conference ministry. He is the author of more than one hundred books and has compiled twenty. For ten years Wiersbe was a Bible teacher on "Back to the Bible" broadcast and for five years was general director. Previous to that, he served as senior pastor of The Moody Church, Chicago, from 1971 to 1978.

Robert L. Wise, Ph.D., is author of eleven books, including *When the Night Is Too Long, The Dawning, The Exiles,* and *The Fall of Jerusa-*

lem. A long-time student of the Hebrew language and of Jewish culture, Robert has traveled extensively in the Holy Land, as well as across the world.

Wise lives in Oklahoma City with his wife, Margueritte.

Andrew Young, an ordained minister, was deeply involved in the civil rights movement of the sixties with his mentor and friend, Martin Luther King, Jr. Since then, Young has served as a member of Congress, ambassador to the United Nations, and as the mayor of Atlanta. He is now cochairman of the 1996 Olympics in Atlanta and vice-chairman of Law International Engineering Company.

BIBLIOGRAPHY

Anderson, Ann Kiemel.
And with the Gift Came Laughter. Wheaton, IL: Tyndale, 1987.
I Gave God Time. Wheaton, IL: Tyndale, 1984.
Open Adoption: My Story of Love and Laughter. Wheaton, IL: Tyndale, 1990.

and Jan Kiemel Ream.
Struggling for Wholeness. Nashville: Oliver-Nelson, 1991.

Anderson, Dr. Neil T.
Bondage Breaker. Eugene, OR: Harvest House, 1990.
Overcoming. Eugene, OR: Harvest House, 1993.
In Search of the Source. Sisters, OR: Questar Books, 1992.
Living Free in Christ. Ventura, CA: Regal, 1990.
Victory Over the Darkness. Ventura, CA: Regal, 1990.
Winning Spiritual Warfare. Eugene, OR: Harvest House, 1991.

and Steve Russo.
Seduction of Our Children. Eugene, OR: Harvest House, 1991.

Blaylock, Betty Lively.
and Cynthia Spell Humbert, and **Dr. Frank Minirth.**
One Step at a Time. Nashville: Thomas Nelson, 1991.

Bright, Vonette Zachary, ed.
The Greatest Lesson I've Ever Learned. Nashville: Thomas Nelson, 1993.

and Bill Bright.
Managing Stress in Marriage. San Bernardino, CA: Here's Life, 1990.

Cadmus, Ronald W.
God's Loving Embrace. Nashville: Thomas Nelson, 1993.

Card, Michael.
The Name of the Promise Is Jesus. Nashville: Thomas Nelson, 1993.

Dunn, Ronald.
The Faith Crisis. Pasadena, CA: Living Spring Publications, 1985.
When Heaven Is Silent. Nashville: Thomas Nelson, 1993.

Dyer, Bob.
The Man Within. Nashville: Thomas Nelson, 1991.

Heavilin, Marilyn Willett.
I'm Listening, Lord. Nashville: Thomas Nelson, 1993.

Hendricks, Jeanne.
A Mother's Legacy. Colorado Springs, CO: NavPress, 1988.
A Woman for All Seasons, rev. ed. Nashville: Thomas Nelson, 1990.

Humbert, Cynthia Spell.

and **Betty Lively Blaylock** and **Dr. Frank Minirth.**
One Step at a Time. Nashville: Thomas Nelson, 1991.

Littauer, Florence.
After Every Wedding Comes a Marriage. Eugene, OR: Harvest House, 1981.
Blow Away the Black Clouds. Eugene, OR: Harvest House, 1986.
Blow Away the Black Clouds: A Woman's Answer to Depression, large type ed. New York: Walker & Co., 1988.
Dare to Dream. Dallas: WORD, 1991.
Hope for Hurting Women. Dallas: WORD, 1985.
How to Get Along with Difficult People. Eugene, OR: Harvest House, 1984.
It Takes So Little to Be Above Average. Eugene, OR: Harvest House, 1983.
I've Found My Keys, Now Where's My Car? Nashville: Thomas Nelson, 1994.
Out of the Cabbage Patch. Eugene, OR: Harvest House, 1984.
Personalities in Power: The Making of Great Leaders. Lafayette, LA: Huntington House, 1988.
Personality Plus. Old Tappan, NJ: Revell, 1992.
Raising the Curtain on Raising Children. (Write for information.) Dallas: WORD, 1988.

Silver Boxes. (Write for information.) Dallas: WORD, 1989.
Your Personality Tree. (Write for information.) Dallas: WORD, 1986.

and **Fred Littauer.**
Get a Life Without the Strife. Nashville: Thomas Nelson, 1993.

and **Marita Littauer.**
Personality Puzzle: Understanding the People You Work With. Old Tappan, NJ: Revell, 1992.

Meier, Paul, M.D.
Don't Let Jerks Get the Best of You. Nashville: Thomas Nelson, 1993.
The Third Millennium. Nashville: Thomas Nelson, 1993.

and **Dr. Frank Minirth, Dr. Paul Meier, Dr. Richard Meier, Dr. David Congo,** and **Dr. Allen Doran.**
What They Didn't Teach You in Seminary. Nashville: Thomas Nelson, 1993.

Minirth, Frank, M.D.
Beating the Odds: Overcoming Life's Trials. Grand Rapids: Baker Books, 1987.
Happy Holidays: How to Beat the Holiday Blues. Grand Rapids: Baker Books, 1990.
The Healthy Christian Life. Grand Rapids: Baker Books, 1988.
Taking Control. Grand Rapids: Baker Books, 1988.
You Can Manage Your Mental Health. Grand Rapids: Baker Books, 1980.

and **Betty Lively Blaylock,** and **Cynthia Spell Humbert.**
One Step at a Time. Nashville: Thomas Nelson, 1991.

and **Dr. Les Carter.**
The Anger Workbook. Nashville: Thomas Nelson, 1993.

and **Dr. Richard Fowler,** and **Dr. Brian Newman.**
Steps to a New Beginning. Nashville: Thomas Nelson, 1993.

and **Dr. Robert Hemfelt, Dr. Paul Meier,** and **Dr. Sharon Sneed.**
Love Hunger: Recovery for Food Addiction. Nashville: Thomas Nelson, 1990.
Love Hunger Weight-Loss Workbook. Nashville: Thomas Nelson, 1991.

and **Dr. Robert Hemfelt, Dr. Richard Fowler,** and **Dr. Paul Meier.**
The Path to Serenity. Nashville: Thomas Nelson, 1991.

and **Dr. Robert Hemfelt, Dr. Paul Meier, Dr. Brian Newman,** and **Don Hawkins.**

Love Is a Choice. Nashville: Thomas Nelson, 1989.
Love Is a Choice Workbook. Nashville: Thomas Nelson, 1991.

and **Paul Meier, M.D.**

Counseling and the Nature of Man. Grand Rapids: Baker Books, 1989.
Happiness Is a Choice. Grand Rapids: Baker Books, 1978.
Free to Forgive. Nashville: Thomas Nelson, 1989.

and **Paul Meier, M.D.,** and **Don Hawkins.**

Worry-Free Living. Nashville: Thomas Nelson, 1989.

and **Paul Meier, M.D., Dr. David Congo,** and **Janet Congo.**

A Walk with the Serenity Prayer. Nashville: Thomas Nelson, 1991.

and **Mary Alice Minirth, Dr. Brian Newman,** and **Dr. Deborah Newman, Dr. Robert Hemfelt,** and **Susan Hemfelt.**

Passages of Marriage. Nashville: Thomas Nelson, 1989.
New Love. Nashville: Thomas Nelson, 1993.
New Love Study Guide. Nashville: Thomas Nelson, 1993.
Realistic Love. Nashville: Thomas Nelson, 1993.
Realistic Love Study Guide. Nashville: Thomas Nelson, 1993.
Renewing Love. Nashville: Thomas Nelson, 1993.
Renewing Love Study Guide. Nashville: Thomas Nelson, 1993.
Steadfast Love. Nashville: Thomas Nelson, 1993.
Steadfast Love Study Guide. Nashville: Thomas Nelson, 1993.
Transcendent Love. Nashville: Thomas Nelson, 1993.
Transcendent Love Study Guide. Nashville: Thomas Nelson, 1993.

and **Pam Vredevelt, Dr. Deborah Newman, Harry Beverly.**

The Thin Disguise. Nashville: Thomas Nelson, 1992.

and **Dr. Paul Warren.**

Things That Go Bump in the Night. Nashville: Thomas Nelson, 1992.

et al.

Ask the Doctor. Grand Rapids: Baker Books, 1991.
Beating the Clock. Grand Rapids: Baker Books, 1986.
How to Beat Burnout. Chicago: Moody, 1986.
One Hundred Ways to Live a Happy and Successful Life. Grand Rapids: Baker Books, 1986.
The Workaholic and His Family. Grand Rapids: Baker Books, 1981.

Morley, Patrick M.
Getting to Know the Man in the Mirror: An Interactive Guide for Men. Nashville: Thomas Nelson, 1994.
The Man in the Mirror. Nashville: Thomas Nelson, 1992.
Marriage Without Walls. Nashville: Thomas Nelson, 1994.
The Rest of Your Life. Nashville: Thomas Nelson, 1992.
Walking with Christ in the Details of Life. Nashville: Thomas Nelson, 1992.

Murren, Doug.
The Baby Boomerang. Ventura, CA: Regal, 1990.
Keeping Your Dreams Alive When They Steal Your Coat. Altamonte Springs, FL: Strang Communications, 1993.

Newman, Dr. Brian.
and **Dr. Frank Minirth,** and **Dr. Paul Warren.**
The Father Book. Nashville: Thomas Nelson, 1992.

and **Dr. Frank Minirth, Dr. Paul Meier, Dr. Richard Meier, Dr. David Congo,** and **Dr. Allen Doran.**
What They Didn't Teach You in Seminary. Nashville: Thomas Nelson, 1993.

and **Dr. Richard Fowler, Jerilyn Fowler, Dr. Deborah Newman.**
Day by Day: Love Is a Choice. Nashville: Thomas Nelson, 1991.

and **Dr. Richard Fowler,** and **Dr. Frank Minirth.**
Steps to a New Beginning. Nashville: Thomas Nelson, 1993.

and **Dr. Robert Hemfelt, Dr. Paul Meier, Dr. Frank Minirth,** and **Don Hawkins.**
Love Is a Choice Workbook.

and **Dr. Frank Minirth.** *Passages of Marriage.*

Ortlund, Anne.
Building a Great Marriage. Grand Rapids: Baker Books, 1984.
Children Are Wet Cement. Grand Rapids: Baker Books, 1981.
The Disciplines of a Beautiful Woman. Dallas: WORD, 1984.
Disciplines of the Heart. Dallas: WORD, 1987.
Disciplining One Another. Dallas: WORD, 1983.
Fix Your Eyes on Jesus. Dallas: WORD, 1991.
My Sacrifice, His Fire. Dallas: WORD, 1993.
Up with Worship. Ventura, CA: 1982.

and **Ray Ortlund.**
   Confident in Christ. Sisters, OR: Questar, 1989.
   You Don't Have to Quit. Nashville: Oliver-Nelson, 1988.

Ortlund, Ray.
   Three Priorities for a Strong Local Church. Dallas: WORD, 1988.

Ream, Jan Kiemel.
   Struggling for Wholeness. Nashville: Oliver-Nelson, 1986.

Scheuermann, Ted.
   The Man Within. Nashville: Thomas Nelson, 1991.

Shurin, Barb.
and **Doug Murren.**
   Is It Real When It Doesn't Work? Nashville: Thomas Nelson, 1992.

Smalley, Gary.
   For Better or For Best. San Francisco: HarperCollins, 1991.
   How to Become Your Husband's Best Friend. Grand Rapids: Zondervan, 1990.
   If Only He Knew. San Francisco: HarperCollins, 1991.
   The Key to Your Child's Heart, rev. ed. Dallas: WORD, 1992.

and **John Trent, Ph.D.**
   A Dad's Blessing. Nashville: Thomas Nelson, 1994.
   The Gift of the Blessing. Nashville: Thomas Nelson, 1993.
   The Gift of Honor. Nashville: Thomas Nelson, 1989.
   Giving the Blessing. Nashville: Thomas Nelson, 1993.
   Home Remedies. Sisters, OR: Multnomah, 1991.
   In Search of the Blessing. Nashville: Thomas Nelson, 1993.
   Language of Love. Colorado Springs, CO: Focus on the Family, 1991.
   The Legacy of the Blessing. Nashville: Thomas Nelson, 1994.
   Love Is a Decision. Dallas: WORD, 1992.
   The Two Sides of Love. Colorado Springs, CO: Focus on the Family, 1990.
   The Two Sides of Love. Colorado Springs, CO: Focus on the Family, 1990 (2 90-minute tapes).

Stanley, Charles.
   Eternal Security. Nashville: Oliver-Nelson, 1990.
   Forgiveness. Nashville: Oliver-Nelson, 1987.

Handle with Prayer. Wheaton, IL: Scripture Press, 1992.
How to Handle Adversity. Nashville: Oliver-Nelson, 1989.
How to Keep Your Kids on Your Team. Nashville: Oliver-Nelson, 1986.
How to Listen to God. Nashville: Oliver-Nelson, 1985.
A Man's Touch. Wheaton, IL: Scripture Press, 1992.
The Source of My Strength. Nashville: Oliver-Nelson, 1994.
Temptation. Nashville: Oliver-Nelson, 1988.
Thoughts on Listening to God. Nashville: Oliver-Nelson, 1993.
A Touch of His Wisdom. Grand Rapids: Zondervan, 1992.
Winning the War Within. Nashville: Oliver-Nelson, 1988.
The Wonderful, Spirit-Filled Life. Nashville: Thomas Nelson, 1992.

Stephens, Dr. Larry.
Please, Let Me Know You, God. Nashville: Thomas Nelson, 1992.

and **Ted Scheuermann, Dr. Brian Newman,** and **Bob Dyer.**
The Man Within. Nashville: Thomas Nelson, 1991.

Taylor, Kenneth N.
Almost Twelve. Wheaton, IL: Tyndale, 1989.
Bible in Pictures for Little Eyes. Chicago: Moody, 1956.
Big Thoughts for Little People. Wheaton, IL: Tyndale, 1983.
Giant Steps for Little People. Wheaton, IL: Tyndale, 1985.
The Good Samaritan. Wheaton, IL: Tyndale, 1989.
Jesus Feeds a Crowd. Wheaton, IL: Tyndale, 1989.
The Living Bible. Wheaton, IL: Tyndale, 1975.
The Living Bible Story Book. Wheaton, IL: Tyndale, 1993.
The Lost Sheep. Wheaton, IL: Tyndale, 1989.
McGee's Favorite Bible Stories. Wheaton, IL: Tyndale, 1992.
My First Bible for Tots: Creation. Wheaton, IL: Tyndale, 1992.
My First Bible for Tots: David & Goliath. Wheaton, IL: Tyndale, 1992.
My First Bible Stories in Pictures. Huntington, IN: Our Sunday Visitor,
    1990.
The Old Testament in Pictures for Little Eyes. Chicago: Moody, 1993.
The Prodigal Son. Wheaton, IL: Tyndale, 1989.
What High School Students Should Know About Creation. Wheaton, IL:
    Tyndale, 1983.
What High School Students Should Know About Evolution. Wheaton, IL:
    Tyndale, 1983.
Wise Words for Little People. Wheaton, IL: Tyndale, 1987.

Thurman, Dr. Chris.
If Christ Were Your Counselor. Nashville: Thomas Nelson, 1993.
The Lies We Believe. Nashville: Thomas Nelson, 1990.
The Twelve Best Kept Secrets for Living an Emotionally Healthy Life. Nashville: Thomas Nelson, 1992.

Trent, John, Ph.D.
The Treasure Tree. Colorado Springs, CO: Focus on the Family, 1993.
There's a Duck in My Closet! Colorado Springs, CO: Focus on the Family, 1993.

and **Gary Smalley.**
A Dad's Blessing. Nashville: Thomas Nelson, 1994.
The Gift of the Blessing. Nashville: Thomas Nelson, 1993.
The Gift of Honor. Nashville: Thomas Nelson, 1989.
Giving the Blessing. Nashville: Thomas Nelson, 1993.
Home Remedies. Sisters, OR: Multnomah, 1991.
In Search of the Blessing. Nashville: Thomas Nelson, 1993.
Language of Love. Colorado Springs, CO: Focus on the Family, 1991.
The Legacy of the Blessing. Nashville: Thomas Nelson, 1994.
Love Is a Decision. Dallas: WORD, 1992.
The Two Sides of Love. Colorado Springs, CO: Focus on the Family, 1990.
The Two Sides of Love. Colorado Springs, CO: Focus on the Family, 1990 (two 90-minute tapes).

Whiteman, Thomas A., Ph.D.
The Fresh Start Single Parenting Workbook. Nashville: Oliver-Nelson, 1992.
Serenity Devotional. Nashville: Oliver-Nelson, 1993.

and **Randy Petersen.**
Becoming Your Own Best Friend. Nashville: Oliver-Nelson, 1993.
Love Gone Wrong. Nashville: Oliver-Nelson, 1993.
Innocent Victims. Nashville: Oliver-Nelson, 1992.

and **Dr. Robert Burns.**
The Fresh Start Divorce Recovery Workbook. Nashville: Oliver-Nelson, 1991.

Wiersbe, Warren.
In Praise of Plodders. Grand Rapids: Kregel, 1991.
Integrity Crisis. Nashville: Oliver-Nelson, 1991.

Living with the Giants. Grand Rapids: Baker Books, 1993.
Meet Yourself in the Psalms. Wheaton, IL: Scripture Press, 1983.
On Being a Servant of God. Nashville: Oliver-Nelson, 1993.
Prayer, Praise, & Promises: A Daily Walk Through the Psalms. Grand Rapids: Baker Books, 1993.
Wiersbe's Expository Outlines on the Old Testament. Wheaton, IL: Victor Books, 1993.
Be series, all by Scripture Press, Wheaton, IL.
Classic Sermons, all by Kregal, Grand Rapids.

Wise, Robert L.
The Dawning. Nashville: Thomas Nelson, 1992.
The Exiles. Nashville: Thomas Nelson, 1993.
The Fall of Jerusalem. Nashville: Thomas Nelson, 1994.
Healing the Past. Black Mtn., NC: Presbyterian Renewal Publications, 1984.

Young, Andrew.
A Way Out of No Way. Nashville: Thomas Nelson, 1994.